OAKLAND COMMUNITY COLLEGE

3 2355 00250037 9

Agnès Varda

D1596075

MANCHESTER
UNIVERSITY PRESS

FRENCH FILM DIRECTORS

DIANA HOLMES and ROBERT INGRAM *series editors*
DUDLEY ANDREW *series consultant*

Luc Besson SUSAN HAYWARD

François Truffaut DIANA HOLMES and ROBERT INGRAM

forthcoming titles

Claude Chabrol GUY AUSTIN

Jean-Luc Godard STEVE CANNON and ELIANE MEYER

Eric Rohmer HOWARD DAVIES

Georges Méliès ELIZABETH EZRA

Bertrand Blier SUE HARRIS

Jean Renoir MARTIN O'SHAUGHNESSY

Jean-Jacques Beineix PHIL POWRIE

Robert Bresson KEITH READER

Coline Serreau BRIGITTE ROLLET

Diane Kurys CARRIE TARR

FRENCH FILM DIRECTORS

Agnès Varda

ALISON SMITH

Manchester University Press

MANCHESTER AND NEW YORK

distributed exclusively in the USA by St. Martin's Press

Copyright © Alison Smith 1998

The right of Alison Smith to be identified as the author of this work has been
asserted by her in accordance with the Copyright, Designs and Patents Act
1988.

Published by Manchester University Press
Oxford Road, Manchester M13 9NR, UK
and Room 400, 175 Fifth Avenue, New York, NY 10010, USA

Distributed exclusively in the USA by
St. Martin's Press, Inc., 175 Fifth Avenue, New York,
NY 10010, USA

Distributed exclusively in Canada by
UBC Press, University of British Columbia, 6344 Memorial Road,
Vancouver, BC, Canada V6S 1Z2

British Library Cataloguing-in-Publication Data
A catalogue record is available from the British Library

Library of Congress Cataloging-in-Publication Data applied for

ISBN 0 7190 5060 X *hardback*
     0 7190 5061 8 *paperback*

First published 1998

05 04 03 02 01 00 99 98   10 9 8 7 6 5 4 3 2 1

PN
1998.3
.V368
S65
1998

Typeset in Scala with Meta display
by Koinonia Limited, Manchester
Printed in Great Britain
by Biddles Ltd, Guildford and King's Lynn

Contents

List of plates

All stills courtesy of Ciné-Tamaris

Series editors' foreword

To an anglophone audience, the combination of the words 'French' and 'cinema' evokes a particular kind of film: elegant and wordy, sexy but serious – an image as dependent upon national stereotypes as is that of the crudely commercial Hollywood blockbuster, which is not to say that either image is without foundation. Over the past two decades, this generalised sense of a significant relationship between French identity and film has been explored in scholarly books and articles, and has entered the curriculum at university level and, in Britain, at A-level. The study of film as art-form and (to a lesser extent) as industry has become a popular and widespread element of French Studies, and French cinema has acquired an important place within Film Studies. Meanwhile, the growth in multi-screen and 'art-house' cinemas, together with the development of the video industry, has led to the greater availability of foreign-language films to an English-speaking audience. Responding to these developments, this series is designed for students and teachers seeking information and accessible but rigorous critical study of French cinema, and for the enthusiastic filmgoer who wants to know more.

The adoption of a director-based approach raises questions about *auteurism*. A series that categorises films not according to period or to genre (for example), but to the person who directed them, runs the risk of espousing a romantic view of film as the product of solitary inspiration, On this model, the critic's role might seem to be that of discovering continuities, revealing a necessarily coherent set of themes and motifs which correspond to the particular genius of the individual. This is not our aim: the *auteur* perspective on film, itself most clearly articulated in France in the early 1950s, will be interrogated in certain volumes of the series, and throughout the director will be treated as one highly significant element in a complex process of film production and reception which includes socio-economic and political determinants, the work of a large and highly skilled team of artists and technicians, the mechanisms of production and distribution, and the complex and multiply determined responses of spectators.

The work of some of the directors in the series is already well known outside France, that of others is less so – the aim is both to provide informative and original English-language studies of established figures, and to extend the range of French Directors known to anglophone students of cinema. We intend the series to contribute to the promotion of the formal and informal study of French films, and to the pleasure of those who watch them.

DIANA HOLMES
ROBERT INGRAM

Acknowledgements

Very many thanks to Agnès Varda and Ciné-Tamaris (Bernard Bastide particularly) for their inestimable support with documentation and films otherwise difficult of access, as well as for the iconography, and especially to Agnès Varda for kindly agreeing to look through the manuscript.

Thanks also to the editors of *Nottingham French Studies* for permitting the reproduction of my article 'Strategies of representation in *Sans toit ni loi*' (*NFS* vol. 35, no. 2); and to Pat Mines and Sara Poole for drawing my attention to documents, and Di Holmes for having patiently read much of the first draft. For any errors that remain, the responsibility is entirely mine.

Agnès Varda's book *Varda par Agnès* (Cahiers du cinéma/Ciné-Tamaris, 1994) provided an enormous amount of source material and is an indispensable research document for approaching Varda's work.

To my mother
Vivienne Smith

Who is Agnès Varda?

Who is Agnès Varda and what justifies her inclusion in a series of major French film-makers? Her reputation in Britain rests largely on a handful of major films, which are far from indicative of the scope of her work. It has been said of her that once a decade she makes a film which calls attention to her, and to date this is not inaccurate. Her first film, *La Pointe Courte* (1954), an evocation of a Mediterranean fishing community which also explores the contradictions of a relationship, made her a modest name as a young director at the fringes of Italian neo-realism (although she was totally ignorant of the movement at the time). A few years later *La Pointe Courte* was to be heralded as an early forebear of the Nouvelle Vague. *Cléo de 5 à 7*, appearing in 1961 as the Nouvelle Vague reached its peak, followed a glamorous Parisian singer across the city during two hours filmed (almost) in real time. Also in the 1960s came *Le Bonheur* (1964), a deceptively sunny contribution to the corpus of the Nouvelle Vague broadly defined, which made a considerable impression at the time. In the 1970s, *L'Une chante, l'autre pas*, the story of two women whose friendship spans ten years of the development of the women's movement, suited the politically active taste of the period. In 1985, *Sans toit ni loi* (English title *Vagabonde*) followed the wanderings of a young female tramp across the South of France, during an unspecified but clearly delimited few weeks of winter. In 1991, there was *Jacquot de Nantes*, a film about Varda's late husband, the film-maker Jacques Demy. These five films may be considered the landmarks of Varda's career, but the work between them, though more difficult of access, is no less interesting.

Agnès Varda's filmography is both long and varied, and, unusually, her career has alternated between fiction and documentary, with some films hovering somewhere between the two (*Jacquot de Nantes* being the most recent and the most ambiguous). Varda's best-known films, mentioned above, come into the category 'fiction' with the exception of *Jacquot de Nantes*, and indeed they represent her entire fictional output with the exception of two fiction films released in conjunction with documentaries (described below) and of *Les Créatures*, made in 1965 with Michel Piccoli and Catherine Deneuve and now practically invisible even in France. This fact reflects interestingly on the status of documentaries. Among the latter, Varda's feature-length tribute to hippie California, *Lions' Love* (1969), is also nearly inaccessible now. *Daguerréotypes* (1975), about the people of Varda's street in Paris, is perhaps her best-known full-length documentary. Most recently *Les Demoiselles ont eu 25 ans* (1992) and *L'Univers de Jacques Demy* (1993) are both concerned with the legacy of Demy. *Les 100 et 1 nuits* (1995) is hard to classify as documentary or fiction. It was made as part of the commemorative celebrations for the centenary of cinema, and therefore tends to the documentary; it has a fictional plot thread but this serves mainly as an excuse to bring together a medley of evocations of the cinema of the past and its possible effect on the spectator, and a galaxy of guest stars.

Varda has twice made a pair of films, a documentary and a fiction film, released simultaneously, which explore a related theme. These two pairs are: in 1981, the documentary *Mur Murs* and a 'fiction' film which includes reference to the making of *Mur Murs, Documenteur*; in 1987 *Jane B. par Agnès V.*, a portrait of the actress Jane Birkin, followed by *Kung-Fu Master*, a scenario from an idea suggested by Birkin during the former film and quickly brought to fruition.

In addition to these full-length films Varda has made several short films, some of which are absolutely central to an understanding of her work. Among the most significant of these are

L'Opéra-Mouffe (1958), *Réponse de femmes* (1976) and *Ulysse* (1982), which will be considered in detail in this book. A full list of all Varda's films, short and long, appears in the Filmography.

In 1994, Varda published a book about her life and work, *Varda par Agnès*, in conjunction with *Cahiers du Cinéma*. It is a series of articles and reflective essays, loosely chronological but treating themes which interest the director as and when they appear most prominently in her film-making career. As complicated and personal in structure as her films, the book reflects Varda's continuing interest in the written word as well as the image, and is indispensable to a study of her work.

It is startling that in 1954 the author of this rich and varied selection of films had had practically no contact at all with the world of cinema. The young Agnès Varda, born in Ixelles, Belgium, in 1928, studied art history at the Ecole du Louvre. Not satisfied with theoretical studies, she resolved to take up a more creative career, and settled on photography, which she studied at evening classes in the Ecole de Vaugirard. Her early interest in art history has, however, had a great influence on her vision, as will be discussed in Chapter 2. After qualifying as a photographer, she collected a number of assignments as well as the inevitable freelance work.

From 1951 to 1961 she worked as *photographe de plateau* (official photographer) at the Théâtre National Populaire (TNP). The TNP was an immensely significant institution. Established in the huge Palais de Chaillot in Paris, as the crowning theatrical glory of a very active cultural policy in France in the years after the Liberation, its aim was to attract large audiences to an intelligent and vital theatre. It was placed in the charge of Jean Vilar, who had already founded the great theatrical festival of Avignon. Vilar was an adventurous director, and the TNP attracted young, popular, dynamic actors such as Gérard Philipe and the débutant Philippe Noiret. Vilar was born and brought up in Sète, on the Mediterranean coast just west of Montpellier, where Varda's family had moved during the upheavals of the war. His wife was a long-standing friend of Agnès'.

It was through the TNP that Varda came into contact with the actors who were to play the couple in *La Pointe Courte*: the cinema was a novelty for them as for Varda. The first idea for the film seems to have come from a few days spent filming in La Pointe Courte, a fishing-village just outside Sète, with a borrowed camera in order to record the area for a terminally ill friend (Varda 1994: 39). However, the move from still photography to cinema seems a natural development of Varda's creative concerns at the time. The tension between recording and creating reality, between the objective and the subjective, documentary and imaginative invention, before becoming one of the major themes of Varda's cinema, was a problem which occurred to her in her approach to the still image. Photography, she felt, left too little scope for exploring the all-important matter of reaction to the image: 'la photographie me semblait par trop muette. C'était un peu *Sois belle et tais-toi*'[1] (Varda 1994: 38). She badly wanted to introduce words to match her images. She also wanted to explore the dimension of time, especially – so she has said – in the damage it causes: 'la sensation aiguë du temps qui passe et de l'érosion des sentiments qui nous infligent moisissures, rouilles, humiliations pas digérées et blessures qui ne se ferment pas ... Pour les blessures de l'âme, la photographie ne suffisait pas'[2] (Varda 1994: 39). Time and decay, and the struggle of life against time and decay, are again themes which recur throughout her work, from *La Pointe Courte* and *L'Opéra-Mouffe* to *Sans toit ni loi* and indeed *Jacquot de Nantes*. In order to treat such a subject satisfactorily the idea of progress and regress, and therefore of movement, is fairly obviously essential.

La Pointe Courte was made with the encouragement of friends and the help of a small legacy. The professional actors were, naturally enough, chosen from Varda's acquaintance at the TNP, but the vast majority of the cast of the film are Sétois fishermen

1 'Photography seemed to me much too silent. It was a bit "Be beautiful and keep quiet".'
2 'the sharp sensation of time passing and the erosion of feelings which inflict on us mould and rust, undigested humiliations and wounds which don't close. For the wounds of the soul, photography wasn't enough.'

playing themselves. Throughout her career Varda has retained a pleasure in the use of non-professional actors, or actors in roles which reveal parts of their off-stage lives. From the 1960s onwards this choice became more common – although always marginal – but in 1954 it was almost unheard of in the French cinema, at least that part of it which pretended to some commercial existence.

Non-professional actors and working environments had, however, become the mainstay of the Italian cinema, which just after the war was probably the most innovative national cinema in Europe. The so-called neo-realist movement in Italy had 'begun' in 1945: by 1954 the most influential French critics of the time, including André Bazin, credited with inspiring the Nouvelle Vague, were lauding it as the future of European cinema.³ Neo-realism used largely non-professional actors in situations which reflected the lives of the ordinary Italian people, with a strong emphasis on location shooting and the influence of locality on human action. One of the major films of the movement, Visconti's *La Terra Trema* (1948), about a fishing village in Sicily, has obvious affinities with *La Pointe Courte* both in its theme and in its filmic choices. Alain Resnais, then a rising star of documentary, was the editor of *La Pointe Courte* and he commented on the relation between the two films. Varda wrote:

> Il faisait des remarques comme:
> – 'Ce plan me fait penser à *La Terra Trema* de Visconti'.
> – 'Qui est Visconti?', disais-je ...⁴ (Varda 1994: 46)

In fact Varda had seen very few films before 1954. If she recalls the experience of the 'poetic realist' work of Carné and Prévert, and especially *Les Enfants du Paradis*, she was on the whole more interested in literature.

> J'avais la sensation que le cinéma s'était fourvoyé dans une fiction

---

3 See, for example, 'Le Réalisme cinématographique et l'école italienne de la Libération', in André Bazin, *Qu'est-ce que le cinéma?*, pp. 257–93.
4 'He would make comments like:
  "This film makes me think of Visconti's *La Terra Trema*".
  "Who's Visconti?", I'd say.'

cinématographique et qu'il n'abordait ni les problèmes traités par le roman, ni les problèmes de l'existence ... J'avais la sensation qu'on ne parlait pas de choses vivantes, importantes, que d'autre part le cinéma n'était pas libre, surtout dans sa forme, et ça m'énervait.[5] (Varda 1961: 8)

The greatest influence that she quotes for *La Pointe Courte* was William Faulkner's novel *Wild Palms*.

La Pointe Courte, however, was to prove her entry into the world of cinema. The contact with Resnais proved a revelation. Like her, he had strong roots in the fine arts and an interest in the Surrealist movement; his constant filmic references persuaded her to widen her limited knowledge of cinema, and to revise her poor opinion of the medium. It was through Resnais initially that she encountered the team of young critics writing at the time for the magazine *Cahiers du Cinéma* under the editorship of the legendary André Bazin. These young critics were later to become the initiators of the Nouvelle Vague. Varda has described her first encounter with these confident and cinema-crazy young men as somewhat intimidating to the cinematic novice that she felt herself to be:

Comme je ne connaissais pas ces jeunes gens, c'est seulement sur un vague souvenir de leurs visages (mieux identifiés plus tard) que je pourrais dire que Chabrol, Truffaut, Rohmer (qui avait un autre nom), Brialy, Doniol-Valcroze et Godard étaient réunis ce soir-là. Je suivais mal la conversation. Ils citaient mille films et proposaient je ne sais quoi à Resnais, tous parlant vite, bavardant avec animation, assis partout y compris sur le lit. Moi j'étais là comme par anomalie, me sentant petite, ignorante, et seule fille parmi les garçons des *Cahiers*.[6] (Varda 1994: 13)

5 'I had the feeling that the cinema had got lost in cinematographic fiction and that it didn't approach either the problems which the novel did, or the problems of existence ... I had the feeling that living, important things weren't discussed, and on the other hand that the cinema wasn't free, especially with regard to its form, and that irritated me.'

6 'As I didn't know these young men, only a vague memory of their faces (which I knew better later) allows me to say that I think Chabrol, Truffaut, Rohmer (who had a different name), Brialy, Doniol-Valcroze and Godard were there that evening. I had trouble following the conversation. They quoted thousands of films and suggested all sorts of things to Resnais, they all talked fast, chatted

La Pointe Courte was very well received by the group, however, especially by Bazin whose taste for the neo-realists no doubt predisposed him to like it. With hindsight it has been cited as one of the most important precursors of the Nouvelle Vague. Varda's connection with the Cahiers group continued and became more equal; Jean-Luc Godard takes the starring role in a comic silent film-within-the-film in her second feature, Cléo de 5 à 7. Made in 1961, Cléo is generally counted among the films of the Nouvelle Vague, even if Varda was always outside its inner circle. For one thing she never worked for Cahiers, for another she turned, after La Pointe Courte, to documentaries and to an interest in questions of form and the nature of the image and largely abandoned narrative until 1961. Along with Resnais and the documentarist Chris Marker, she formed part of a subset of the Nouvelle Vague which has sometimes been called the 'Groupe Rive Gauche' (Left Bank Group), although they never formed anything like the coherent group based at Cahiers.

After La Pointe Courte, Varda made two commissioned documentaries, on which she managed to impose a personal touch, as well as a very personal, subjective, avant-garde short, L'Opéra-Mouffe. It was while presenting the second of the commissioned works, Du côté de la côte, at a festival in Tours that she met Jacques Demy. They remained together until Demy's death in 1990, although it was a working partnership only in the loosest sense. The two never collaborated on a film, with the exception of Jacquot de Nantes, made when he was already dying. Explicit mutual influence is minimal or absent, although they admired each other's work. However, events in Demy's career undoubtedly influenced Varda and vice versa, in the casual sense of engendering encounters, dictating places of work, introducing locations and experiences. The conditions of their mutual work were not without an influence on the scenario of Les Créatures, as Varda admits in Varda par Agnès. More significantly, Demy obtained a

brightly, and sat everywhere including on the bed. I seemed to be there by mistake, feeling small, ignorant and the only woman among the guys from Cahiers.'

firm contract with Columbia Pictures in 1967, as a result of which the couple spent three years in California. Varda herself never secured a major studio deal, despite a number of efforts and near misses; the disappointment was probably mitigated by the relative liberty that she had in her work. San Francisco was effervescent, flower-powered, idyllic, and Varda's contacts there read like a catalogue of the well-heeled counter-culture. (Jim Morrison was an honoured guest at her daughter Rosalie's eighth birthday party.)

Within that world she made two short films and one feature, *Lions' Love*, document or tribute to the American sixties pheno-menon although officially a French film. These are films that are hard to find these days (although *Lions' Love* was shown on the art-house circuit in Britain in 1992). In general the period between 1964 (*Le Bonheur*) and 1974 (*Daguerréotypes*) for Varda was one of considerable activity which remained or has become marginal. Much of her work espoused the prominent political causes of the time (*Black Panthers, Salut les Cubains, Loin du Vietnam*, the latter a collectively made film in which she partici-pated). More unusually, a film critical of the contemporary fascist regime in Greece, *Nausicaa*, was withdrawn by the French television which had commissioned it, and was never shown. The obscurity of the films from this period is sometimes hard to explain. Only *Loin du Vietnam* is well known. The Californian films may have suffered because of their uncertain anchorage, neither quite American nor quite French. Short films are a form of cinema which tends to slip more easily into the shadows, and most of Varda's films between 1964 and 1974 are shorts. *Lions' Love* is an exception, as is *Les Créatures*, whose subsequent invisibility is extremely hard to fathom, given the profile of its stars and its promising subject.

By the early 1970s Varda was back in France, and in the mid-1970s a series of short films and one major feature, *L'Une chante, l'autre pas*, reflected the long-standing interest which the film-maker had for the French women's movement. Agnès Varda is one of very few French women film-makers who have identified themselves as feminist. In this as in most fields of interest she has been committed rather than militant; the commitment dates from at least the early 1950s (when she took part in a delegation sent to question Mme Thorez, wife of the Communist leader of the time, about the French Communist Party's decision to oppose legal contraception). During the 1960s and 1970s the most urgent questions for the nascent feminist movement were the legalisation of contraception and later of abortion; Varda took part in the network of support groups organised in France to combat the dangers of illegal abortions, and her experiences have been transposed into those of Pomme and Suzanne in *L'Une chante, l'autre pas*. The film was conceived of as a celebration of the vitality of the 1970s' women's movement; it is more loosely structured than most of Varda's films, but the politics of reproduction emerges as a unifying theme for the progress of the two characters. Varda's own experience of motherhood has by no means been irrelevant to her films: the short film *L'Opéra-Mouffe*, made while she was pregnant with her first child, Rosalie, illustrates her great skill at exploring the subtleties of her own experience and translating it into a visual experience both subjective *and* objective. (*L'Opéra-Mouffe* will be discussed further later.) In *L'Une chante, l'autre pas* she investigates the possible implications of pregnancy and motherhood for women from a great variety of angles, treating both the emotional and the social aspects. Although undoubtedly fictional, its large quotient of social documentary and even of autobiography illustrate the way in which fiction and non-fiction interpenetrate in Varda's films.

Varda's second child, Mathieu, was born in 1972, and his effect on his mother's career has been more visible to the extent that he has appeared in her films since *L'Une chante, l'autre pas*, most notably in *Kung-Fu Master* in 1987 where he plays the leading role alongside Jane Birkin (whose own daughters Charlotte Gainsbourg and Lou Doillon also appear – but Gainsbourg was already a child-star with two leading roles to her credit).

Varda returned to America during 1979–81, but her stay this time proved less idyllic. Temporarily separated from Demy, she gained a contract with EMI for a film based on a Californian news story, to be called *Maria and the Naked Man*. The script was written and accepted, but the studio wanted a star in the leading role, and none could be obtained. Although even at the end of 1981 Varda still had hopes of making *Maria* with Theresa Russell and Simone Signoret, the project was finally abandoned. *Mur Murs* and *Documenteur* are a direct result of the frustrations of this period, with very small budgets extracted painfully from the institutions of the French industry. Varda assumed some of the costs, and all the production work, herself, and her interviews at this period suggest a degree of discouragement. She told *Positif* that she felt that with regard to her career she was 'en panne. Pas en panne d'inspiration, en panne de courage' (Varda 1982: 41) ('at a standstill. Not of inspiration, but of courage'). However, in 1985, *Sans toit ni loi* obtained greater recognition than any other of Varda's films, winning the Golden Lion at the Venice Festival (one of the three most prestigious European film festivals, the others being Cannes and Berlin. Varda had received a Silver Bear at Berlin in 1964 for *Le Bonheur*). *Sans toit ni loi* also won a César (a 'European Oscar') for best actress for Sandrine Bonnaire. In fact the 1980s were an extremely productive decade for Varda. *Mur Murs* and *Documenteur, Sans toit ni loi, Jane B. par Agnès V.* and *Kung-Fu Master* are all major films, and in the realm of the short film *Ulysse* won a César in 1982.

The 1990s have so far been overshadowed, as far as Varda's work is concerned, by the death of Demy. After *Jacquot de Nantes*, she has made two films directly concerned with his memory and his influence. Her only other film so far in the 1990s is also a work of commemoration, made in honour of the centenary of the cinema but released only for a short time and at a considerable financial loss.

Agnès Varda has lived for more than forty years on the rue Daguerre, in Paris, where she set up first a photographer's studio and later the headquarters of her production company, Ciné-Tamaris. The shopkeepers and inhabitants of the rue Daguerre are the subject of the 1974 film *Daguerréotypes*, and the street and the buildings she occupies have become associated with her. Her establishment there has some of the atmosphere of the local artisan's workshop – Agnès Varda as *cinéaste du coin*. Given the constant importance in her films of work which links people to their community and their locality (*La Pointe Courte, Daguerréotypes, Sans toit ni loi, Jacquot de Nantes, ...*) I do believe that she would appreciate this view of the film-maker's trade.

References

Bazin, André (1981) *Qu'est-ce que le cinéma?*, Paris, Cerf

Varda, Agnès (1994) *Varda par Agnès*, Paris, Cahiers du cinéma

Varda, Agnès (1961) 'Agnès Varda', interview with Jean Michaud and Raymond Bellour, *Cinéma 61*, pp. 4–20

Varda, Agnès (1982) 'Entretien avec Agnès Varda', interview with Françoise Audé and Jean-Pierre Jeancolas, *Positif*, no. 253, April, pp. 40–4

2

Cinécriture and the power of images

Varda and film technique

Varda's background, before *La Pointe Courte*, was in the still image and the theatre. She first studied history of art, then trained as a photographer. 'J'ai découvert la capitale et le milieu dans lequel j'ai évolué ensuite, celui du théâtre, de la peinture et des artisans ... j'atteignis l'âge de faire mon premier film à vingt-cinq ans, sans avoir vu vingt-cinq films, ni même dix'[1] (Varda 1994: 22). Her approach to the construction of moving images was thus formed neither by learning from the professionals, as was considered almost indispensible for an aspiring film-maker in the years before the eruption of the Nouvelle Vague, nor from a stock of admired or despised precedents as was the case with the *Cahiers* group. Her cultural references were literary and artistic. The Surrealists were an early discovery, Kafka had impressed her, Faulkner's narration was inspirational at the time of *La Pointe Courte*, and Nathalie Sarraute has been a pervasive influence throughout Varda's work – *Sans toit ni loi* is dedicated to her and borrows part of the plot of her novel *Le Planétarium*.

Also pervasive in Varda's work is a sense of the power of the image – the still image – and the significance of its every part. The paintings of the fourteenth and fifteenth centuries, where every

1 'I discovered the capital and the circles I moved in afterwards, those of the theatre, painting and craftspeople ... I reached the age when I made my first film at 25, without having seen twenty-five films, nor even ten.'

detail has a potential narrative or symbolic function, are clearly present in her mind and echoes of such images occur throughout her films. As a photographer her consciousness of the power of significance of every element of an image was developed. Varda's photography always gives central importance to the subject, by which I mean that she does not treat photography as a formal exercise privileging light, colour and texture, but the conjunction of elements and the relationships between them are carefully chosen in order to produce meaning from the interplay between them. In 1982, when a request to string together a series of photos in a mini-film for a photography festival led her to look back over this aspect of her work, she identified the keys to the pictures which she regarded as most successful. On the one hand, significant detail, 'un détail, que j'ai vu ou pas au moment du déclic'; on the other, the exchange between elements of the image and especially between the glances or gazes of people photographed: 'c'est cet échange de regards, c'est cet échange de désirs de regards'[2] (Bergala 1982: VIII).

Still image and moving image often meet in Varda's films, and we will return to this aspect after a brief consideration of how this woman from a non-cinematic background approaches the craft of film-making generally. How do her literary interests, her artistic and photographic experience affect her concept of the film, and what, indeed, does the act of film-making imply for Agnès Varda?

Certainly, her approach to cinema is based on a comprehensive consideration for every detail of the film. This includes, of course, both image and sound-track, but she rejects the idea that the cinema should be dependent on words to convey its meaning. The sound-track in Varda's films – and I refer here especially to documentary films where the temptation to a direct, explanatory

2 'a detail, that I saw or not at the moment that the shutter clicked' ... 'it's that exchange of glances, that exchange of the desire of glances' (both quotes p. VIII). Both comments relate to specific images. The first recalls Barthes' analysis in *La Chambre claire*, locating the heart of a successful photo in an unexpected detail or *punctum*. (Varda denies having read this.) The second of course extends to the relation between image and the world outside the frame, photographer or spectator. All this is applicable to much of Varda's approach to the moving image.

voice-over may be great – is never simple, and never detachable from the image. However, the way in which she describes the visual construction of a film is in some ways literary. She constructs a film, she says, as a writer constructs a text, and she has coined the term *'cinécriture'* (ciné-writing) to describe her work. What she means by this is best described in her own words:

> J'ai lancé ce mot et maintenant je m'en sers pour indiquer le travail d'un cinéaste. Il renvoie à leurs cases le travail du scénariste qui écrit sans tourner et celui du réalisateur qui fait sa mise en scène. Cela peut être la même personne mais la confusion persiste souvent. J'en ai tellement assez d'entendre: 'C'est un film bien écrit', sachant que le compliment est pour le scénario et pour les dialogues.
>
> Un film bien écrit est également bien tourné, les acteurs sont bien choisis, les lieux aussi. Le découpage, les mouvements, les points de vue, le rythme du tournage et du montage ont été sentis et pensés comme les choix d'un écrivain, phrases denses ou pas, type de mots, fréquence des adverbes, alinéas, parenthèses, chapitres continuant le sens du récit ou le contrariant, etc.
>
> En écriture c'est le style. Au cinéma, le style c'est le cinécriture.[3]
> (Varda 1994: 14)

What this means, when considering Varda's work, is that every aspect of the film is by definition chosen with a view to an intended effect, message, meaning. It is of course a commonplace of film studies that every choice made is potentially to be decoded for analysis. However, the director who declares herself so committed to instilling meaning in all details is not so universal.

3 'I invented the word and now I use it to mean the film-maker's work. It puts the work of the scriptwriter who writes but does not film, and of the director who does the mise-en-scène, back in their respective boxes. The two may be the same person, but there's often lasting confusion. I am so fed up with hearing: "It's a well-written film", when I know that the compliment is meant for the scenario and the dialogue.

A well-written film is also well filmed, the actors are well chosen, so are the locations. The cutting, the movement, the points-of-view, the rhythm of filming and editing have been felt and considered in the way a writer chooses the depth of meaning of sentences, the type of words, number of adverbs, paragraphs, asides, chapters which advance the story or break its flow, etc.

In writing it's called style. In the cinema, style is *cinécriture*.'

If we take Varda's definition of *'cinécriture'* seriously, as we must, it means that her films will repay the closest reading possible, because the film-maker herself is aware of the implications of everything she does. Very little in Varda's films is 'merely' functional or narrative. As well as getting us from point A to point B of the story, each shot will have implications of its own, as will the ways in which the shots are joined, possible changes of rhythm between shots and so on.

This attention to detail is evident in all interviews that Varda has given about her work. The choice of the actress Silvia Monfort to play the young wife in her first film, *La Pointe Courte*, was guided not only by Monfort's availability (although Varda's choices were actually limited, her inexperience not appealing to most established actors), but by her resemblance to Renaissance Italian portraits. In *Sans toit ni loi*, the tracking-shots of Mona the vagabond walking through the country, which punctuate the film, are not merely a device to link the episodes of the film into a narrative. Each begins and ends on some wayside object: the object where each shot starts being the same or of similar nature to that which ended the previous one. Thus the tracking-shots become a continuous walk – the incidents punctuate Mona's journey, rather than glimpses of the journey being used to link the incidents. The direction of tracking, from right to left, was chosen because Western cultures read from left to right, and so left-to-right movement becomes associated with a sense of moving 'forward', 'in the right direction', 'with the culture'. Mona is moving in the wrong direction, against the culture, against the tide. The direction she travels is part of the general refusal which Mona embodies. Similarly the movement of the camera which is not synchronised with Mona's walking, but either overtakes her or is overtaken by her, underlines her independence and her transience. The theme-music which accompanies these shots connects them, but was also commissioned especially for the film and created to add to the portrait of Mona. Varda supplied the composer, Joanna Bruzdowicz, with a notebook in which 'j'écris, séquence par séquence, pas seulement les minutages mais des suggestions liées à des sensations que je décris, ou bien je cite un

poème ou j'indique des œuvres de la même famille musicale ...
Elle [the music] paraphrase la solitude de la vagabonde, qui va en
s'accentuant'[4] (Varda 1994: 209).

This example illustrates the care with which Varda selects every
aspect of a shot. Many of these subtleties may escape the notice of
the average spectator of the film entirely – others, such as the
music, will create their effect *en douce*. It would take several
viewings to unravel all the implications above – in this case Varda
has helpfully drawn attention to the construction of the 'Grande
Série' (as these shots were called during filming) in interviews and
discussions of the film.

Such interviews and discussions with Varda always give pride
of place to the craft involved in the making of the film, and to the
significance of choices of detail. Rather than discussing theme,
characters, scenario, she emphasises the dominant colours, the
frequency and direction of tracking-shots, the appearance of the
actors. We might remember the Nouvelle Vague credo expressed
by Jean-Luc Godard (who of all the *Cahiers* group remained the
most consistently concerned with the significance of all filmic
elements), 'les travellings sont affaire de morale' ('tracking-shots
are a moral choice'). It is perhaps not coincidental that among the
Cahiers group it is Godard to whom Varda was closest, as his role
in *Cléo de 5 à 7* suggests.

Agnès Varda's consciousness of her creation means, not that
her films make more formal sense than anyone else's, but that she
remains firmly in control of every aspect of the sense that can be
gleaned from them. The visual effect is always calculated and
therefore often particularly striking. Although there are no doubt
implications which can be read into Varda's formal choices which
she may not have intended to put there, such readings will always
be an extra dimension to add to the rich stock of meaning of which
the film-maker is aware.

It is thus hard to deny to Varda's work that rather over-used

4 'I wrote, sequence by sequence, not only the timing but suggestions linked to
the sensations I was describing, or I'd quote a poem or suggest other musical
works of the same family ... It [the music] paraphrases the vagabond's ever-
increasing solitude.'

title of *cinéma d'auteur*. Her visual sense determines the appearance of the film in every detail, even if she does not herself hold the camera. There are images, notably in *Jane B. par Agnès V.*, or in a television documentary made in 1964 while she was making *Le Bonheur*, where she does appear behind the camera. In *Jane B.* there is a shot where the camera and the cameraman are seen briefly, before Varda's face replaces them. She speaks of the camera here as 'un petit peu moi' ('in some ways me'). The title of *Jane B.* itself is clearly a claim of authorship (though a complex one, as we shall see in Chapter 4). As photographer and as art historian Varda's background has emphasised personal creation, and the literary metaphor which she uses to explain her idea of film-making further puts her approach to her work on a personal level of creation of her *own* meaning. Through her production company Ciné-Tamaris she has largely produced her own films since the mid-1960s, a heavy burden of work and financial worry which has nonetheless left her creatively free. She has indeed shown little patience with institutional restraints, even during her first stay in Hollywood having, she claims, refused a studio contract unless she was allowed final cut. She denounces on screen the censorship to which the TV companies subjected *Réponse de femmes* (incidentally turning that misfortune to the advantage of her theme). She has rarely made commissioned films since the very beginnings of her career, choosing subjects to coincide with her current preoccupations. She has, in other words, a high degree of control over her work as well as an alert consciousness of its complications and of the significance of every part of it, and it is not surprising that, as we shall see, themes and creative choices recur in changing forms throughout her career.

It should be clear from the above that Agnès Varda's films repay detailed study of all the aspects cited as significant to film construction in basic texts on cinema language.[5] I would like now to concentrate on one specific aspect of this, characteristic of Varda's work for reasons hinted at above; the ways in which, in

5 For a detailed and very structured general discussion of the subtleties of film-language, the best textbook is still Bordwell and Thompson (1993).

her films, the *still* image is engaged with and called into question using the resources of cinema. I would like to concentrate particularly on three questions. First, the use that Varda makes in her films of the resources of the creative photographer, colour and light, position and structure: in other words of *mise en scène*, as Bordwell and Thompson define it. Secondly, the vital importance in her films of significant or even symbolic objects intercalated as brief still close-up images in the flow of the narrative (the use of this technique in a documentary context is more widespread). Thirdly, the appearance in her films of what might be called cultural icons. By this I mean, on the one hand, reproductions of identifiable images from the Western cultural bank, as befits a former art history student. The *tableaux vivants* in *Jane B.* are perhaps the clearest and the most extended examples, but from *La Pointe Courte* onwards Varda has flirted with the history of art (the history of images) – as when she chose Silvia Monfort because she could have been painted by Piero della Francesca. On the other hand, there are 'cultural icons' of less precise origin, visual clichés which we recognise as if they are self-evident, timeless images. Such is the picnic of *Le Bonheur*, a version, in its subject, its colour scheme, the arrangement of its human and natural elements, of an eternal Kodak ad (plate 1). In French, *cliché* means 'snapshot' as well as having its English meaning. Such instant images are a fruitful starting point for visual exploration, for someone who moved from photography to cinema in order to allow movement into her representations of the world.

The photograph itself figures in a number of Varda's films. The introduction of actual still images into the stream of the film interests her, usually as a collection of images which her protagonists contemplate and which have some clear or obscure significance for them. Varda (1994: 130) lists three instances – stamps in *Le Bonheur*, for the post-office worker; postcards in *L'Une chante, l'autre pas* and in *Sans toit ni loi*, where, however, their nature and their function seem very different. The Tarot cards in *Cléo* have a more obvious function, and may be a key to the mysteries of other such series. In *Jane B.* this procedure recurs – in the sketch with Philippe Léotard, art-books are everywhere and their contents are sometimes shot in close-up, photos of the past are used as a backdrop to spoken memories (not unusual) and also adorn Birkin's house. In fact in *Jane B.* Varda uses the combination of still image and film in practically every possible way. In *Ulysse* the photograph is much more central and more explicitly in question. Varda returns to a photograph taken twenty-eight years previously, in order to compare its significance then and now and to find the people pictured in it and confront them too with the frozen moment. The protagonists, Varda herself whose voice is heard on the sound-track, and eventually the spectator, are thus faced with issues connected with time and memory which are immensely important to Varda's work. It will recur in our consideration of the function of the still image, although this aspect of her films, and *Ulysse*'s contribution to it, merits a chapter of its own (Chapter 6).

Mise-en-scène

Mise-en-scène is the stock-in-trade of the photographer – the elements which together make up a striking and hopefully significant still image. It is undeniable that all Varda's films are filled with very striking images. However, rarely if ever does one find an image which does no more than impress us by its immediate beauty. The use which she makes of colour, of light and shadow, and especially of structure (the arrangement of objects, of centres of interest in the picture) almost always take on meaning only in the context of the whole film. Varda describes the relationship between photography and cinema thus: 'Ces deux saisies de la vie, l'une immobile et muette, l'autre mouvante et parlante, ne sont pas ennemies mais différentes, complément-aires même. La photographie, c'est le mouvement arrêté ou le mouvement intérieur immobilisé. Le cinéma, lui, propose une série de photographies successives dans une durée qui les anime'[6]

6 'These two snatches of life, the one immobile and silent, the other moving and speaking, are not enemies but are different, even complementary. Photography is movement stopped or inner movement frozen. Cinema for its part presents a sequence of successive photographs given life over time.'

(Varda 1994: 130). This last sentence is key. The meaning of the light, the colour and the structure of the images in Varda's films comes from the way in which these change over time, throughout the film or even throughout a shot.

A good example of this is the shots in *La Pointe Courte* which show the young couple, Philippe Noiret and Silvia Monfort, walking on the beaches of *La Pointe Courte* as they discuss their relationship. These shots are all very strikingly structured. Any still from these sequences supplies, first, a striking image where the human figures are dramatically lit and arranged around intriguingly shaped marine debris, and secondly an image which has, in itself, a certain narrative content. The position of the couple can be read in terms of their relations of the moment. They may be in the same plane, or one – usually the woman – may be distant and small; they may be together or separated by a breakwater or a sharply pointed spar, they may both be lit, or, very often, one is in bright light and the other in shadow. As Frank Curot (1991a: 89) has pointed out, these shots often begin or end with camera and characters motionless, so that there are moments when the image is as still as a photograph.

But the importance of these 'photographs' is in their relation to each other. As the characters talk, they move, changing the balance of forces in the picture. The structure of the image and the dialogue provide a mutual commentary. Neither is unambiguous – the dialogue given to the couple in *La Pointe Courte* is poetic and allusive and skirts around the 'central' issue of whether or not she will leave. The different visual elements which can separate the couple are complex and the sequences play with them subtly – they approach each other, but with a breakwater between them, even when they seem closest they are still divided by the contrast of light and shade. However, the two elements together allow the spectator to follow the meanders of their discussion, which progresses slowly, indirectly, to an eventual accord. It is the progress that is the point of the sequences where the couple appear: no single stage of it matters in itself, and each structured, definable moment is important precisely because it will not last. Their thoughts move on, their relationship alters again – but at every point one could stop the film and look at a visual representation of 'the state of play at the moment', and occasionally the film pauses for just that purpose.

La Pointe Courte, Varda's first film, is the most clearly photographic in the sense that practically every still would stand alone as a structured, readable image. But it is not alone in constructing such images, temporary summaries of the characters' situation which could be extracted from the films and read as mini-narratives in their own right. Take, for example, the sequence where Cléo tries on a hat, fairly early in *Cléo*. A still shot of her at this point provides an elegant photographic image of the situation of this woman, behind glass, separate from the world which is reflected against her without touching her. Her glamour is obviously visible, so is her status as an object, to be looked at but who does not look out. The mirrors which surround her indicate her narcissism. Even the way in which the reflections on the glass lie across her makes her appear less than solid, and the presence in the background of a white gown displayed on an invisible body-frame adds to the ghostly atmosphere (plate 5). If one was conditioned to look for symbolism – if, for example, one read the photograph as one would a Renaissance painting – intimations of mortality appear in this one image. We have, in short, in one still image a masterly summary of Cléo at this moment.

However, it is at this moment only. The meaning of any such image *within* the film is distorted by an analysis which ignores its fragility. The film as it continues will obliterate the image and modify the situation. Cléo at 6.45 is no longer the Cléo of 5.37. An image detached from its filmic context, on the other hand, becomes unchangeable. If this picture, for example, was really a still photograph – as it easily could be, and a successful and eloquent one – Cléo would become in a sense irredeemable, her subjectivity for ever fixed, narcissistic, the epitome of what can only be called alienation. Sometimes Varda illustrates in the film what happens when the still image persists. In *Sans toit ni loi* the image which Yolande holds in her head of Mona and David is literally a still photograph. It fixes what is a very transitory situation, which to Yolande becomes permanent and representative. The uses which Yolande makes of this 'still' are considered in much more detail in Chapter 4; it is a valuable image to her, and her reactions to it develop over time. However, the development of the image in her head and the development of Mona and David coincide not at all. This episode provides an example of the dangers of believing such still summaries of a situation, even – or especially – when they are visually highly readable. They do allow other meanings to enter the narrative though. The Mona in Yolande's 'cliché' loses her individual identity, but she inherits a more universal one. She and David become an illustration of love, irrespective of the contingencies that have placed them there; and Yolande needs an illustration of love, it helps her to understand what is lacking between her and Paolo. The problem arises in confusing the illustration with reality. An illustration is by definition permanent, reality by definition temporary. Mona is not an exemplar of perfect love, but as we shall see this does not devalue the image. On the other hand, the illustration of perfect happiness represented by the picnic in *Le Bonheur* is devalued to the extent that its protagonists are committed to its preservation, permanent and unchanging.

Decisions regarding colour for a film-maker are twofold. First, since the 1950s (in France), whether to use it at all; secondly, given its use, what strategy to adopt – should colours simply be 'realistic' and left largely to chance or are they to be given prominence and significance, and if so, how. It should not be surprising that Varda chooses to impute significance to colour, and also to use black-and-white and colour sequences in the same film.

The first film in which the choice of black-and-white or colour becomes an issue is *Cléo*. *Cléo* is largely shot in black-and-white, like the majority of the Nouvelle Vague films up to that time. Only Godard had so far turned to colour (*Une femme est une femme*, made the same year). Varda, however, does use colour for the introductory sequence – the Tarot cards which prefigure Cléo's fate. This immediate announcement that the film had the option of colour, makes the return to black-and-white, as well as the introductory colour, significant, and intriguing. Varda has explained the choice:

Dès les premières images de *Cléo de 5 à 7*, les tarots colorés de la cartomancienne racontent l'avenir de Cléo en virtuel, en mensonge ou en prémonition. ...

Comme un court prologue inséré dans le récit, ce début de *Cléo de 5 à 7* est en couleurs. Ou plus précisément le tapis de table et les tarots. Le générique s'y inscrit. On annonce en couleurs le film, ce que voit la cartomancienne est une fiction, puis on voit le visage affolé de Cléo, en noir et blanc comme la suite du film.[7] (Varda 1994: 62)

The distinction between colour and black-and-white carries at least two connotations. First a distinction between fiction and not-fiction which allows the film to approach the tragic but not quite to become so. The story in the cards is 'virtual' while Cléo's subsequent actions are 'real', and the one may have no connection with the other whatever our (and Cléo's) suspicions. Secondly, the coloured sequence illustrates the obsession which comes literally to 'colour' Cléo's outlook. Its bright colour reflects its over-whelming importance to the rest of the film; the following images take on their full significance only when seen in the context of the threat represented by this sequence. The incidental third advantage to the image-maker of the striking primary colours of Tarot cards is thus used to produce significance.

In *Jacquot de Nantes* (and to a lesser extent in *Jane B.*), colour and black-and-white take on more definitely cinematic reference. There is a well-used premise, which has become an accepted piece of cinema shorthand, that black-and-white can be used to indicate the past, the era when film would be black and white. In *Jacquot de Nantes* the main story-line is concerned with Jacques's childhood in Nantes in the 1930s and 1940s: these sequences, thus filmed in black-and-white, reflect the period but also the influence of the cinema in Jacques's formative years. However, the use of colour is complex. There are two 'series' of coloured images in *Jacquot de*

7 'From the first images of *Cléo de 5 à 7*, the card-reader's coloured deck tells Cléo's future virtually, as a lie or a premonition. ...

Like a short prologue inserted in a story, this beginning of *Cléo de 5 à 7* is in colour. Or rather the tablecloth and the cards are. The credits appear over them. The film is announced in colour, what the card-reader sees is a fiction, then we see Cléo's terrified face, in black-and-white like the rest of the film.'

Nantes: first, close-ups and extreme close-ups of Demy in 1990; secondly, extracts from his films. The first series corresponds to the usual use of this temporal shorthand – black-and-white = past, colour = present – but the agonisingly intimate shots are in a totally different register from the narrative 'past' sequences. If the black-and-white past spreads diffusely over time, the 'present' sequences are a concentrated, extended instant. They are cinema, not photography; the camera moves along Demy's body, explores his face. He remains in the same position, so that each return to this series of images is a return from a different point in the past to the same, momentary present. The colour in extracts from Demy's films is of course an inevitable given, since most of Demy's films were in colour (clearly, extracts from the others are in black-and-white). However, Varda uses the contrast. The extracts are inserted in the black-and-white reconstruction of the past, and take up a moment from Demy's supposed childhood, indicating how he used his own memories in his – largely fantastic – films. Such a transposition of memory into a fictional/ magical setting inevitably changes the everyday reality into something more powerful and therefore gives the instant, taken out of its context and made significant, intensity. Colour is associated with concentrated significance, but also with fiction and fantasy. Further, there are even within the narrative of childhood one or two sequences in colour, which portray stage shows which Jacques saw at the time. Again, the colour reflects the intensity of the experience, but also its unreality. Like the Tarot cards, it is 'virtual'. The choice also, like the black-and-white images, reflects cinematic tradition – in the early days of colour it was expensive spectacle, not daily realism, which benefited from the new technology (see Chapter 5).

Varda is not an expressionistic user of colour – that is, on the whole the colours in her films strike us as natural (unlike, say, Beineix and the 1980s' *cinéma du look*). Many of her films, especially the early colour films, are noticeably dominated by brilliant light – *Le Bonheur, Lions' Love, L'Une chante, l'autre pas* are all under the sign of the sun. This gives to the colour and light of the films connotations which are specifically photographic. In all three films there is a common desire to take Utopian images of sunny happiness – whether in suburban France or bohemian California – and put them into a temporal context which reveals the idyllic moment to be somewhat less idyllic. In *Le Bonheur* it is fundamentally flawed, in *Lions' Love* carefully constructed and maintained, in *L'Une chante, l'autre pas*, the most optimistic of the three, the result of hard work and underpinned by a serious purpose. In the sequences of *L'Une chante, l'autre pas* where Pomme (the one who sings) leaves for Iran with her partner Darius, the connotation deepens and broadens – no longer the individual idyll of the snapshot but the more universal cliché of the postcard from exotic locations.

In *Lions' Love* and *Le Bonheur* the brilliant light is a distinguishing sign of the films, but in *L'Une chante, l'autre pas* it is not universal. The sequences at Suzanne's house in Soissons, particularly, are of a different quality, of very restrained colour – browns and earth-colours are mostly contrasted with a greyish-white sky. This episode uses the colour-scheme and lighting which later typify *Sans toit ni loi*, which is a dark film (although even here Varda occasionally makes use of a pervading whitish light – this time a blank and wintry light). Both the Soissons episode of *L'Une chante, l'autre pas* and *Sans toit ni loi* represent anti-idylls. In the earlier film these colours correspond to one character's season in hell, from which she escapes to a brighter, and eventually a sun-drenched, world. *Sans toit ni loi* is a sustained exploration of the dark side of *L'Une chante, l'autre pas*.

In her choice of colours Varda does occasionally make use of specific connotations, although these are intentionally vague and may well be multiple. On the predominance of white, for example – important to her films, as we have seen – Varda has said: 'tout ce qui est lié à l'amour se concrétise dans la blancheur ... Ce n'est pas symbolique ni systématique. Ce sont des images qui s'éveillent seules, qui s'imposent à moi'[8] (quoted Prédal 1991: 37) but also 'Quand j'imaginais Cléo en danger, la menace était blanche

8 'Everything connected to love is concentrated in whiteness ... It isn't symbolic or systematic. These are images which form of their own accord and impose themselves on me.'

comme serait la mort. J'avais lu qu'en Orient la couleur du deuil est blanche. ... J'ai utilisé le blanc comme une sensation. C'est un fond qui menace d'envahir et les éléments noirs s'y dessinent'[9] (Varda 1994: 62). In other words, white for Varda is connected to both love and death, a double connotation where the elements may of course vary in significance, even before we take into account the quite different reactions which the audience may have to a white image.

> Si le blanc a cette connotation pour elle [Varda], il n'en est pas forcément de même pour tous les assistants. Sa répétition, en relation avec le thème de l'amour, finit néanmoins par toucher plus ou moins consciemment le spectateur, d'autant plus que l'auteur aime aussi l'associer fréquemment à la mort. Dès lors la signification du blanc est à la fois double et purement personnelle.[10] (Prédal 1991: 37–8)

Clearly, Varda's apparent naturalism conceals careful thought about the palette to be used in each film. In other cases, it is the combination of colours which has been selected in its entirety, for example the palette of *Le Bonheur* was selected in order to evoke the Impressionists' use of colour. In *O saisons, ô châteaux*, gold was associated with the 'living' (Varda 1965: 48).

As with the structure of the images, the significance of colour and light in the films includes, indeed is defined by, the way they change in the course of the work. As a coda to these two sections this quote, relative to colour but applicable to all aspects of the image, sums up this point:

> Dans un film la couleur circule comme le sang, régulièrement. Soudain l'on sent battre le sang plus fort, les couleurs nous ont fait

---

9 'When I imagined Cléo in danger, the threat was white like death is. I had read that in the East the colour of mourning is white. ... I used white like a sensation. It's a background which threatens to be invasive and the black elements stand out against it.'

10 'If white has this connotation for her [Varda], that does not necessarily go for all the audience. Its repetition in relation to the theme of love ends up, however, by affecting all the audience consciously or unconsciously, all the more as the film-maker also likes to associate it frequently with death. From then on the signification of white is both double and purely personal.'

impression, l'espace d'un instant. J'aime l'irrégularité des sensations, colorées ou pas. Le cinéma, c'est le mouvement des
sensations. Montrer des photos de films, dans ce livre ou ailleurs,
c'est déjà les trahir.[11] (Varda 1994: 62)

The inserted object

From *La Pointe Courte* onwards, Varda has integrated stray objects
into her films in a way which becomes one of the more striking
characteristics of her style. A shot will move from her protagonists
to end with a close-up on some near-by piece of debris (*La Pointe
Courte*, *Sans toit ni loi*); sometimes the object is introduced
following a character's gaze, explicitly (*La Pointe Courte*, *Cléo*) or
implicitly (*L'Opéra-Mouffe*).

In the early films, these objects become images of the
characters' sensations. The savagely pronged fork picked up by
the young woman in *La Pointe Courte* is easily read as a metaphor
either for the couple's relationship, or for the woman's feelings
about their relationship at that moment ... exactly how it is read is
left to the audience but the context makes the connection
inevitable. Varda's use of this technique is effective because the
objects she chooses, while visually striking and sometimes
unfamiliar – especially in *La Pointe Courte*, are perfectly in place in
the context of the film. The fork may seem like an exotic
implement to the average spectator, but we accept it as part of the
business of the fishery which we accept as unfamiliar. A similar
use is made of a dead cat – not this time unfamiliar, but shocking
and easily susceptible to connotations, and also quite naturally
present in the scene.

In *L'Opéra-Mouffe*, the first short film which Varda made
entirely freely, this process is central to the film. *L'Opéra-Mouffe* is
a film of impressions of the rue Mouffetard in Paris through the

11 'In a film colour circulates like blood, regularly. Suddenly we feel our blood
   racing, the colours have impressed us for a moment. I like irregularity of
   sensations, coloured or not. Cinema is the movement of sensations. Showing
   stills from films, in this book or anywhere, is already a betrayal.'

eyes of a pregnant woman. The film is organised in series of shots around several related themes: faces of the Mouffetard down-and-outs, a Christmas carnival, glimpses of the meat-and-fruit market which is still the main feature of the rue Mouff'. It is in the latter that we see how Varda uses the strangeness of everyday objects. For instance, in the first sequence after the credits, a glimpse of the pregnant woman is followed by a series of shots of fruit, foremost among them a watermelon being cut open to remove the seeds. This shot is close up: we are obliged to concentrate on the form of the action since there is no narrative yet, so that it functions like a still image. Its connotations are, however, determined by the previous shot of the woman. Subsequent shots of less obviously suggestive forms in turn acquire connotations because of the expectation which has been created.

The connotations here are certainly not, as the Soviet montagists (with whose ideas this technique has a superficial affinity) would have had them, rational or didactic. They correspond to much more visceral reactions, and a more precise, though non-cinematic, connection would be with the Surrealist approach to the object-*trouvaille*. According to André Breton's description in *L'Amour fou*, the *objet trouvé* may be a powerful catalyst which crystallises the unconscious or semi-conscious preoccupations of the finder (Breton 1992: 697–705). To perform this function the object obviously has to be appropriate, to 'chime' with the observer. If this is so the *objet trouvé* becomes analogous to an object seen in a dream, a metaphor giving form to hitherto unformed anxieties and desires and permitting their expression: 'La trouvaille d'objet remplit ici rigoureusement le même office que le rêve, en ce sens qu'elle libère l'individu de scrupules affectifs paralysants, le réconforte et lui fait comprendre que l'obstacle qu'il pouvait croire insurmontable est franchi'[12] (Breton 1992: 700). The metaphor is strictly to be found in the appearance of the object. The Surrealists created many such appropriate objects,

12 'The finding of the object here fulfils strictly the same function as the dream, in the sense that it frees the individual from paralysing affective inhibitions, reassures him and makes him understand that the obstacle which he thought insurmountable is crossed.'

whose forms make it clear that the chief interest of the process was to approach a non-rational expression of anxieties produced by the body and sexuality.

In *L'Opéra-Mouffe* the objects are found in the street where they are in their element, but the relevance of this concept is obvious. Varda said in 1961: '*L'Opéra-Mouffe* est un film de panique. C'est au fond un film tendre, ce qu'on a appelé sa cruauté ne relève que de l'affolement'[13] (Varda 1961: 12). The Surrealists are a constant reference when she discusses her literary influences, and although her interviews on the specific subject of *L'Opéra-Mouffe* do not call attention to the parallel, this film could bear the description of a (rare) example of Surrealism *au féminin*. *Cléo* uses a similar process, casually glimpsed objects and events being imbued with new and powerful meanings by Cléo's sense that death is at work inside her body. Here the narrative flow leads inevitably to a more restricted selection of images, and the metaphors are somewhat less subtle – but it is easier in *Cléo* than in *L'Opéra-Mouffe* to see how the short, still close-up on the object-catalyst corresponds to the *glance* of the protagonist, which imprints a still image on her mind and allows it to become a symbol. Comparing this with the way in which Yolande's glance creates a still image of Mona in *Sans toit ni loi*, as described above, indicates the way in which Varda's films show the still image to be connected to the object. A person captured in a still image becomes an object, significant only in the way that she or he 'chimes' with the preoccupations of the observer. These themes are found together in the sequence in *Jane B.*, discussed in Chapter 4, which advances the ultimate portrait-image as the equivalent of the anonymous death-mask known as 'L'Inconnue de la Seine', and asks Birkin, among the many masks which she adopts for Varda, to pose in an – almost – still image modelled on this one. L'Inconnue de la Seine was an object which intrigued the Surrealists, and makes an appearance in Aragon's novel *Aurélien* (1944) although Varda presents it as a personal memory.

Exploration of still images is a more obvious technique for

13 '*L'Opéra-Mouffe* is a film of panic. At bottom it's a tender film, what has been called its cruelty is only alarm.'

documentary than for fiction, especially in that many of Varda's documentaries have been specifically concerned with analysis of significant objects. Her documentaries on 'street art', *Mur Murs* and the 1984 short *Les Dites Caryatides*, put the murals and statues, exposed to the casual gaze of the passers-by, on the dividing-line between art and *objet trouvé*. In *Daguerréotypes* (1975), the issue of the still image inserted in the moving one is central, as is the significant object although the two aspects are largely separate. Close-ups of everyday objects used by the shopkeepers of the rue Daguerre are here set against similar close-ups where the same objects are used in a different context, as props in a conjuring show. The result is to open a crack in the rigid everyday context and give the objects new possible functions. However, the concentration on the *functions* of the objects requires them to be seen in use, and these close-ups are not still images. It is in fact not the form of the object which is significant but its purpose. The primary audience for the conjuring show is made up of the people who use these objects daily, and the camera is interested in their reactions. The form of the objects is much too familiar to them to act as a catalyst for anything, it is their unfamiliar context which creates new connections. This process and its effect on the audience will therefore be considered later.[14] The still image is announced by the title of the film, like most of Varda's titles many-layered but designating as its recognised meaning the first form of photograph, invented by Louis-Jacques-Mandé Daguerre in 1839. Daguerreotypes required sitters to remain immobile for several minutes, so that this kind of still image is far from instantaneous. The film *Daguerréotypes* mostly watches its protagonists at work, and therefore in moving images, in glimpses which last a few seconds or minutes each – about as long as it would take Daguerre to photograph them. The movement, however, is in one sense illusory. Apart from the gestures of work, or leisurely strolls in the street, the people move very little – the camera explores the space around them. At the end of the film there is a series of shots which correspond exactly to the procedures of the daguerreotype; that is,

---

14 However, it is perhaps appropriate to mention here that this process too has affinities with Surrealist practice, as Dr Silvano Levy has pointed out to me.

the protagonists pose facing the camera, motionless, for several seconds each. Although they are filmed, not photographed, the result is a still image. Throughout *Daguerréotypes*, as well as in interviews connected with it, Varda insists on the immobilism of the world of the rue Daguerre. The false still images which she creates indicate this much more than reproductions of the implied old photographs would do. These people can, it is implied, actually be represented by still images, because they will not change. The century-old form of the images (implicit in the name and the procedure but also in the poses) only intensifies the effect. The baker and his wife, facing the camera with their elaborate decorative loaf held up between them, are a convincing group for a portrait of the 1830s (plate 2).

By *Sans toit ni loi*, the still glimpse of the everyday object has acquired a subtle function, deeply integrated into the narrative and into the punctuation of the film (see the remarks on the Grande Série of tracking-shots of Mona, above). It is no longer so clear that the stray objects are interpreted through the feelings of the protagonist – it is not even certain that Mona notices the punctuating objects, and we certainly have no hint that they act as a catalyst to her self-perception in any way. The objects in question are almost all abandoned attributes of the working life of the area: a stack of tyres, a rusty tractor, or a pile of cement-sacks. Their only visible significance to Mona is practical, although not the practicality they were designed for. Mona's reaction to every object she encounters is in terms of immediate need, and we may pick up this way of seeing. In this perspective, most of the punctuating objects are little more than potential shelters. However, even this approach requires a sense of the form of the object coupled with a perception of it, as it were, through the body, and if the spectator adopts it the objects acquire a chilly intensity.

On the other hand we may automatically associate these images of abandonment, of work no-longer-in-progress, with Mona rather than perceiving them from her position. Again, they function as metaphors, although how we read them will no doubt differ between spectators, and their intensity may be a function of the degree to which one finds Mona herself disturbing. One can create parallels without too much difficulty – she is potentially functional in society but has abandoned it and largely been abandoned by it, she is gradually being worn down by the action of wind and weather, her space is waste-ground, corners of fields. They are also emblematic of the environment she is moving through, in its wintry state of suspended animation. These are only suggestions based on personal reaction; in brief, these objects are more likely to find their resonance in the gut reaction of the audience to Mona and her world, rather than in the presumed emotions of that indefinable young woman herself. Nonetheless, resonate they do, undoubtedly intentionally. In common with preceding films, their position in the film is akin to a series of still photographs intercalated in the narrative, their significance largely dependent on their own immediate qualities of form and association, but our associations are guided by their position as stages in an ongoing journey (the still ends of long tracking-shots) and by their association with the narrative which surrounds them.

The art-image

Varda began her career as an art history student. Having watched even a small sample of her films, one cannot help being struck by the degree to which the classic images of Western art pervade her work. They appear sometimes explicitly and in their own names, but even more frequently as echoes and references which could pass unnoticed – many undoubtedly do. Varda has drawn attention to some in her writings and interviews which perhaps otherwise would have been ignored or treated as coincidental – the moral no doubt is that given Varda's visual culture any possible reference should be assumed intentional!

Frank Curot (1991b: 170) has attempted a typology of the appearances of painting in film. First, as an object, framed and hung on the wall or otherwise susceptible to being handled within the diegetic space, as in the case of the *Dame à sa toilette* in *Jane B.* or the paintings to be seen in the painter's studio in the sketch with Philippe Léotard, in the same film. Secondly, in individual close-up which retains the identity of the picture but gives it full status as a frame of the film, hence integrated into the narrative. This is less frequent in Varda's work than in Godard's – the frequent use of references to painting links Varda, again, with Godard especially among French film-makers – although an example from *L'Une chante, l'autre pas* will be mentioned below.

The third of Curot's forms of filming an art-image is the *tableau vivant*, reconstituted by actors; this is clearly central to *Jane B.* which provides the most complete example in Varda's work. Fourthly, there is the visual or even thematic reference which may concern only one element of the image (Silvia Monfort's face, for example) or even remain unseen. In *Varda par Agnès* Varda describes the influence of a painting by Baldung Grien, *Death and the Maiden*, on the conception of *Cléo*. She even says that during filming the picture was hanging in the studio, but it never appears in the film.[15]

The constant reference to *Jane B.* in the above list is only natural since the film is the subject of Curot's article, but it is not fortuitous; no other of Varda's films is so consistently, variously and vitally supported by the reference to art. Elsewhere in Varda's work pictorial references are mostly of the first and the fourth type. As Curot observes, the first, while the most precise, leaves little scope for exploring the image. Its most intriguing aspect is its capacity for reducing the image, raw material of the film itself, to the level of any other object which can be bought and sold – or not sold – or used 'out of context' because of properties which have nothing to do with its rich meaning. In two of the sketches in *Jane B.* paintings are an object on the market. In one they sell well, and as such are directly translatable into money, and for Birkin's character, a venal art agent, this is indeed all they are useful for. In the 'Laurel and Hardy' sketch they do not sell – indeed, they apparently don't represent either – so are not translatable into money. In both cases they are of no help to the artist. Léotard-the-

15 At least not in the versions I have been able to see, but copies seem to vary. The sub-titles which Sandy Flitterman-Lewis analyses in *To Desire Differently* were cut from the version shown on British television in 1994!

successful-artist refuses to see his paintings as mere merchandise, and the agent shoots him. 'Maurel' cannot make a living from them at all. To treat paintings as objects of transaction seems in both cases to rob them of any value; they must be allowed to exist as representations or they are nothing.

The painting which Mona steals in *Sans toit ni loi* can only be inserted in the narrative in conjunction with the collection of postcards – another kind of still image – which she carries with her. The sequences of Mona with these portable images are comparable – in both cases one shot shows her crouching, on the left of the frame, looking down at the image which is dark and rather unclear, in front of her on the ground. The following shot shows the image in close-up, but it remains obscure: we do not get a clear idea either of her postcards or of her painting and so the images themselves are less important to the audience than the fact that Mona has some use for them. The painting appears to be a landscape, the postcards are both of places and of objects, but more than that we cannot see. The painting is damaged, and eventually Mona puts it on her fire. It has at least three possible functions for Mona. By analogy with the postcards it may reflect a need for images, which is incompletely shown like most aspects of her life (does her movement include travel into imaginary spaces? Does she feel a need for some form of representation? We do not know enough to say). By analogy with the silver spoons which she takes from Tante Lydie it may represent something saleable – her disappointment when she finds it damaged could easily be explained this way. Finally, its value is that of its canvas and wooden frame which burn acceptably.

These paintings are not well-known images, which is reasonable enough since their content is not at issue – although the tone of the paintings in the Léotard sketch (the work of Jean Dewasne) sets the colours, and the atmosphere, of the whole episode. In *L'Une chante, l'autre pas*, the pictures on Pomme's wall in the later sequences, after her return from Iran, are significant primarily for their content. They are twentieth-century portraits of women, remarkable for their frontal gaze and their air of calm reflection. They provide a still model against which to see Pomme who is in a state of flux, reassessing her life; at one point the camera cuts to a shot of one of these paintings which fills the frame, integrating the image fully into the narrative. The woman is hesitant, reflective, and she becomes a substitute for Pomme which is able to represent her state of mind in a *general* sense, freed from ties to any particular moment or stage in her thought-process. When Emilie in *Le Bonheur* contemplates a stamp showing reproductions of a Chagall, the painting-as-object becomes also a painting-representation. Chagall's wedding-scene where bride and groom float in the air backed by a cock and surrounded by an inverted angel and a goat/violin has an obvious thematic relevance to the film, but it is a complex image and the interpretation is not inevitable. Unlike most of the images of *Le Bonheur*, it is a representation of marriage which is not a cliché, and therefore not easily read. All the filmic images in *Le Bonheur* are visually simple – it is not only the picnic which is apparently complete and self-explanatory. Chagall's bizarre metaphors are disturbing as no single image in *Le Bonheur*, not even the suicide, can ever be. And yet it is reduced to a very everyday object performing a useful function within the framed and clichéd world, and reproduced so small that there is no need for it to be considered in its fullness, and to Emilie it is, once again, the object of a transaction.

At the other extreme, the pictorial reference slipped into a film so subtly that the viewer is not even obliged to see it is so common in Varda's work as to be almost a trademark. The choice of Silvia Monfort for *La Pointe Courte*; the Impressionist palette which Varda chose for *Le Bonheur*; the grotesque characters of *L'Opéra-Mouffe* irresistibly reminiscent of Bosch; in the later sequences of *L'Une chante, l'autre pas*, as Pomme reassesses her married life with Darius, a series of 'holy family' compositions; in *Kung-Fu Master*, an image of Birkin nursing her sick child lit and constructed like a Flemish interior; the barren earth-coloured landscapes of *Sans toit ni loi*, especially that of the credit sequence, constructed like the background landscapes of the more barren kind of Renaissance imagination. The emergence of Mona from the sea has been compared to Botticelli's *Birth of Venus* (Hayward

1990: 290-1),[16] although it certainly is not a reconstruction of the painting, quite the contrary.

The reasons for such references often depend, even more than in the use of paintings themselves, on subjective reactions to the images. For Varda (1994: 44), Piero della Francesca's women are notable for 'leur regard absent dans des visages ronds et calmes que prolongent des cous paisibles' ('their absent gaze in a round calm face prolonged by a tranquil neck'). This calm is what Varda sought in Monfort, but she could no doubt have expressed that without use of the reference. On the one hand, knowledge of Piero della Francesca seems to have helped Varda to formulate what she wanted (the use of the artistic image as a catalyst, as with significant objects and the glimpse/still, see above) – in which case it hardly matters whether the audience notices the reference. However, if we do, it enriches the film, adding a series of connotations which link the Monfort character to a 'type', to earlier centuries and to a world of established images that have acquired their own mythical charge. This rich background, which makes of the transitory filmic image something with a tradition and a significant structure, is common to all such references.

Sometimes the connotations may be more precise – although they are always open to the vagaries of different audience tastes. Thus the Impressionist palette in *Le Bonheur*. Varda has described her pleasure in 'playing with the colours', knowing that the transitoriness of film was the very effect that the Impressionists sought, with enormous difficulty, to fix in painting (Varda 1994: 62). Opposition between the fleeting and the apparently stable is central to *Le Bonheur*. One might also retain, however, the association of Impressionist painting with happy days, sunshine and holidays, or on the other hand a certain celebration of the conventional which has increased with the enormous popularity of reproductions of their work. More than any other artistic movement, Impressionism has become a cliché, so often seen that it is taken for granted. The Chagall mentioned above provides a striking contrast.

16 Hayward's article is rich in painterly references. See also the analysis of the introductory shot, p. 292.

The contrast between the permanent archetypes of painting and the fluctuations of real life lie behind the images of Pomme, Darius and her new baby in *L'Une chante, l'autre pas,* since the group which visually seems the picture of unity discusses how best to break up that unity. There are two such family groups, but the more strikingly referential is the later one, when the family is on the very brink of separation. It is hard to link to any *specific* painting, referring more to a corpus which has acquired its connotations through its familiarity as a whole, but the reference is inescapable. The preceding shot, of the baby's basket and a suit-case standing together as if exhibited in a museum or set up for a still life, is also very painterly although (to my knowledge) not referring to any specific picture. It serves to announce the imminence of Darius' departure and also to create a structured, artistic atmosphere in a film which is perhaps Varda's most 'realist'.

With the reference to Botticelli in *Sans toit ni loi,* something more complex is introduced. The reference in fact is really to the myth: 'il me semble qu'elle venait de la mer' ('I believe she came from the sea'), the narrator of the film says of Mona. That sentence, being impossible to take literally, sparks a set of connected ideas – it was Aphrodite/Venus who came from the sea, and that recalls the painting because its fame is such that myth and painting have grown together. This is not the case with all of Varda's references, but this one depends on it, as there are no visual clues. The image is in fact directly contrary to the painting. Venus is in the foreground of a very shallow-focus image – if one may call it that. Mona is in the far distance in deep focus. Venus is bright, Mona is dark. Venus is facing the viewer, displaying her nakedness to be gazed at: Mona is practically invisible (although she is being looked at, by Paolo and his friend who seem to see more clearly than we do) and certainly is not seeking the gaze. One could go on: Botticelli's Venus (like Cléo in *Cléo de 5 à 7*) is slim, blonde and pristine – an over-used ideal of female beauty now if not when she was painted; Mona is smelly, dark and of undefinable shape. Venus, again like Cléo, is surrounded by a throng of subsidiary figures whose function is to *present* her as a spectacle; Mona is alone, and the people who are asked to present her to the narrator and the spectator will fail at the task. She is, in other words, an anti-Aphrodite. The first image of her establishes this at a glance: what Venus is is what Mona is not, and most of all she is not presented to the gaze, we have to catch fleeting voyeuristic glimpses.

The most extended and complex of Varda's artistic references, however, must be the sequences in *Jane B.* reconstructing, and analysing, a portrait based on a composite of Titian and Goya. *Jane B.* is filled with paintings. It is itself compared to a portrait in an early sequence. In the course of its intricately combined and very various threads Jane will appear as an art dealer, surrounded by abstract paintings and by reproductions of all art history; she will riffle through a book of reproductions which contains an Arcimboldo, a Delvaux, a Bosch, a Dali, and then reproduce the Dali in another *tableau vivant*. But the central painting-metaphor is provided by the play which, in the course of four sequences, Varda makes with a *tableau vivant*, a coherent combination of the *Venus d'Urbino* (Titian), Goya's *Majas*, clothed and naked, and an anonymous French painting entitled *Dame à sa toilette*. Frank Curot's article (1991b) provides a careful analysis of the way in which Varda deconstructs the picture in the context of a discussion of the hidden mechanisms of representation. Jane takes the role of the servant and the technicians and camera appear in the film, either in immediately subsequent shots, or in the case of the final credit sequence within the same image. Surprisingly, although Curot notes that the technicians usually appear in mirrors, he does not connect this with the appearance of the painter in a mirror in many paintings of the period (for the possible significance of this see Chapter 4).

These picture-sequences give the film its frame. Varda uses them to explore the contrast between foreground and background, and also to consider the status of female representation and the paradox which she elsewhere reveals in Jane, the simultaneous desire to be seen and to be anonymous. The contradictions of that simultaneous desire are acted out by the oscillation in the roles Jane takes in the picture. The first and the last sequences of the film have Jane set in a reproduction of the background scene only, where she is dressed as the young servant. However, she is sitting with her face to the camera (while the servant is always seen from the back) and she speaks as Jane Birkin. At this point the artistic reference is, as Sandy Flitterman-Lewis (1993: 313) observes, not entirely clear, and its effect is general and atmospheric. It presents the actress in a costume – throughout the film she will try a series of costumes and personae – and we read the image as one that is constructed for the viewer (as of course all Varda's images are, but here we cannot miss the point; this is not Jane as she is but a representation). There is an incongruity between image and monologue: we see a composed Renaissance woman and hear her describing how she got drunk and vomited in her hotel room on her thirtieth birthday. This too reminds the viewer that a portrait is a composition which has a calm not necessarily reflecting the anguished emotions of life.

In the second picture-sequence the emphasis has changed. As Varda's voice-over proposes to paint a portrait in the manner of Titian or Goya, we see the whole composition. In the background is the young servant, now in the form she has in Titian's painting, her back to the viewer and bent over a chest. Jane lies in the foreground, displayed to the camera in the clothes of Goya's *Maja*. The composite picture allows women to be portrayed both in foreground and background, but it is clear who is the subject of the painting, the one we are meant to look at. However, the camera leaves her, for a brief close-up of the window at the back and the head of the servant girl. When it returns to the full composition, Jane has been transformed into the *Maja desnuda*, even more displayed to the camera which then moves slowly up her body from toes to eyes in an intimate, caressing tracking-shot. We may recognise this profoundly intimate way of filming the body from *Documenteur* and will find it again in *Jacquot de Nantes*. Such intimacy is a response to the implied invitation of the painting. The *Maja desnuda*, looking at the viewer with her arms thrown behind her head, is not merely displayed, she is displaying herself; not merely offered to the gaze but inviting it. And yet the close look is singularly uninformative – seen in such close range Jane's body becomes anonymous, at times even unidentifiable. If as Flitterman-Lewis (1993: 315) says this is the woman's body considered as a landscape, it is a landscape in which one sometimes needs landmarks – the nipple, the mouth – to work out where the camera is. The music on the sound-track also offers no clue, instead acting as a kind of auditory frame, presenting the woman to the gaze.

From this sequence the camera cuts abruptly to a close-up of Philippe Léotard's face, in his role as the exploited painter in his sketch with Jane, accusing her violently: 'You only think about money'. The contrast of atmosphere is startling and salutary, the first explicit reminder that such self-display as the Maja's goes with wealth and privilege. Within this scene the initial painting reappears, catching the painter's attention as he leafs through his art-books looking for his misplaced money. He draws attention to the servants in the background, a device common to several portraits. Varda shows a montage of three; we are invited to concentrate on the background, and in the background the woman working, with only her back – or, at most, an undistinguished profile – visible.

After a long sequence of images and aspects of Jane have been tried, considered, and sometimes rejected, the film returns to the painting. Jane is once again the servant, but in close-up, facing the camera: 'on a glissé' she says 'du gros-plan à l'arrière plan' ('we have slipped from the close-up to the background'). The housekeeper and the maid are now shown in close-up, in a way which equates them to the foreground of the portrait when the camera tracks from the face of the housekeeper to a painting on the wall (here *Dame à sa toilette*): the heads are at much the same scale. Varda 'dramatis[e] le conflit latent que peut suggérer le tableau' (Curot 1991b: 165) ('dramatises the latent conflict which the picture seems to suggest') between mistress and servants, and it is important that she dramatises it in terms of the right to be seen. The two female servants criticise their mistress: 'la dame de ces lieux est de toutes les humaines, l'humaine la moins humaine' ('The lady of this place is of all humans, the most inhuman human'), says Jane as the maid, and the housekeeper agrees: 'she has everything' including 'the right to live naked, voluptuous, idle'. At this point the camera tracks from housekeeper to the naked close-up of the 'lady' of the Fontainebleau portrait, displaying her nakedness in front of her obscure – and clothed – servant.

Jane, too, as Varda has previously pointed out in conversation with her, has the right to be seen, through the privileges of stardom; but, paradoxically, she occasionally rejects it, claiming instead the desire to be anonymous – or rather, to be seen to be anonymous, to have a feature-film made of her in her everyday clothes. In having her play the part first of mistress, then of maid, in a portrait taken from a rigidly class-structured world, Varda dramatises this conflict. Jane-the-maid expresses towards the lady of the portrait the same ambivalence as Jane Birkin herself feels towards her star-image. On the one hand she reviles it – inhuman, over-privileged, and pretending to a status of universal beauty which excludes others. 'Elle croit dérober la beauté du ciel avec ses nichons' ('she thinks she's the owner of heaven's beauty with her tits'). On the other hand she desires it; the maid dresses up in her mistress's clothes. Thus disguised, she reads a poem while a voice-off (her own?) sings: both music and poem are of the period, and yet the suggestive words and the music may relate to Birkin's first introduction to stardom, previously shown in the film, as a singer with Serge Gainsbourg.

She is called to order by the housekeeper – she is dressed in a costume not hers, and out of place. The maid returns to obscurity and turns her back to the camera, before in the last sequence letting loose a swarm of flies (which crawl out of her hands like the ants in the famous Surrealist film-image from *Un chien andalou*) to cover the naked foreground figure and, as the camera tracks backwards, the whole composition. In this last appearance of the whole composition, the naked Maja is played by an extra, but an extra chosen to look as like Jane as possible. The maid thus expresses her jealousy and hatred of her own double, in the name, not of the actual greater perfection of her body (the extra in question notably has the same flat chest as Jane) but of the right she has to display it and make claims for it.

In the final sequence as in the first Jane, seated facing the camera in the maid's costume, is talking about herself, Jane. The intervening examination of the structure of the picture and its implications has, however, added to the meaning. The subject of the film-portrait has, it would seem, faced a choice between the roles of mistress or of maid. Birkin's contradictory desire to be a star and to be an average woman is not easy to resolve. The framing sequences now take on the appearance of a choice, expressed metaphorically in terms of the roles provided in the painting. She has chosen the maid rather than the mistress, but she has chosen to allow the maid to be the subject of the painting, looking out as if inviting the gaze but demanding attention not by the offered beauty of the body – exemplary or not – but through what she says, her attitude to life.

Thus it seems to me that the politics of the painting are to be interpreted, as is so much else in the film to which we will return in Chapter 4, in terms of Varda's continuing interest in the representation of women and their relation to the gaze. The Renaissance portrait implies a desire for the gaze; the woman puts herself on show – but as a stereotypical figure who finally reveals nothing of herself. The only other alternative offered in the portrait is a background role, in context but fleeing the gaze, turning the back on it. There is a search throughout the film for ways to reconcile the two, as there is also for a way to reconcile the person and the role, the 'je' (I) and the 'jeu' (game) as Gainsbourg's song says. The framing image illustrates a form of synthesis: the maid is given the right to the gaze, the person speaks in the costume of the role.

The extended consideration given to this is surely merited by the importance of the sequence to the film. Apart from *Mur Murs* it is the most extended essay devoted to the art-image which Varda has made, and it illustrates many of the ways in which she uses art for social connotation and to enquire into representation, especially the representation of women. The images in *Mur Murs*, much more explicitly intended as social comment, will be discussed in the next chapter.

The cliché and the myth

Apart from the recognisable artistic image, Varda also uses more diffuse cultural images in her work, almost always for purposes of deconstruction. We have already touched on this subject, which involves apparently instantly readable images which we referred to earlier in the chapter as clichés. Not surprisingly they are not entirely unconnected with the art-image, which was often their earliest medium. Thus the family group formed by Pomme, Darius and their child, which we discussed above in terms of the Holy Family, is also, more simply if less richly, 'the Family'.

Le Bonheur is of all Varda's films the one most concerned with such images. It is made up of a sequence of scenes all of which are carefully structured to be apparently instantly understandable. We see man, woman and children picnicking in an idyllic landscape, or man and woman making love, or family at the window of their house, or man (or woman) at work in different environments. With the single exception of the discovery of Thérèse's body, every image from the film, taken singly, could be read as an epitome of stable happiness. It is the way in which they are linked, the progression between them, which dislocates the apparent stability, reconstructing the image of the beginning, at the end, but with a different character substituted. The process is violent in proportion to the amount which the spectator has invested in the cliché. A cliché, as Pascal Bonitzer has suggested, is essentially an image to be *consumed*:

> Entre le photogramme et le cliché, entre l'image quelconque comme instant quelconque de la durée, ou photo instantanée, et l'image de masse comme cliché, il y a une différence qui est celle de la production à la consommation, mais un lien qui se déduit de la conversion automatique de l'image produite en image consommée. On n'appelle pas pour rien les clichés des tartes à la crème ... la preuve de la tarte à la crème, c'est que quelqu'un la reçoit sur la figure. Elle se prouve en éclatant, en s'étalant, en s'émiettant, en dégoulinant.[17] (Bonitzer 1987: 27–8)

17 'Between the still and the cliché, between the random image taken as a moment in time, or snapshot, and the mass image, the cliché, there is a difference which is that between production and consumption, but a link which can be followed

The clichés of *Le Bonheur* burst over the spectator's face, and by the time we see them reconstituted we are wary.

Le Bonheur is in some ways an exception among Varda's films in that these clichés are not attached to any subjectivity. Indeed they are radically detached from any locatable source, either the characters in the film or the film-maker. *Le Bonheur* is simply a sequence of images presented for the viewer, who observes their appearance, and, gradually, the ways in which their content fits together to reveal unexpected patterns; or at least patterns that do not fit the messages of Happiness in Work, Happiness in Conjugal Love and so on that the images denote. There is no authorial voice in this process. Because of this Varda was criticised – at the time and later – for approving François; she has always denied this and indeed it is hard to see how one can read the film this way, as François as much as the two women is merely a puppet in the hands of the cliché. The final resolution is not his choice, but simply a fact which he accepts. It is the all-powerful cliché which has reproduced itself, as if the characters, so long as they are alive, have no choice but to reconstitute the same patterns. Varda considered the film to be an examination of the nature of happiness, and especially of the 'aptitude' which certain people (François) have for attaining and retaining it. That aptitude seems to pass through living entirely in the present and in the appearance, but the film largely accepts – or takes as given – that the 'happiness' in question *does* amount to the preservation of the cliché. The one attempt to introduce – only on sound-track – an alternative image leads to tragedy. Thérèse has to disappear in order to avoid the appearance of an idyllic family image containing two women, and she does so unhesitatingly and discreetly. Since there is no subjectivity (unless we are seeing through François's eyes when we see this sequence of sunny images) there is no sense of a decision on her part, very little even of pain. Emilie equally seems to make no decisions, replacing

---

through the automatic conversion of image produced into image consumed. Clichés are not called "tartes à la crème" [custard pies, a French idiom for clichés] for nothing: the proof of the custard pie is that someone gets it in the face. It proves itself by bursting, spreading, crumbling, dripping.'

Thérèse as if inevitably and reconstituting the family group.

The only moment when the characters become more than figures in the image is when, for one reason or another, they are set in opposition to the image and obliged to conceive of another one. Since this only occurs between François and Thérèse, Emilie never becomes more than a prop. When François puts forward the possibility of happiness with both Thérèse and Emilie, he evokes a new image, but it never materialises and on its failure he returns effortlessly to the old image with a new partner. Thérèse – whose very work involves the perpetuation of the Image of Marriage, since she designs wedding dresses – simply retires from the scene rather than step out of the sequence. Emilie is never challenged by the possibility of an unusual pattern; but when the moment comes to reconstitute the usual one, she does so as if necessarily, and, again, with no hint of subjectivity or reaction to what has gone before.

Thus *Le Bonheur* seems to end with the conclusion that the necessary component of happiness is the appearance of happiness, which is itself entirely conventional and coded into a number of stock situations: 'L'apparence du bonheur, c'est aussi le Bonheur' (Varda 1965: 48) ('The appearance of happiness is also happiness'). *Le Bonheur* is undoubtedly a very clever film, and it is almost perfectly constructed, but it is most untypical of Varda's work in that it totally ignores any desire on the part of characters or film-maker, presenting a practically mechanistic universe dedicated to re-creating a few unvarying images from a set of human chesspieces. Despite – or because of – its sunniness (and despite Varda's youth at the time and apparently cheerful approach), it is a very chilly film; I admit that I find it hard to like, but this is perhaps a gauge of its success in exploring the power of the image above and beyond any individual perception, endorsement or refusal of it.

Along with cliché and art-image, we should mention Varda's use of mythology, a constant, and enigmatic, element of her work. Still images are abstracted from time, and as such, they can easily become representative of a very large swathe of general ideas to which time and context may seem to be irrelevant. In the discussion of art-images, we are also dealing with images which have been presented to large numbers of people, and have therefore become a collective representation. In other words, such images are naturally related to the myth. This is true to some extent of photographs, and we see this process in action in *L'Une chante, l'autre pas*, when Jérôme expounds on how Pomme represents the essence of woman as he tries to find a satisfactory pose for her. It is even more clearly true of paintings, especially fifteenth- and sixteenth-century paintings, many of which announce themselves as representations of classical myths. Jane Birkin as the Venus d'Urbino's servant girl reveals how a woman has been transformed into a goddess. All direct comparisons of a character with a painting evoke the potential which the character has for representation, for becoming a myth, at the cost, however, of losing her (it is usually her) position in time and history, her social identity.

This extends to the references which recur throughout the films to myth even when there is no obvious iconography attached, as in the connection between Mona the woman from the sea and Aphrodite. There are other examples in *Sans toit ni loi*: the credit sequence, for example, labels Mona's boyfriend David 'the wandering Jew'. *Jane B.* is filled with mythical characters whose roles Jane is asked to act out, sometimes with reference to existing images, sometimes not. In the documentary *Mur Murs*, one of the most striking murals is a modern version of the fall of Icarus and Varda at first intended to use this as the title of the film. *Ulysse* of course evokes mythology by its title, and Varda's commentary weaves the story into her explanations. Although the still image which has immortalised Ulysse to Varda (plate 7) has very little to do with the myth, it *would* in fact be possible to see it as an illustration of an episode, and the dead goat provides a suitably mysterious Mediterranean ambience.

Still images of all kinds are thus frequently associated explicitly with mythology. Their role in the films is an extension of that which Bernard Bastide (1991: 82) identified as the function of myth: 'A côté de son rôle de simple moteur d'une inspiration, la mythologie retrouve ici sa fonction originelle: fournir des modèles pour la conduite humaine, nous inciter à réfléchir à quelques questions essentielles: la mort, la liberté, la passion.'[18] As Barthes recognised in his study of the modern myth, the function of a mythological model is to negate time and context and to present itself as universal. Varda's mythological references, however, as one might expect, are not to be simply accepted: the characters fit them only up to a certain point, if at all. In *Sans toit ni loi* and in *Ulysse* , the mythological reference is given by the voice-over of the film-maker/narrator. The attraction of the story is given as personal: the words 'Mythologies vous me faîtes rêver', (Mythology you make me dream), used by Bastide as the title for his article, are spoken by Varda-the-image-maker in *Ulysse* , and in *Sans toit ni loi* the narrator introduces her reference with 'it seems to me'. The spectator can therefore take them or leave them, and there is much in the films which suggests that perhaps they should be left, since their living models diverge from them. Earlier in *Ulysse* , in fact, the same voice-over rejects all myths as ways of interpreting the goat.

And yet such image-interpretations can be attractive for their own sake, and Varda does not necessarily criticise this, especially with regard to mythology proper. Her voice-over, after all, valorises the stories, and emphasises not only their links with the image, but also their attractiveness. The narrator's words in *Sans toit ni loi* make us aware that she has placed her subject within a pre-existing frame of reference of her own, deciding that she shall be mysterious, powerful and desirable. Certainly, since this is apparently documentary, we might argue that she should be 'neutral', but without mystery and desirability, where is the impulse for the narrator to start the enquiry, or for the spectator to follow it?

The attraction of the myth is also a lure in *Ulysse* . There is so much that is unexplained, both in the photograph and, almost by definition, in the myth, that the tenuous connection between image and title produces curiosity. In fact, the explanation hinges

18 'Besides its role as a mere engine of inspiration, mythology here recovers its original function: to provide models of human behaviour, to incite us to reflect on essential questions: death, liberty, passion.'

on something quite different, but the association remains. At the end of the film it is recognised, described (the voice-over mentions several aspects of the story of Ulysses, some of them easily associable with the picture), but never explained. Its function is to make the spectator, as well as the narrator, dream, by suggesting other possible meanings which are never going to be confirmed.

The myth in fact provides Varda with an anti-cliché – a reference which is generally recognisable but which is extremely hard to read. It does not break down on investigation, as the cliché does, but when used (as it always is) as an approach to under-standing something more concrete – be it a tramp-woman or a photograph – it is useless as a source for a fixed meaning. All it does is raise more questions and possibilities. It is a creative approach for the spectator, especially in films which – like many of those of the 1980s, and certainly *Ulysse* , *Sans toit ni loi* and *Jane B.*, also rich in mythological references – are structured as investigations rather than narratives. To conclude with a myth is not to conclude: the spectator can follow the connotations she or he chooses, and any significance which is especially appealing will attach itself to the images which Varda has provided. Thus the myth's ambiguity as a model of human behaviour is a condition of its other function, as source of inspiration. Unlike the cliché, which is not ambiguous and is therefore suspect, or even the art-image which sometimes has to be deconstructed in order to reveal its ambiguity, the myth is not a fixed model so much as a guarantee of potential significance. Its danger comes in attaching it to one image. When Aphrodite becomes *The Birth of Venus*, and nothing else, the myth becomes a cliché, when it is in fact a complex knot of possible meaning which part of Varda's work is concerned to restore to its full power.

The photo

The still photo, when it appears in Varda's films, appears, inevi-tably, as an object, and quite frequently as a collection of objects. Mona amasses postcards, so do the women in *L'Une chante, l'autre pas*. In this latter film Jérôme displays a collection of photographs, and Pomme collects photos of her past life. Jane Birkin decorates her walls with photos of 'me as a baby, my babies, everyone as a baby', she also has childhood photographs and a number of publicity shots of herself. The daguerreotypes, although not real photographs, follow the plural pattern – the different couples are 'fixed' one after the other in a series. Such sets of still images derive at least some of their meaning from their number and relationship to each other. It seems a fitting way in which to introduce the still photograph into a film, which is after all a number of still images in temporal series. Sets of photographs such as Jane's babies or Jérôme's sad women (a series taken by Varda herself to suit the needs of the film) insert into the time-series of the film another possible link between images, formal and thematic. Clearly, the mass presence of a particular kind of image may raise again the problem of the cliché, the image designed for mass-consumption. Photographs in Varda's films are not exactly repeated; it is the theme rather than the image which appears *en masse*, but – in the case notably of Jérôme's photos – it is the sheer number of similar representations which arouses a query. It is as if Jérôme is trying to demonstrate his version of truth by the weight of numbers of examples.

A photograph, of course, also represents a 'frozen instant' of time, preserved when the moving world of the film (in a narrative) or of the life of the people concerned has moved on. The effect of these fossilised relics of the past – the only visible trace which remains of that time – on the inhabitants of a moving present is explored in several of the films. A shot of Jane Birkin standing in front of an enlarged portrait of herself as a child places together two Janes, one of which can now only exist as a still image. In narrative films particularly this function of photographs is linked to a sense of loss and lack. After Pomme's husband Darius and her first child have returned to Iran without her, Pomme looks at photographs of two, or three, of them together; in the following shot she gazes out tearfully at the camera. We understand that, like Yolande in *Sans toit ni loi* considering her image of Mona and David (plate 4), Pomme when looking at the camera is gazing at an image in her mind, and her sadness shows that she feels a sense of loss: unlike Yolande, however, she holds the image physically in her hand, as tangible proof that what she now lacks was once part of her life. Tante Lydie's photographs in *Sans toit ni loi* also represent an irretrievable, fixed past, part of the accumulation of objects around Lydie who seems to be beyond any further development in the present. Mona's arrival breaks up this fossilised existence, and hurls Lydie into the present – she sleeps in the carefully preserved bedroom, asks Lydie about the photographs (thereby reducing them to objects to be handled, explained and commented on), and then brushes them aside as she and the old lady settle down with the cognac. The effect seems to be salutary, but it is really destructive, since as soon as Lydie shows a sign of detaching herself from her vegetative life and interacting with her surroundings, Jean-Pierre and Eliane seize on the evidence of her 'senility' to put her in a home.

Sometimes the photograph becomes emblematic of the past not only through its subject but by its very appearance. Thus the *idea* of the daguerreotype, recognisable by its artificial pose even when it is simply a reconstruction, is a metaphor for the kind of society which Varda describes in the rue Daguerre, which has not developed at the same pace as 'the world outside', or even the other end of the street. If these people were to be photographed, it is this style of image which would be appropriate.

A similar stylistic connotation is obtained by several montages of postcards in *L'Une chante, l'autre pas*. The presence of the cards is easily explained, since the women communicate mostly in this brief way. However, several of the images on these montages are much too old-fashioned credibly to represent their correspondence. In the first and most important case, three consecutive groups of images are shown mounted as if on display boards, as Varda's voice explains the nature of the pen-friendship which develops between Suzanne and Pomme. The first group of images are largely of Paris (where Pomme is), the third of Hyères (Suzanne's home). These images are varied, although all are recognisable postcards, and particularly there are one or two on each board which are clearly of pre-war style. The intermediate group is of three cards, with the names of Suzanne and Pomme written on the backing mount. These are montages of dried flowers, more reminiscent of the 1870s than the 1970s. Perhaps Varda is illustrating in this way the persistence of the need for female friendship, which was catered for by the production of such cards. Despite their involvement in new and exciting developments through the women's movement, Pomme and Suzanne are also carrying on a tradition.

A montage of postcards appears once again as the image which closes the Iranian episode. This time there is no commentary: the shot follows Pomme's departure to have her baby in England, and remains silently on screen for a short time. As before, the images are of mixed periods, but all of Iran: they include a nineteenth-century photograph of a veiled woman, and a very twentieth-century one which shows a man's head in profile as he walks in front of a modern glass building. The image here has the effect of a summary of Pomme's Iranian excursion, but the link with Suzanne is less obvious – at this point, Pomme is no longer communicating by postcard with her, but about to rejoin her. It is perhaps another tradition which is here at issue; that of the Western vision of the exotic East. It is a tradition in which Pomme has implicated herself, as she admits (standing in front of an elegant building with Darius during this episode, Pomme in voice-off reflects that 'she feels as if she is in a postcard') and as Darius will later turn into an accusation: 'Mademoiselle voit un étranger qui lui plaît, alors allons-y: l'exotisme, le grand voyage, le grand jeu.'[19] Pomme on the other hand refuses to return to Iran because 'false images, clichés ... oh no, that's over'. The last we actually see of Iran, in fact, is a tracking-shot from right to left ('against the grain', therefore) across an unremarkable and shabby housing estate, which contrasts strongly with the beautiful, if highly stylised images which have previously illustrated Pomme's and Darius' life there.

Thus through the postcard – an image designed for communication, for mass-production and mass-consumption, we

19 'Mademoiselle sees a foreigner she likes, so, let's go: exoticism, foreign travel, the great game.'

rejoin once more the issue of the cliché. The existence of postcards from many periods illustrates that the cliché has a temporal existence of its own. Contact with the moving reality which they represent may destroy them for any individual consumer (as Pomme's false images of Iran are destroyed) but the images persist.

The danger of such clichés, as *Le Bonheur* showed, lies in their apparent simplicity – they are easy to read, their meaning is obvious. A picture-postcard vision of a place, such as Pomme starts out with in Iran, similarly implies that the country is seen as easy to interpret, because pre-existing readings are stamped on it arbitrarily. Such instant reading could be seen as a form of instant possession, and Jean-Luc Godard, in *Les Carabiniers*, used the postcard famously to illustrate this. Godard's two protagonists return from war laden with postcard images of objects and landmarks, which they leaf through and lay out proudly, claiming ownership of all the objects represented in the name of the cards and of pre-war propaganda which had promised them 'possession of occupied country'. This famous sequence is mentioned here because of its conceptual similarity to the enigmatic shot in *Sans toit ni loi*, where Mona lays out a series of postcards on a wall. I cannot say whether the reference is conscious, but Varda and Godard frequently show similar preoccupations in their treatment of the still image. Mona, defined by her radical lack of possessions, keeps this set of images for no apparent reason and she seems to lay them out for consolation, but unlike the images in Godard's film their subjects are not clear and Mona makes no claims for them. If they do represent symbolic possession, it remains symbolic. Of all Varda's films, *Sans toit ni loi* is perhaps the one which goes furthest in refusing instant understanding; Mona's is by definition an image which cannot be seized, at least not without fatally distorting it. Her apparent fondness for these image-objects is therefore rather startling, and it is maybe in this context that they should be read.

This chapter has moved from general remarks on Varda's approach to film-form to a detailed analysis of the importance of the construction and significance of single images and their relationship to the movement of the film. In the following chapters we will look at a number of themes which Varda's work treats in detail. Inevitably, we will concentrate in each chapter on the films most intensely concerned with the subject at hand. If this chapter has ranged widely from film to film, perhaps at the expense of detailed analysis, this is because the formal questions treated are, obviously, not simply frequent but omnipresent in her work, and it is through the film-form (and only through this) that it is possible to analyse the themes to which we will now turn.

References

Barthes, Roland (1980) *La Chambre claire*, Paris, Gallimard Seuil

Bastide, Bernard (1991) '"Mythologies, me vous faites rêver", ou mythes cachés, mythes dévoilés dans l'œuvre d'Agnès Varda', in *Etudes Cinématographiques: Agnès Varda*, Paris, Lettres modernes, pp. 71–83

Bergala, Alain (1982) 'Agnès Varda joue et gagne', *Cahiers du Cinéma*, no. 340, October, pp. VII–VIII

Bonitzer, Pascal (1987) *Peinture et cinéma: décadrages*, Paris, Cahiers du cinéma/ Etoile

Bordwell, David and Thompson, Kristin (1993) *Film Art: An Introduction*, 4th edition, New York, McGraw Hill

Breton, André (1992) *Œuvres complètes II*, Paris, Gallimard Pléiade

Curot, Frank (1991a) 'L'Ecriture de *La Point courte*', in *Etudes Cinématographiques: Agnès Varda*, Paris, Lettres modernes, pp. 85–99

Curot, Frank (1991b) 'Références picturales et style filmique dans *Jane B. par Agnès V.*', in *Etudes Cinématographies: Agnés Varda*, Paris, Lettres modernes, pp. 155–72

Flitterman-Lewis, Sandy (1993) 'Magic and wisdom in two portraits by Agnès Varda: *Kung-Fu Master* and *Jane B. par Agnès V.*', *Screen*, 34:4. winter, pp. 302–20

Flitterman-Lewis, Sandy (1996) *To Desire Differently*, New York, Columbia UP

Hayward, Susan (1990) 'Beyond the gaze and into *femme-filmécriture*: Agnès Varda's *Sans toit ni loi*', in S. Hayward and G. Vincendeau (eds), *French Film, Texts and Contexts*, London, Routledge, pp. 285–96

Prédal, René (1991) 'Agnès Varda: une œuvre en marge du cinéma français', in *Etudes Cinématographiques: Agnés Varda*, Paris, Lettres modernes, pp. 13–39

Varda, Agnès (1994) *Varda par Agnès*, Paris, Cahiers du Cinéma

Varda, Agnès (1961) 'Agnès Varda', interview with Jean Michaud and Raymond Bellour, *Cinéma 61*, no. 60, October, pp. 4–20

Varda, Agnès(1965) 'La Grâce laïque', interview with Jean-André Fieschi and Claude Ollier, *Cahiers du Cinéma*, no. 165, April, pp. 42–50

1 The image of family harmony (*Le Bonheur*, 1964)

2 The baker and his wife with the symbol of their trade (*Daguerréotypes*, 1975)

3 To gaze beyond the camera, I: Emilie (Sabine Mamou) in her office (*Documenteur*, 1981)

4 To gaze beyond the camera, II: Yolande (Yolande Moreau) recalls her first sight of Mona (*Sans toit ni loi*, 1985)

5 Cléo (Corinne Marchand) in the hat-shop, between the mirrors (*Cléo de 5 à 7*, 1961)

6 The start of the rehearsal of 'Sans toi' (*Cléo de 5 à 7*, 1961). Note the strong dividing-line between Cléo and her listeners (Dominique Davray, Michel Legrand, Serge Korber); she seems already to be in a different space

7 Man, boy and goat – the photo at the heart of the film (*Ulysse*, 1982)

8 An old-fashioned framed mirror shows Varda the film-maker facing her subject, Jane Birkin (*Jane B. par Agnès V.*, 1987)

9 On the set of *Jacquot de Nantes* (1990). Demy (far right) and the three actors (Philippe Maron, Edouard Joubeaud, Laurent Monnier) who play him at different ages. Varda is standing beside the camera

10 Jacquot (Philippe Maron) and his brother Yvon (Clément Delaroche) prepare for the first performance of 'Cendrillon' (*Jacquot de Nantes*, 1990)

11 Angels from the cemetery are used by Jacquot (Philippe Maron) to decorate a puppet theatre (*Jacquot de Nantes*, 1990)

3

People and places

The sense of place is a constant throughout Varda's films. At different times she has explored the South of France and the châteaux of the Loire Valley, the streets of Paris or of Los Angeles. Even where the surroundings seem least important (for example, in *L'Une chante, l'autre pas*) passages of the film rejoin the lyrical engagement with place which is elsewhere so noticeable. Varda believes that place has a profound effect on character and perception, and this was a guiding principle in her work as far back as 1961: 'Je crois que les gens sont faits des endroits non seulement où ils ont été élevés, mais qu'ils aiment, je crois que le décor nous habite, nous dirige [...] en comprenant les gens on comprend mieux les lieux, en comprenant les lieux on comprend mieux les gens'[1] (Varda 1961: 14, 20). One strand of Varda's film-making consists in presenting the subjectivity of a principal character through her perceptions of her surroundings: this is the procedure adopted in *L'Opéra-Mouffe* and *Cléo de 5 à 7*, both films which could be described as 'the experience of being a woman in Paris' and, much later, in *Documenteur*, 'the experience of being a woman in Los Angeles'. If this is a disturbing experience, this reflects the film-maker's attitude to the capital at the time as well as her understanding of the protagonists' situations. 'Qu'évoquait

---

1 'I believe that people are made not only of the places where they were brought up, but of those that they love, I believe that the environment [le décor] lives in us, directs us [...] By understanding people you understand places better, by understanding places you understand people better.'

pour moi Paris? Une peur diffuse de la grande ville et de ses dangers, de s'y perdre seule et incomprise, voire bousculée',[2] she said of her approach to *Cléo*, in 1961 (Varda 1994: 48). Indeed, the subject of *Cléo* was in part decided on because the film had to be made in Paris, and Paris for Varda meant anxiety. Her pet project at the time, *Le Mélangite*, which was never made, was also structured, according to her contemporary description, in part on a perception of places. The protagonist is 'divided' (played by five different actors), according to contradictory elements of his character or his life. Among the terms of this division are his feelings for Sète (the town of *La Pointe Courte*) and Venice, and it is this division which Varda expands on most often when she talks about the film, in 1961 as in 1994 (Varda 1961: 13–14; 1994: 122).

In fact, all Varda's work up to *Le Bonheur* is posited on the relationship between protagonists and place, or, in the case of the two documentaries which she made for the Office Nationale du Tourisme, between film-maker and place. These were made to order, and the subject was chosen by the Office: Varda professed to dislike both the Loire châteaux and the holiday resorts of the Côte d'Azur, and could only find the inspiration to make the films by displacing the subject-matter to deal with her own reactions, which were critical in the first instance. The most important early film in this context is surely *La Pointe Courte*. The village of La Pointe Courte is here the *primary* subject; individual protagonists are secondary and the film approaches them almost entirely through their reactions to the place. *La Pointe Courte* does contain the seeds of the wandering subjective explorations which were to succeed it, but the fishing community and its surroundings are a centre in their own right, and much more than a series of metaphors for the couple's problems. The definition of the place is inescapably a human one. La Pointe Courte is primarily a community, and the physical surroundings which are important to the film are those which belong to the community – boats, nets, fishing implements and so on.

Although the spirit of the place where she is working remained

2 'What did Paris evoke for me? A vague fear of the big city and its dangers, of getting lost in it alone and misunderstood, or even brushed aside.'

important to Varda throughout the 1960s, her major films after *Le Bonheur* turned more towards smaller spaces and smaller groups, with the exception of a little-seen documentary, *Salut les Cubains* (1963), the fruit of a photographic expedition to Cuba. In 1974, however, she returned to the description of a community in its home-place at feature-film length with *Daguerréotypes*, this time a documentary. Although Varda is present in the film here (she is not, at least not explicitly, in *La Pointe Courte*), *Daguerréotypes* like *La Pointe Courte* is concerned with the way in which the place lives through, and in the minds of, all its inhabitants – of whom, of course, Varda is one.

In the films made in the early 1980s in Los Angeles the possibilities of a different relationship to place are explored. The film-maker in Los Angeles is no longer in her own community, and the authorial position in both *Mur Murs* and *Documenteur* is that of an outsider, but nonetheless both films are imbued with the sense of place. In *Mur Murs*, there is a documentary focus, the mural paintings which caught Varda's artistic eye. The film-maker treats the murals, however, not as exercises in form and colour or even iconography, but as clues to the functioning of the community which they overlook and which they also express. In *Documenteur* the place is seen through the private world of a lonely and preoccupied French woman living in this strange town with her small son, but her preoccupation does not cut her off from her surroundings, instead she uses the surroundings to find expression for her preoccupation, and thus Los Angeles becomes literally the matter of which the film is made.

This chapter will look at these films in some detail.

La Pointe Courte (1954)

La Pointe Courte is the name of a *quartier* of Sète, the fishing port on the Mediterranean coast where Varda grew up. *La Pointe Courte*, the film, has two distinct strands, which alternate in a series of nine sequences. One strand concerns all of La Pointe Courte and its community; the other only two people, a young man from the village and his Parisian wife (Philippe Noiret and Sylvia Monfort), visiting for the first time the place where her husband grew up. These two strands are so very different from each other that it has been said that *La Pointe Courte* consists of two films joined together; and it is perhaps tempting, in analysing the film, to concentrate on the coherent, concentrated, and very subtly filmed story of the couple. La Pointe Courte, however, is very much more than a background to the personal story, as the title of the film should make clear. To Varda the place was the central theme of the film, a theme experienced very intensely: 'je peux voir les lieux comme dans *La Pointe Courte* avec une telle force d'amour, complètement avalés enfin, sans humour'[3] (Varda 1961: 5). Not only are the two strands of equal importance, but the village is the central theme of both of them; they simply present different ways of relating to it, two alternative portraits of a place which, despite what the young husband says to his wife on her arrival, would probably appear to metropolitan audiences as 'picturesque' or even 'exotic'. The 'Pointe Courte' strand has a story-line bound up in the working life of the village, while the story of the young couple hinges on the husband's intense feelings for a place which is alien to his wife. Despite her best efforts, this precipitates a crisis in their relationship. He feels she is slipping away from him, she feels unable to penetrate his world. Resolution of the problem depends on the woman's ability to respect the importance of this new element in the husband she had been convinced she knew, and on his willingness in turn to recognise her difficulties with a world which to him is quite natural. Their reconciliation (which does come) therefore hinges on their reconciliation with La Pointe Courte.

Of the film's nine sequences, the two strands account for four each, while one – the *joutes* – is important to both stories and fits coherently into both filmic schemas. However, it is the Pointe Courte series which begins and ends the film. After participating

---

3 'I can see places, like in *La Pointe Courte*, with such a force of love, completely devoured in the end, without humour.'

   She contrasts this approach with her mischievous treatment of the tourist honeypots in *O saisons, ô châteaux* and *Du côté de la côte*.

for a while in the life of the place, we watch the couple – at least the wife – arrive; at the end of the film we see them both leave, but without following them once they have passed through the village street where a dance is taking place: the final images show the dancers going back to their homes, while the musicians play on. Thus the couple are surrounded and framed by La Pointe Courte, in the life of which their story is no more than an incident. This establishes a hierarchy, which may also be inferred from the fact that the couple have no effect on the events in the Pointe Courte series, although the place is so vital to their relationship: the subject of their conversation, a factor they must resolve, and also an influence on the course of that conversation and even a means of communication.

The Pointe Courte sequences deploy two or three narratives of their own, around the major, intensely filmed narrative of the couple. The principal one, in terms of the film-time spent on it, concerns the visit of government sanitary inspectors and the efforts the community makes to outwit them – in spite of which one young man, Raphaël, is caught fishing in a forbidden area and sentenced to three days in prison. Linked to this is the narrative of Raphaël's romance with Anna, which her parents oppose. Meanwhile in one of the houses a sick child dies. Clearly, any of these three narratives contains as much potential drama as does the couple's relationship, if not more. Varda's treatment of them, however, while always sympathetic, is resolutely undramatic. In contrast, the couple's sequences seem exaggeratedly dramatised.

The film opens with a tracking shot down the main street of the village. Throughout the film the camera moves in strong tracking-shots, as if better to explore the place it is in; although the kind of exploration varies with the sequences. *La Pointe Courte* starts with what is apparently a straightforward establishing shot, commanded by the film-maker to unveil the place to the audience. However, the situation soon becomes more complicated. We cut to a man standing in shadow at a corner of the street, and the camera circles him suspiciously before moving off again following the direction of another man who has just crossed the frame. From here on the camera's progress, in a series of tracking-shots and brief close-ups, is linked to the movements of a number of different people. A man climbs across the roofs of the outbuildings at the back of the row of houses; a face looks from a window further down the street. Then there are two cuts to the interiors of the houses; at the window of the first, where a meal is in progress, a small boy appears. Cut to the second interior, just as a young woman comes in whom we recognise from the meal in the previous shot. Rather than simply revealing the street, the camera is now moving down it in company with a rapidly changing sequence of its inhabitants. At last we return to the early shot of the man standing in shadow; this is the dreaded inspector, and the camera's progress down the street has followed the jungle-telegraph warning of his presence.

Thus we are introduced to La Pointe Courte from the point of view of its inhabitants, in the plural. By and large the camera remains at human eye-level; there are no dramatic angles. The movement is purposeful, even urgent, although it is not until the end of the sequence that we understand its purpose. Nothing is lingered on, and yet Varda introduces many important aspects of the place in this rapid sequence of shots. The camera passes through the house where the sick child lives. There are brief close-ups of objects, such as a woodpile or a cat in its basket, which have a certain charge of information (for example, woodpile = a self-sufficient community without modern conveniences); but the brief concentration on these could be justified with reference to the fleeting glances of a hurried messenger, or even to practical considerations such as how to negotiate the woodpile.

So far, no individual has emerged as particularly significant. In the last interior shot we for the first time see faces in close-up, briefly, as the reason for the agitation is revealed. After we return to the inspector on the corner, however, the film becomes more personal: there is a lively discussion between the official and a belligerent fisherman, and close-ups of the protagonists are provided; but not for long. This is a constant of the Pointe Courte sequences. Although there are occasional close-ups, the majority of the key scenes are filmed from a certain distance. Here, the outcome of the discussion is viewed first from a high angle, then from outside the courtyard where it takes place so that a fence intrudes between the camera and the protagonists. The interrogation of Raphaël by the inspectors, the death of the little boy, the encounters between Raphaël and Anna, are all filmed with the camera at a discreet distance: there may be nothing in the frame but the protagonists, but the camera is not so close as to scrutinise their faces. It is the view of a sympathetic observer; and it is a view which never lasts long. Just enough time for comprehension of what has taken place, and the film moves elsewhere. The dramas of La Pointe Courte are glimpsed, not gazed at.

The source of the glimpse is often hinted at: most of the incidents are preceded or immediately followed by a shot which establishes somebody, usually anonymous, in the position of observer. The arrival of the boats in port before the inspector's launch comes in – which leads to Raphaël's misfortune since he has delayed his return – is intercut with shots of two women on the quayside cleaning oysters and watching proceedings. The fishermen earlier arrived are of course also in a position to watch their colleague's discomfiture. The drama of the sick child can be observed by its uncomprehending brothers and sisters in the front room, or, more tellingly, by the neighbours who congregate round the mother's door as soon as the keening of one of their number announces what has happened. The arrival of this woman and her reaction on looking at the child, as observed from the door of the room, is the way in which Varda announces the child's death: the point of view of the neighbour, not of the protagonist.

This position of the camera is enough to impose on the viewer an attitude to events in La Pointe Courte which assumes human involvement, but remains detached. It also contributes to the sense of an interlinked community, in which there is no such thing as an isolated drama. The momentous events are shared by all the uninvolved neighbours. This could of course easily be portrayed as oppressive, but Varda presents it as entirely positive. There is no such thing as a judgemental glance within the community; and where the situation might make judgement inevitable, all concerned band together to avoid such embarrassment – thus the gendarmes sent to arrest Raphaël agree to meet him outside the village so that he won't be seen by his neighbours (or the spectator) under police escort. This is not, incidentally, to avoid publicising an embarrassing *fact* – Raphaël has several friendly chats about prison which the film relays to us while following him as he leaves the village. It is simply the image which is avoided. In fact, Raphaël's arrest makes him something of a local hero, and contributes to his girlfriend's parents' eventual decision in his favour.

La Pointe Courte is thus a traditional community which has a coherence gained from the way in which it looks at itself. The villagers band together to expel the outsider (the inspector). The camera enters the network by which the village communicates and binds together: it moves with the villagers and also follows their glances, looking at the community as they do. The eye of the camera is not of course always on the local dramas. Incidental conversations also feature, as – more importantly – do the everyday activities of the village. Here, in the course of work, the people and the objects that surround them are in continual, practical contact. Apart from their documentary role, these shots of the community at work provide interesting links within the film. First of all they allow the spectator to understand how the objects in this environment fit into place, which is important to appreciating the other strand of the film, as we shall see in a moment. Secondly, Varda arranges them in order to make the social structure of the community visible. Early in the film, for example, there are a series of very striking shots of washing hanging on the backyard lines. The last shots of the first Pointe Courte sequence show the village women bringing in this washing. After the first sequence concentrating on the couple, we return to the village with a series of equally striking shots of nets drying in front of the harbour. Nets and washing create a visual rhyme which is also a division: within this community there is the women's and the men's domain, separate but intimately related. This is never allowed to become an opposition; indeed, there is no suggestion that any hierarchy is involved. Varda seems to see La Pointe Courte as an almost idyllic example of co-operation. There is no desire to exchange work regimes. In an emergency everyone co-operates, as in the system for dealing with the inspectors. The division does not even follow all the usual stereotypes – we see a father taking responsibility for consoling his little boy whose playmate has just died. The exclusively male ritual celebrations following the *joutes* are broken up ritually by the women before the two groups mingle in the street dance. And, in discussion, both sides have equal weight. The longest and most intimate shots of the Pointe Courte sequence are those in which Anna's parents and their extended family discuss Anna's relationship with Raphaël. The arrangement of the male and female groups is shown, so that the spectator can appreciate their symmetrical opposition. The discussion is on equal and amicable terms, and the women carry the day.

Apart from the rhyming between male and female domains, the shots of the community at work provide a link between the Pointe Courte sequences and those of the couple. We have already discussed in Chapter 2 the way in which Varda uses objects in the scenes between Monfort and Noiret in order to illustrate their state of mind. As metaphors, the props of the Pointe Courte environment are very effective, but they owe some of that effect to our certainty that they are not *merely* metaphors. In the village sequences, we see objects and places with practical eyes. If they are unfamiliar, we can thus understand their function. Those that are more familiar have their presence accounted for – for example the omnipresent cats which could quite easily become intrusively symbolic (although Varda simply says that she films cats because she likes cats!).

These same objects in the couple's sequences are filmed quite differently because they are seen quite differently. The object-metaphors, at least those shown in close-up, are almost exclusively connected with the wife's gaze, the wife's state of mind. To her these things are quite unfamiliar. In these sequences, they are shown stripped of their practical function, and invested with another – to be a concrete image of her feelings. The viewer shares this way of seeing which is made inevitable by the editing (as we have seen) but thanks to the preceding sequences we are also aware of the 'objective' *raison d'être* of these objects, and can therefore appreciate the *process* by which we come to see them differently. This process is also central to films such as *L'Opéra-*

Mouffe and *Cléo de 5 à 7*, but in these films there is no alternative vision. *La Pointe Courte* provides an *illustration* of the way the external becomes an image of the internal.

That is not, however, the only way in which La Pointe Courte impinges on the couple's story. The first point to note is the difference which Varda establishes between the couple and every other person in the film, *even before* they begin their dialogue. At his first appearance the husband (Noiret) is not so differentiated. He appears through the washing which two village women are gathering in and walks on down the road. The camera follows him as does the gaze of the two women. He is part of the community, object of the neighbourly gaze described above. However, the image of him walking down the road is not quite comparable to those that have gone before. He walks well beyond the bounds of the community (no other character is seen outside this social space). He becomes far distant – while the discreet medium long-shot is a constant feature of the village gaze. The camera besides does not remain exactly at the point where the two women are watching, and so we are no longer looking at him through the eyes of the villagers. As Noiret walks off to meet his wife, he leaves the close comprehension of La Pointe Courte, and enters a much more isolated universe. As the couple walk back from the station the camera which follows them keeps its distance, sometimes an immense distance (as at the point where they hail the ferry, their figures no more than two distant dots in the picture). Apart from the distance, they are also filmed from dramatic – especially high – angles. The camera's position is no longer that of a neighbourly gaze. Throughout the couple's scenes, filming is either from great distances and strong angles, or fully close-up, an intimacy which also isolates them from their surroundings. The only exceptions to this occur in their bedroom, where no outside gaze can penetrate.

The couple are thus excluded from the integrated community of La Pointe Courte. However, they are not oblivious of it, indeed they talk about it incessantly. The essence of their conversation is the nature of his loyalty to and identification with a place which is alien to her. Her way of seeing the village is important, not least because it is probably close to the reaction of many spectators: she

does not understand it or feel close to it – indeed feels threatened
by its community closeness of which her husband is a part and
she is not – but by the same token she looks at it, and sees more
detail perhaps than her husband does. There is a significant piece
of dialogue as the couple walk for the first time down the main
street.

> She (with mild reproach): 'Tu m'as toujours dit qu'il n'y avait rien
> à voir.'
> He (as if this proved his point): 'C'est vrai. Regarde ...' (the camera
> moves from spread nets to look straight along a road lined with
> weeds and old boxes).
> She: 'Moi j'aime voir des choses.'[4]

At first accepting his description, and resenting his attachment
to the place which excludes her, she will come to see the
unfamiliar in the village and look at it with something of the eye of
a tourist (albeit a tourist with an urgent interest in becoming more
deeply familiar with the place). He on the other hand feels that
there is nothing to see, because the images of the village are part of
his life. Their further conversation pursues this theme which is
not unlike the famous dialogue at the opening of Alain Resnais's
Hiroshima mon amour between a foreign woman and a local man:
'J'ai tout vu à Hiroshima ... Tu n'as rien vu à Hiroshima'[5] (Resnais,
of course, edited Varda's film). The woman claims at one point
that she knows her husband so well that she could take his place;
he responds that although she can imitate his gestures and
reactions she cannot 'know what he knows'. This reflection on the
relationship between man and woman is also a reflection on the
relationship between people and place. Both depend on an
understanding which goes beyond simple observation however
careful the observation may be. *La Pointe Courte*, the film, is
perhaps an attempt to film a place in such a way that the camera
can do more than simply observe. Varda's attempt to 'know' the
place makes use of an alternation of different types of gaze – the

4 'You always told me there was nothing to see.'
   'That's true. Look....'
   'I like to see things'
5 'I've seen everything in Hiroshima ... You have seen nothing in Hiroshima'.

familiar which sees without looking, in pragmatic practical terms; the unfamiliar which looks with a stranger's eye at the 'picturesque'; the subjective which sees in the features of the place metaphors for an internal turmoil. The couple's conversation about their relationship with La Pointe Courte and with each other puts these different ways of seeing into words, albeit allusive and poetic words; their dialogue is that of the reflective intellectual, radically different from the language of the rest of the community and even from the 'natural' dialogue of a non-cinematic man and woman. Varda said: 'Je voulais que le couple soit une chose parfaitement abstraite ... je voulais qu'il soit un homme et une femme qui n'avaient pas de nom, pas de métier, je voulais, et c'est évidemment une idée littéraire, qu'ils soient abstraits, qu'il n'y ait pas un dialogue réaliste. J'ai donc fait un dialogue théâtral'[6] (Varda 1961: 9).

It is important, too, that the different types of gaze are associated with images which seem naturally to call for the contrary reaction. Thus the highly picturesque scenes of the *joutes* are filmed largely from the point of view of the jousters, involved in the action and not preoccupied with the image. The one 'picture-postcard' image (necessary perhaps to give the audience an idea of what is going on) does not espouse the gaze of any of the spectators, but shows the scene from a distant, high angle which creates a painterly landscape – the image might have been made by Canaletto. By contrast, when Silvia Monfort looks at 'things', her eye dwells on a row of dilapidated houses, a tar-barrel or a dead cat.

La Pointe Courte was in Varda's mind made by and for the local community. There are no professional actors other than Philippe Noiret and Silvia Monfort (friends from the TNP; Noiret's brilliant film career began here). The film was first shown in the cinéma Colisée in Sète, and Varda returned there to show it every ten years thereafter until it came out on video, when cassettes were distributed to all those who had appeared in the film and still lived in the village. An alleyway in La Pointe Courte was named after Varda.

6 'I wanted the couple to be something completely abstract, ... I wanted them to be a man and a woman with no name, no job, I wanted them – and it was obviously a literary idea – to be abstract, and I didn't want there to be a realistic dialogue. So I wrote theatrical dialogue.'

Daguerréotypes (1974–5)

When Varda undertook the filming of *Daguerréotypes* in 1974–5, it was with a similar intention of involving the community, although her attitudes towards her subject were more ambivalent even as her links with it were even closer. Varda had lived in the rue Daguerre, in the 14th arrondissement in Paris, since the 1950s (in 1997 she still lives there). In 1974–5 she was looking after the 2-year-old Mathieu and unwilling to undertake a film which demanded long periods away from home. A study of her own home-base seemed ideal, practically speaking, and corresponded thoroughly with her sensibility to place, to community, to the evocative detail of the everyday. The restricted range also provided a symbol for the confinement in the domestic sphere which was the traditional lot of the woman, and which Varda was currently experiencing in her own life. The 1970s were Varda's most politically active period, as they were for a large number of French film-makers and intellectuals. Her awareness of activism in general, and feminist activism in particular, had been sharpened during her period in California. She was active in women's protest movements from her return (see Chapter 4), and between 1975 and 1977 she was to make a handful of militant feminist films. However far it may seem at first glance from such concerns, *Daguerréotypes* cannot be separated from this atmosphere.

Although *Daguerréotypes* is a documentary presentation, there is a narrative of sorts provided by the announcement, the arrival and the performance of a conjuror in the corner café. This allows Varda to 'crystallise' the insights which she has about the community (she even uses the word when describing what the conjuring show will do) around a single event which brings everybody together in one place and confronts them with events which are unexpected but which nonetheless relate very closely to their normal lives. The conjuring show was not arranged for the film, although Varda did ask as many people as possible to go, so that the unity of the whole community in front of the spectacle is an artefact.

The environment of the rue Daguerre, even more than that of La Pointe Courte, is entirely defined by its community. It is a profoundly *un*picturesque spot, in comparison not only with the fishing-village but even with the rue Mouffetard: this is a point that Varda makes in her voice-over commentary, and accordingly, long-shots or 'sweeps' of the street are almost non-existent. The place is constructed through close-ups – of the small shopkeepers who inhabit the upper end of the rue Daguerre, and, to a lesser extent, of the objects which surround them and which they either sell or make use of for their craft. Even the objects rarely stand alone. They are not used as they were in the 'couple' sequences of *La Pointe Courte*, or in *L'Opéra-Mouffe*, as images or symbols of the protagonists' state of mind – they appear only as a function of the human reality of the street. They change hands, they appear in their daily function, as tools or as products of a creative process.

Construction through close-ups serves to underline the restricted space available to the protagonists, and to the film-maker, in *Daguerréotypes*. Restriction and constraint were guiding principles at the moment of conception of the film:

> J'étais un peu coincée dans la maison. Et je me suis dit que j'étais un bon exemple de créativité des femmes, toujours un peu coincée, étouffée, par la maison, par la maternité ... Je me suis bien demandée ce qui pouvait sortir de cette contrainte-là ... Je me suis moi-même attachée à la maison. J'ai imaginé un nouveau cordon ombilical. J'ai fait tirer une ligne électrique du compteur de ma maison, et le fil mesurait 80 mètres. J'ai décidé de tourner *Daguerréotypes* à cette distance-là. Je n'irais pas plus loin que mon fil.[7] (Varda 1975: 39–40)

Thus Varda's movements are artificially restricted; but so too are those of her characters, confined in the cramped interiors which the camera's constant close presence indicates. The discreet distance at which the camera watched goings-on in the village in *La Pointe Courte* has considerably closed in, and the gaze has

---

7 'I was a bit stuck in the house. And I thought that I was a good example of women's creativity, always a bit stuck, a bit smothered, by the house, by motherhood ... I wondered what could come out of that constraint ... I voluntarily tied myself to the house. I thought up a new umbilical cord. I stretched a flex from the meter in my house, and the lead measured 80 m. I wouldn't go any further than my lead. I would find something to film, there – and no further.'

become, at least potentially, oppressive. The spatial confinement is made literal in the person of Marcelle, 'Mme Chardon Bleu', the wife of the druggist, the first person on whom the camera lingers and the last whom it leaves. Ancient, vague, her eyes constantly wander off the camera to look slightly desperately round the tiny shop, or to stare through the glass of the door into the street (the very first image of the film). The narrator – clearly Varda in this film, but at this early stage the identification is not perfect – refers over the earliest images of her to her 'douceur de captive' ('prisoner's gentleness'). She is an amnesiac and unable to do any work in the shop in which she drifts around; unlike the other characters she is not (cannot be) shown in action, but at the end of the day and nearly at the end of the film she briefly goes out into the street and her husband explains that 'in the evening she often goes out ... or rather she wants to go out'. Varda said of her 'elle est amnésique, et de ce fait, parfaitement captive dans ce monde clos [...] Elle est le fantôme du petit commerce. Elle m'a toujours fascinée'[8] (Varda 1975: 39).

The community in *Daguerréotypes*, then, has tensions within it which do not appear in La Pointe Courte. Its coherence is too tight-knit, it produces the desire to escape. Varda's attitude to the traditional community here is much more ambivalent than it was to the fishing village. The existence of the community as an entity, however, is in this film as much as in *La Pointe Courte*, or even more, the fact which defines the film and gives it coherence, and the film is as fascinated as the other with the links which hold that community together and with its relationship to its surroundings, even if these are more limited and practically restricted to interiors. Varda's filming is calculated to express these links and relationships. Although the camera rarely makes broad movements, changes of angle within the small shops are mostly effected by movements rather than cuts. Thus the space inside the shop is united even though we mostly see only close-ups of small portions of it: the frame moves from full concentration on the shopkeeper to an angle on his client and on to scan the shelves, shuttling

---

8 'She's amnesiac and, because of that, totally captive in this closed world [...] She's the ghost of small shops. She has always fascinated me.'

between the available points of view in the shop and at the same time providing 'interim' frames where shopkeeper and customer appear together, at least in part.

As the film progresses, we come to recognise the faces of the customers, frequently the other shopkeepers or their families. The same people appear in different roles, showing how inter-dependent is the small world of this street. The narrator is integrated in this from the start. She does not talk about the making of the film (simply using the phrase 'tout a commencé' to denote the decision to make it), but she defines herself as a neighbour and a regular customer. She does not herself appear on screen, but the first customer in Le Chardon Bleu is introduced as 'my daughter Rosalie', and Rosalie is thoroughly integrated into the image. The camera stares at her in close-up as it stares at Léonce and Marcelle, trapping her in the same suffocatingly small space. By the last sequences of commercial activity, we recognise nearly everyone in the frame and can attribute to them their appropriate function in the life of this small portion of Paris. *Daguerréotypes* thus establishes a bounded community, which as an entity withstands the occasional appearance of an unfamiliar face or an unexpected voice. It is a paradox which is striking when *Daguerréotypes* and *La Pointe Courte* are compared that the much looser physical boundaries of the rue Daguerre (in La Pointe Courte a stranger is seen by all the inhabitants as an intrusion) go along with tighter and more restrictive bounds within the community.

While the voice-over establishes from the outset that the narrator has a place in this community, she remains detached from it by the manner of her commentary, and the camera is also detached. Unlike *La Pointe Courte*, *Daguerréotypes* rarely attributes the camera's gaze to an onlooker who is identified before or after the shot – with the exception of the conjuring show, where the onlooker is the entire community. Most often, we see the activity in a shop from a fixed point which corresponds to no-one's position in the image, but which reflects very accurately the procedure which the film-makers perforce used; that is, to set up their equipment in a corner and wait as inconspicuously as possible for something to happen. Movement is restricted to pans from a fixed base. Freer shots are obtained by filming shop-fronts from the other side of the street, which allows the camera to follow the protagonists' movements. A good example is the sequence showing the opening of the ironmongers' shop. The camera moves backwards and forwards a good deal, following the movements of one or other of the owners, changing from one to the other or even briefly following a passer-by. However, it moves to keep them in frame, watching them, and not *with* them, and there is no watcher in the community, as far as we know, positioned thus across the road. On one occasion the camera does undeniably move with the protagonists, watching out of the window of a car in which a driving lesson is in progress, but neither instructor nor pupil is likely to be looking out of a side window as the camera is doing.

The camera then is largely identified with the controller/narrator, and the latter's establishment of her credentials as a 'Daguerréotypesse'[9] is thus essential if we are not to feel that we are sharing an outsider's, even a tourist's, uncomprehending vision. However, the Mystag sequences are a quite complex exception.

Once the Mystag show starts – about halfway through the film – there are inevitably going to be shots where the community is looking at the same things as the camera. These are cut alongside shots of the audience; this establishes that the camera is according to its usual habit installed in a corner to watch what goes on, but its angle of view is probably not vastly different from the rest of the audience, and we see (and hear) reactions to what camera and audience both see on stage which establish a community of gaze. Some of the reactions on the sound-track come from behind the camera, so it is clear that it is among the audience. Here then the camera is accepted as it were among the community.

Apart from the reactions of the people in the audience, Mystag's tricks are intercut with images from the daily routine of the shops. The choice of images is guided by Mystag's current trick; and indeed during these sequences (there are usually several

9 Untranslatable. 'Type' is French slang for 'guy' and 'typesse' enjoyed a certain fashionable usage (cf. 'chaps and chapesses'). Daguerreotypes have already been explained. Varda's punning titles can only lose in another language.

quite short shots cut together) Mystag takes over the sound-track. We hear his patter as if it was a commentary on the images, which indeed it matches very closely, if allusively. The associations between sound and image which are made by the camera defy the logic of place which has hitherto been well kept – we 'know' that the camera/narrator is in the café watching the show, and not moving into, say, the baker's shop. The viewpoint is obviously associative/psychological (on hearing what Mystag says, the baker's shop is evoked or imagined); it could be the narrator's association, but the narrator has never appeared as a human presence at the Mystag show, while we have been watching clearly defined reactions from the rest of the *audience*. Thus I think that the associations are read as mental images evoked by Mystag's chat in the audience, probably as a whole, or in some one member of the audience who can be taken as representative of the whole. They are never attributed to anyone in particular, for example by a shot of one face gazing to camera.

Thus, through the spectacle, we are allowed entry into the imagination of the community seeing itself in a somewhat new light, or alongside unexpected alterations of the normal behaviour of things. However, this is strictly an imaginary space, and we never really experience the real space in the way that the community does. We never learn the positions of the shops in relation to each other. Geographically each is a self-sufficient entity, its own little world, even though the people circulate. The community is defined not by space but by common experience and familiarity of every part with every other part, which allows imaginary representations to be shared by everyone (it is not necessarily the baker who associates the fire-eating metaphor with his work in the oven).

The containment of the community is emphasised several times by the narrator. Over some rare outdoor shots, which come and go across the street following the movements of a mechanic, then of two elderly women doing their shopping, the voice evokes 'the other end' of the street where 'il y a des vendeurs de journaux politiques, des militants, des discussions: ici rien' ('there are sellers of political newspapers, militants, discussions: here there's nothing'). The image allows us to see 'the other end of the street' in the distance, but the camera does not move, it simply turns from right to left to follow the first woman, then, once she has met the other, retraces its panoramic path from left to right until it is back where it came from, immobile. The words 'ici rien' coincide with a close-up image of a discussion between a mechanic and an elderly man. It is implied that this is not the kind of 'discussion' which goes on at the other end of the street. As the voice-over concludes that 'politics is bad for commerce' (although the other end of the street also holds 'le grand marché') the camera closes in on the men's hands: the mechanic is showing the other the oil on his. The connection of oily hands with a narrow mind recurs in the insensitive garage-owner in *Sans toit ni loi*, and may be a visual symbol for Varda, but it is not an obvious one and the spectator could make other connections. We do not hear clearly what the two men are in fact talking about, but the implication is that it is a local conversation.

However, there are elements in the image which nuance the judgement of the voice, even here. The second woman holds a newspaper, and even glances at it. The contrast between this part of the street and the 'other end', a contrast between a closed community and an open one, is not a staunch divide: the other end is clearly visible and freely accessible, and intimations of the outside world are not a threat: the immediately preceding sequence has followed, in a series of short shots, the progress of the postwoman down the street, at once a cohesive force, as she greets everyone, and one which brings news of the outside. One of her letters goes to a young woman, Isabelle, who is an anomaly within the community to which she apparently belongs. She is associated not with the small shops but with a skating rink outside the area, and during the Mystag show she is shown several times holding a newspaper announcing the political issue of the moment in Varda's mind: 'Avortement: l'heure de la vérité' (Abortion: the moment of truth). This may remind us that three of these 'apolitical' women, including Isabelle, take part in *Réponse de femmes*, Varda's television ciné-tract on behalf of a female look at the female body, which will be described in the next chapter.

Varda's eye in *Daguerréotypes* was from the start more critical than it was in *La Pointe Courte*, where she took the part of the fishing community unreservedly. In her comments on *Daguerréotypes* she insists on the difference between herself and her subject, especially at the level of political awareness, but claims that her aim was to understand and not to question. The difference is not entirely absent from the text: as we have seen the camera does not enter into the movements of the 'characters'. In the first part it does attempt to enter the rhythm of the street, 'le temps du petit commerce' ('small shopkeepers' time'), in the long time between cuts and the strategy of waiting for the action to take place. But the strategy is explained, and it remains an intellectual solidarity, based on observation of what happens in the shops rather than on empathy with them. The voice-over constantly refers to the characters as 'immobile', 'sleeping' (literally at one point, since Varda films the butcher having a nap and interviews a number of people about their dreams or lack of them) or 'silent' (the 'silent majority') before finally consigning them to the record of old-fashioned, motionless, posed photographs. Mystag will both awaken his audience and send it to sleep, or so the voice-over announces, but the last we hear of him, still in voice-off and therefore with some of the authority of the commentary, is his preparations to do the latter, and this concludes the film, as his announcement heralds the series of poses.

Both *La Pointe Courte* and *Daguerréotypes* represent careful descriptions of communities in which Varda is, or was, personally involved. *Daguerréotypes*, like *La Pointe Courte*, was shown to its destined audience immediately on completion. Varda hoped that it would call forth at least a small amount of self-questioning, given the pointers which the commentary provides. Perhaps she even expected some irritation. She seems to have been a little disappointed at the response: 'franchement ça n'est pas allé très loin. Ce qui était le plus évident, c'était d'abord la joie des gens de se voir, à l'écran ... Il y a bien un refus, et qui est exactement celui du film. Le refus de sortir du cliché. ... Personne ne semble s'être remis en question à un degré quelconque. Personne n'avait envie d'apprendre quelque chose sur lui-même'[10] (Varda 1975: 44).

Although at the end of the film the narrator identifies herself as 'Agnès Varda, Daguerréotypesse', she remains outside the visible community of the film, while in *La Pointe Courte* the camera mingles with the village.

Mur murs and *Documenteur* (1980–1)

These two intersecting films (*Mur Murs* 'appears' in *Documenteur*) map Los Angeles in 1980–1, through the eyes of an outsider, French and female but in both cases distanced from Varda. Once again, the place can only be mapped through the lives, the preoccupations, the movements and contacts between its inhabitants, but the approach must necessarily be different. The area is much greater and its boundaries, both physical and human, are more permeable than those of La Pointe Courte or the upper rue Daguerre; to be an outsider is almost a majority condition (as Emilie's landlord tells her when she moves in to her battered new accommodation in *Documenteur*: 'You should be at home ... We have Germans and Israelis and Mexicans here. A lot of foreigners').

In their strategies of approach to Los Angeles the two films are, as might be expected from their format and their close association, in some ways opposites of each other. *Mur Murs*, a documentary, takes as its starting point the eye-catching murals of LA. Even if they are the work of individual artists, by their position in the public street and their sheer size they inevitably form part of the community's space and therefore must have at least the consent of those living beneath them – a consent which suggests that they illustrate preoccupations more collective than the artist's own personality. Hence they seem a good approach to understanding how the community may see and express itself, even more so when we discover – as we very rapidly do – that the artists are for

---

10 'Frankly it didn't go very far. The most obvious thing was the joy people got at seeing themselves on screen ... There was certainly a refusal, the same refusal as in the film. The refusal to come out of the cliché. ... No-one felt that they were in any way called into question. No-one wanted to learn anything about themselves.'

the most part local and responding to the places they have grown up in by the paintings they produce there. Varda says: 'Par quel autre moyen qu'un documentaire aurais-je pu apprendre plus sur cette ville et ses habitants?'[11] (Varda 1994: 146); by choosing to make a documentary on these examples of a community's visual self-expression, she allows the camera to look at images made by the community itself even though it is itself inevitably an 'outsider'. The majority of the words spoken in the film are those of the artists, or of the local owners of the walls who have paid for the paintings – for it is not only the artists who are the product of the community but as a general rule the patrons too. Thus *Mur Murs* sets itself to record as much as possible the expression of local identity, certainly in local words and often also in local images.

In *Documenteur* on the other hand the outsider remains radically outside. The sound-track is occupied mostly by the interior monologue of the protagonist, Emilie, or by her conversations with her little boy, her rare friends, and one or two other contacts. With her friends, the talk is of personal problems; with other contacts exchanges are strictly functional. Alone, Emilie comments on her emotions but rarely on what she sees, and when she does, it is to emphasise how impossible it is to understand the images. 'On ne sait rien d'eux. Même pas s'ils ferment les yeux quand ils font l'amour. Même pas s'ils viennent de le faire. Vont-ils le faire, ou veulent-ils le faire?'[12] There is not even any need to understand the images strictly speaking; Emilie connects her own longings to the indifferent faces of the Los Angeles crowd, and is not seeking to find out what theirs are. If *Mur Murs* sets out, in fairly conventional documentary manner, to understand its surroundings through the mediation of the film-maker, *Documenteur* turns this on its head and sets out to understand the person through the mediation of the surroundings.

11 'By what means other than a documentary could I have learnt more about this town and its inhabitants?'
12 'You know nothing about them. Not even if they close their eyes when they make love. Not even if they have just made love. Or are they going to, or do they want to?'

It is not the light which Emilie can shed on Los Angeles but that which Los Angeles can shed on Emilie which is important. The contrast is not dissimilar to that which *La Pointe Courte* contains within itself – *Mur Murs*, like the 'village' sequences, seeks entry into the community and understanding of the function of its elements, while *Documenteur*, like the 'couple's' thread, uses elements of the community to give form to the woman's subjectivity, which in turn allows her if not to come to terms with her emotions at least to find new terms to express them.[13]

The vision of LA which emerges from *Mur Murs* is mediated through a great many different voices, with different experiences and different visions, and indeed the result may amount to a number of separate communities, with various internal relations. What connection is there between the Los Angeles of the Mexican street-gangs, where the community is bonded against the violence which comes from neighbouring communities (but where the expressions of protest against that violence are nevertheless designed to be read and understood by all parties to all conflicts: the various gangs are all more-or-less 'insiders' who speak the same visual language) and the country singer immortalised by her husband on the wall of their seaside shack? And what is the place of the factory which employs anonymous artists on a project as interminable as that of Sisyphus (to borrow the sort of myth which Varda is fond of), painting an idyllic community of pigs to camouflage a slaughterhouse? This latter could be taken as a metaphor for an alienating, violent, uncaring world of business – the artists are unrecognised, the work is dangerous (the previous artist was killed on the job), the painting does not express the deepest sentiments of the painter who does not particularly care for pigs, nor does it tell the truth about the enterprise. The image of perfect porcine peace covers murderous violence – at least as far as any pigs involved are concerned. And yet the factory workers, who after all are the principal community in the large space

13 Varda has doubts about this formulation, and quite rightly ... 'I love the way you say "coming to terms with your own emotions". Do we ever come to terms ... I mean, do we ever capture them?' (Filmed interview with *Scotland on Sunday*, Glasgow French Film Festival, 1996.)

surrounded by the wall, seem fond of it and see some truth in it.

In *Documenteur* the image of the place is, as we have said, not so much a description of Los Angeles as of the emotions of a character who is faced with a loss and loneliness which she is unused to and the effects of which she cannot foresee. It is therefore not surprising that the camera, following her gaze, selects the bleak, the chilly or the abandoned. Emilie is often shown looking out beyond the camera in the way which has already been described as indicating a concentration on inner images (plate 3), although here the majority of the attached images are external and directly visible to her; we understand that she is adopting and adapting them in her head. However, they are *also* an accurate picture of one side of LA.

The prevalent poverty, illustrated by sequences of images of down-and-outs, tramps, and drunks, is not experienced by the viewer as a surprise: however, it is worth noting that this is a theme which Varda has carried with her everywhere from her earliest films. Even *La Pointe Courte* was in part inspired by 'mon désarroi devant les gens qui meurent de froid, vagabonds dans les champs, clochards dans les rues et vieilles femmes abandonnées dans des logements non chauffés'[14] (Varda 1994: 40). The same lost population frequents the rue Mouffetard (*L'Opéra-Mouffe*) and of course the Provence of *Sans toit ni loi*; but not *Daguerréotypes* or *Mur Murs*, and in *La Pointe Courte* the theme is not insistent. Rather than a specific sign of any one place and community, consciousness of such marginal poverty is a characteristic of Varda's most subjective films, and its significance in the films is primarily the echo which it provides of the protagonist(s)'s fears and desires. In a striking sequence of *Documenteur*, a tracking-shot moves from Emilie and a friend appropriating a sofa from an alley, across a number of skips and dustbins where tramps are rifling through the rubbish. Clearly, Emilie and the tramps are engaged on much the same errand, although she is looking for more substantial booty. Just before this point, a shot of her in her kitchen has revealed walls and sink covered with graffiti. Clearly

14 'my helpless confusion in face of people who die of cold, vagabonds in the fields, tramps in the streets and old women abandoned in unheated houses'.

this reflects her circumstances to some extent, but if she is moving towards the tramps' existence (in some elements only of her life) this seems also an image of her state of mind. As the camera moves from one of the tramps across a series of dustbins and accumulated rubbish, we hear the little boy Martin's voice, off:

> Qu'est-ce qu'il cherche? Les choses à manger, des choses à garder, des choses gaies? C'est sale là-dedans. 'Y a des bêtes. Moi j'ai peur des bêtes. Pas des bêtes qu'on connaît comme les animaux les escargots les chiens les chats le loup [...] mais les bêtes de la nuit, les bêtes qu'on connaît pas, les bêtes qu'on ne voit jamais, les bêtes qui vivent dans le noir.[15]

The move from images of homelessness and poverty to a sense of mysterious fear suggests the function which such impressions have in Varda's films generally.

The image of LA in *Documenteur* is notable especially for one other factor, the sea. Unlike *Mur Murs*, which concentrates on the urban landscape of streets, shops and factories, *Documenteur* presents Los Angeles as a coastal community. Emilie's office overlooks the beach, and there are frequent close-ups of waves – again, a shorthand indication of desires not quite pinned down – but the sea's presence also affects the appearance of the land. The people of this Los Angeles spend their leisure hours fishing from a small unpretentious pier, and groups of cheap low houses are scattered across what is very nearly still duneland. Unlike the presence of urban blight, this element of the setting does carry surprise; LA seems almost a small settlement, shabby but circumscribed, with none of the awe-inspiring scale which the murals alone impose on *Mur Murs*. It is not so far from La Pointe Courte; and Emilie despite remaining an outsider nonetheless appears to have an inclusive vision. She is alone in a dank environment, but not dwarfed by the cosmopolitan city, and if she never allows herself

---

15 'What's he looking for? Things to eat, things to keep, happy things? It's dirty in there. There are creatures. I'm scared of creatures. Not creatures you know like animals, snails, dogs, cats, wolves [...] but night creatures, creatures you don't know, creatures you never see, the creatures that live in the dark.'

to become integrated into the community she is able to take it in and to make sense of the images she forms of it on her own terms.

In neither of these films is the exploration, or the control over the camera, attributed to Varda. In *Mur Murs*, one assumes at first that she has control of the introductory voice-over (which admittedly has a reduced role to allow as much community self-expression as possible), but this is denied within the film by the presence of 'the visitor' on screen. The visitor appears very little, asks one or two timid questions and is otherwise seen looking as she moves through the streets – perhaps the most important thing about her is that she is very visibly not Varda, but she is a French woman exploring the city and therefore in the film-maker's position and a substitute for her. (In fact she is Juliet Berto, and one might regret that she has so little to do.) The voice-over of *Mur Murs* is again divorced from Varda by *Documenteur*, where Emilie is shown reading the voice-over for her employer's new film since the latter is not available to do it. The script is that of *Mur Murs*.

As the above suggests, Varda or someone who may be assimilated to Varda is present in *Documenteur*. It is only a virtual presence, we never see Emilie's employer's face nor do we hear her voice; but we know she is a film-maker before we know that she has in fact made *Mur Murs*. Thus it is made clear, by extension, that Emilie is not a film-maker but a film-maker's secretary; more specifically, she is not Agnès Varda since she did not make *Mur Murs*. Varda is elsewhere, the subjectivity and the approach to the city is therefore, we must accept, not hers. In fact Emilie is played by *Mur Murs*' editor, Sabine Mamou, who is given a position in the film not too unlike her own, but this is not to say that the film is claiming to be about Sabine Mamou. The displacement is simply a distancing strategy with respect to Varda herself, important because in so many of her films she has made a point of her own presence and involvement.

These two films illustrate two ways in which a community can be explored and its images taken in by an outsider who remains such; but LA is not a closed community, and the presence of the stranger excites no defensive reactions. The effect of an outsider in a traditional community, and the possibility – however distant – of that community calling itself into question, is explored again in *Sans toit ni loi*. The film tends to be considered in terms of the individuals concerned, whether they be Mona or Mona's principal interlocutors, but the setting of the film is in fact sharply limited geographically and in some ways socially coherent. Places are never actually identified, but that the area is restricted is clear from repeated shots of recognisable spots (such as the railway line and railway bridge from which David leaves and where Yolande later finds Mona) and even more from the central knot of characters – Mme Landier/Jean-Pierre/Eliane/Lydie/Yolande/Paolo – whom Mona meets independently at several different times.

The way in which these recurring characters act to delineate the small circuit of Mona's wanderings suggests that, once again, place is defined by community, but this is not really so: community in *Sans toit ni loi* is in fact minimal. Apart from that central knot, there are few social interactions between the people Mona encounters. However, everyone is contextualised socially, and almost all take their context from their links with the place. Many are farmers or farm-labourers, working on the land and seen at work during the hardest time of the year. Even Jean-Pierre and Mme Landier, apparently 'bourgeois intellectuals', are investigating the deterioration of the area's trees. Lydie, Yolande and Yolande's uncle Bionnet are anchored not to the land but to its buildings, and their individual case is generalised by Mona's comment to Mme Landier as she travels in her car, that there are many such ramshackle houses across the countryside. The farmers and the service workers (truckers, garage hands, packers, gravedigger) all enter into the dimly earthy colour-scheme of the film. Their clothes and even their bodies blend with the environment, making them even more coherent with it.

The place and the nature of the place thus provide a link between otherwise very isolated individuals. Mona's presence provides another link, of which most are unaware. She meets them all individually because they largely live individually. Even among the central group social contacts are minimal and confined to the necessary demands of family, employment or sex (or a combination of these), and the pattern is even more pronounced outside that small circle. These people share their environment, rather as they share a common acquaintance with Mona, without being aware of it, and yet all are formed by it and coherent with it.

The choice of place in *Sans toit ni loi* is a conscious overturning of cliché. It is the South of France, but in winter, and therefore harsh. Varda concentrates on everything that is most harsh about it. The joining-shots which link the Grande Série of Mona's wanderings, slipping from characters to some object in the environment, have already been mentioned. As the film progresses, it becomes more and more obvious how dilapidated the objects chosen are. Agricultural machinery rusts unused, stacks of sand-bags or tyres wait abandoned by the roadside, buildings are flaking and cracked, and often shuttered, and everywhere is characterised by a dominant mud-colour. Within this landscape the people take on some of the same characteristics simply by association, but they are visually similarly typed: clothes are elderly, shapeless and mud-coloured, many of the people are also elderly and shapeless, and even the young partake of the same colour-scheme. The rootless squatters whom Mona meets at the railway station live inevitably in the middle of the surrounding squalor, and by definition in the least maintained parts of it. Thus the place of *Sans toit ni loi* displays an undeniable coherence, but it is a cracking and fragmenting coherence which can hardly be called a community. Actual malice towards other individuals is relatively rare (and most pronounced in Eliane, of all the characters the least integrated into the nature of the place). The predominant attitude is indifference, each individual or unit continuing its own way with as little interaction with others as it can manage. The final incident of the film is interesting in this regard. A village wine festival might be supposed to be a ritual of social coherence, among the community and between community and place. In fact its community character is more one of ritual fragmentation: the inhabitants shutter their houses and if they meet in the street they run away from each other. If the wine-god figures represent a link between community and land, it is a link with the land's hostility; and, of course, the dominant cold-earth colours continue their reign. The only way in which the festival reaffirms the community is through the expulsion of the outsider, but even this seems to be more by accident and misunderstanding than design. Mona is terrified into flight because she does not understand the rules of ritualised fear, but her pursuers are not targeting her particularly.

It is thus, arguably, the pervading indifference which kills Mona, but she is in this respect anyway entirely at one with the rest of the community. She has in fact simply developed the common characteristics to their extremest degree, and it may not be too fanciful (or at any rate it is tempting, given Varda's tendency to play with the connotations of myth in connection with ordinary characters) to see in her a materialisation not so much of Aphrodite as of the spirit of the place. As far as the prospects for human community go, it is not an encouraging sign.

The community of *Sans toit ni loi* is thus a community in decay, or rather a series of individuals. Many were real individuals, whom Varda met and spoke to in the course of the preparation of the film and even before its final structure was decided, and to this extent the film, like *La Pointe Courte* or *Daguerréotypes*, was made around and by implication for its non-professional cast. However, there is no question in this film either of a dedication, written or spoken, to its participants, nor of a collective viewing afterwards. Varda's memory of the area is an echo of the impression left by the film: 'les vignes du Gard et de l'Hérault avec leur ceps noirs qui ne promettent rien, des paysages sévères, des villages raides comme Lunel et Marsillargues et des fermes peu accueillantes ... La méfiance règne. Une femme seule dans sa cour m'a vue venir de loin et a lâché son jars. Ils mordent. J'ai couru vers ma voiture'[16] (Varda 1994: 166).

Clearly, the filming could have little effect on this community which hardly qualifies as a community, and which is bleakly

16 'The vines of the Gard and Hérault with their black unpromising rootstocks, dour landscapes, stiff villages like Lunel and Marsillargues and unwelcoming farms ... Mistrust reigns. A woman alone in her yard saw me coming in the distance and let loose her gander. They bite. I ran back to the car.'

criticised. However, the idea that to film a place and especially a community is to act upon it has not been entirely abandoned, as can be seen in Varda's commemorative film made in 1992 in Rochefort, *Les Demoiselles ont eu 25 ans*. The film marks the 25th anniversary of the making of Jacques Demy's *Les Demoiselles de Rochefort*, with a combination of extracts from the film, footage taken on set at the time, and present-day images of Rochefort's celebrations and interviews with locals who took part in the film. The film takes its place in a corpus of films around Demy and his work which Varda made in the early 1990s, but in this case the local character of Demy's film stands out. It is a general rule in Varda's work that the way in which a film begins and ends is significant in setting the tone of the whole, and here the film begins and ends with the town of Rochefort. The first sequence begins with a tracking-shot upwards from the surface of the river (over which the credits roll) to the bridge which is one of the town's landmarks. It then cuts to a table on which an unidentified hand scatters old postcards of the town, while a male voice-over announces that 'from the transporter bridge to the place Colbert, the town of Rochefort remembers the filming of *Les Demoiselles*'. The function of a montage of postcards has been discussed in the previous chapter: their use here is interesting in that they clearly pre-date 1966 and the date of the principal subject of the film. Their verbal match appears to be 'la ville de Rochefort se souvient' ('the town of Rochefort remembers'): they have become a sign of the history of a place, into which the film has now been integrated.

Very near the end of the film a young schoolteacher, a newcomer to the town who has previously said that he feels he knows Rochefort better through the film than in reality, claims: 'Ce n'est pas d'abord le film d'un cinéaste, ce n'est pas le film d'actrices, c'est le film des Rochefortais, comme un immense et gigantesque film de famille qui aurait eu une gloire dans le monde entier.'[17] The final credit sequence lines up a number of local pairs of twins in front of another municipal landmark. Thus

17 'It's not first and foremost a film-maker's film, it's not an actress's film, it belongs to the people of Rochefort, like an immense gigantic home movie which had gained fame throughout the world.'

Varda's documentary inserts *Les Demoiselles* firmly in its local context, and although she does not neglect either Demy's role or the actresses', the input of Rochefort into the film, and conversely the effect which the film had on the town, is an all-pervasive theme. Not only do a series of extras share their memories of the film, but we learn that in the opinion of the current mayor the shoot marked a turning-point in Rochefort's fortunes, a renaissance of civic pride. 'On était tous un peu endormis', admits one of the townsmen, significantly, near the beginning of the film, 'et c'était un petit peu comme la fée au bois dormant. ... Ils sont arrivés avec leur film et on s'est réveillés, on s'est levés si vous voulez.'[18] At the end of *Daguerréotypes*, Mystag the Master of Ceremonies sends everyone to sleep. Here it is the impact of a film crew which persuaded the town to put itself on show – even repainting the shutters of the streets – and later to consider its image. The restoration of the derelict arsenal is attributed by the mayor to that impact. In 1992, the 1967 shoot is commemorated by a carnival which takes up the tunes and the images from the film and repackages them for the town's own entertainment – without stars, with the parts of Deneuve and Dorléac played by local teenagers and largely for a local audience. The carnival, participatory spectacle emanating from the local community, plays an important part in *Jacquot de Nantes*. It is significant that here it is so closely linked to the cinema and also to the sense of local identity. Because *Les Demoiselles* is about another film than itself, Varda can discuss openly the ways in which a film can be made into a gift to a community, and indeed can come to belong to it in some real sense: this aim will be considered again in Chapter 6 when we shall consider the notion of the gift of a film to its subject in a wider context.

18 'We were all a bit asleep, and it was a bit like the Sleeping Beauty. ... They arrived with their film, and we woke up, we got up if you like.'

References

Varda, Agnès (1961) 'Agnès Varda', interview with Jean Michaud and Raymond Bellour, *Cinéma 61*, no. 60, October, pp. 4–20
Varda, Agnès (1975) 'Autour et alentour de *Daguerréotypes*', *Cinéma 75*, no. 204, December, pp. 39–53
Varda, Agnès (1994) *Varda par Agnès*, Paris, Cahiers du cinéma

4

Women's images and self-images

Throughout her career Varda's interest in a specifically feminine cinema has been constant. She is one of the very few French *réalisatrices* who have been strongly involved in the women's movement: she has declared this involvement and explored it in her films (notably *L'Une chante, l'autre pas*). An interest in 'film-making in the feminine', however, seems to have pre-dated any political involvement. She told *Cinéma* in 1961 (Varda 1961: 7): 'Il existe un vocabulaire de femme lié à l'univers féminin. Je sens cela par moments dans la mesure où je suis aiguillée par un certain nombre d'attirances, de sujets qui m'attirent toujours un peu plus que si j'étais un homme. [...] Je ne veux pas non plus faire un cinéma féministe, raconter des histoires de femmes concernant les femmes.'[1] Her short film *L'Opéra-Mouffe* (1958) proves clearly enough that her idea of a 'woman's visual vocabulary' was quite sophisticated early on. Her woman's perspective underlies all her films, and the conclusions drawn in this chapter should be borne in mind in the consideration even of works not directly treated here.

I shall explore this theme in Varda's work in relation to four 'major' films – *Cléo de 5 à 7* (1961), *L'Une chante, l'autre pas* (1976),

The part of this chapter dealing with *Sans toit ni loi* is in part an abridged version of an article which appeared in *Nottingham French Studies* (Smith 1996).

1 'A woman's vocabulary exists, linked to the feminine universe. I feel this occasionally in that I am inspired by a certain number of attractions, subjects which always draw me rather more than they would if I were a man. ... I don't want to make feminist cinema either, to tell women's stories about women.'

Sans toit ni loi (1985) and *Jane B. par Agnès V.* (1987) – and two shorter ones, – *L'Opéra-Mouffe* (1958) and *Réponse de femmes* (1975). If *Sans toit ni loi* takes up a large part of this chapter, this I think is a fair reflection both of its exemplary procedure which has relevance to many other films, and to its worldwide fame which makes it probably the most studied of Varda's films. Twenty-five years after *Cléo*, *Sans toit ni loi* (aka *Vagabonde*), shares with the former film its concentration on one woman over a limited period of her life, although in most other respects the two films are sharply contrasted. In the intervening decade, *L'Une chante, l'autre pas*, also a high-profile film on its appearance, has been called a film about feminism rather than a feminist film (meaning that while its subject is the women's movement, its fabrication is conventional and its representation of women unproblematic). I hope to question this somewhat. *Jane B.* has had a rather lower public profile than its predecessor *Sans toit ni loi*, perhaps because it is a documentary which explicitly approaches complex themes which the fiction films incorporate into a relatively user-friendly story.

This chapter will look at these five films chronologically, following Varda's evolving exploration of the questions 1) What does it mean to be a woman and 2) How to represent the feminine. The latter question involves at least three aspects. First, how is a woman seen (and why); secondly, how does a woman see (and why); thirdly, how does a woman see herself, and especially herself *as* a woman. This aspect of Varda's work, up to *Sans toit ni loi*, has been the subject of analysis in Sandy Flitterman-Lewis's fascinating study of French women film-makers, *To Desire Differently* (1996).

L'Opéra-Mouffe (1958)

This short film (17 minutes) consists of a series of groups of images, arranged in 'chapters' – with headings – and linked by a musical soundtrack, hence Opéra. The title is a play on the phrase *opéra-bouffe* (comic opera, but *bouffe* is also slang for food, a connection which the film quickly makes). The images concerned are all of the rue Mouffetard (or rue Mouff as it is often known). This is a narrow, cobbled street in the student quarter of Paris, well known for its fruit and vegetable market. Now full of small restaurants, it was considerably shabbier in the 1950s and haunted by tramps (as indeed it still is at its lower end).

L'Opéra-Mouffe is impressions of the rue Mouff through the eyes of a pregnant woman. We see very little of this woman, although an image of her appears early on in order to 'explain' what follows. She is in fact Varda herself, pregnant with her first child while making the film. However, Varda did not intend the film to be read as *her* experiences of pregnancy specifically: 'Le film garde constamment le ton d'une œuvre écorchée. J'ai eu moi une grossesse très heureuse, j'ai traduit ce qui pourrait être celle d'une femme de la Mouffe. La sensibilité n'est pas ce qu'on éprouve, mais ce qu'on peut éprouver'[2] (Varda 1961: 12).

Although clearly the film presents a specifically feminine point of view, it is perhaps first and foremost an example of the genre that Varda herself has called 'subjective documentary', or even of Surrealist film, as suggested in Chapter 2. The interest lies in the way that the observer both selects what she sees among the variety of a busy market street, and interprets the images selected, so that her vision relates to her current situation – that is, her pregnancy. The situation chosen probably relates more to the fact that Varda's own pregnancy had caused her to notice this phenomenon of selection and interpretation in herself, than to a definite, 'feminist' desire to present a Woman's vision. A similar process underlies Cléo's relation to Paris in *Cléo*, in some ways closely comparable to *L'Opéra-Mouffe*. However, *L'Opéra-Mouffe* is short and has no conventional story, so that the subjective vision is its sole concern.

The two principal series of images concern, on the one hand the contents of the market, on the other the people of the street. Both these themes are introduced in the first few images of the film, both return, pursued at greater length, later under various

2 'The film's tone is constantly that of a work flayed alive. I had a very happy pregnancy, I have translated what that of a woman of the rue Mouff might be. Sensitivity is not what one experiences, but what one can experience.'

titles – 'du sentiment de la nature', 'de la grossesse', 'des envies' in the first case; 'quelques-uns', 'de l'ivresse' in the second.[3] The images of the market are chosen for the very obvious relation they bear to the woman's body, and their implications are for the most part disturbing, sometimes violent. Images of the street people concentrate, more and more as the film progresses, on the old, poor and ragged, the down-and-outs. Varda says of these: 'tous ceux-là, les vieux, les borgnes et les clochardes, tous avaient été des bébés, des nouveaux-nés souvent aimés à qui on avait embrassé le ventre et talqué le derrière'[4] (Varda 1994: 115).

The progression of the film after the introductory sequence takes the subject/viewer into more and more troubling territory. The first 'chapter', 'Les Amoureux' ('The lovers') shows a couple making love. It is a tender sequence which contrasts with the more and more disturbing associations taken on by the sights of the street. The chapter titles indicate this progression, from 'Of the feeling for nature' to 'des angoisses' (of terrors), from 'Some people' to 'Of drunkenness'.

L'Opéra-Mouffe, despite its light-hearted sound-track, is an uncomfortable film; the associations that, guided by the sound-track and the brief glimpse of the watcher, we cannot avoid making are unsettling. With very few exceptions (there are one or two constructed objects later in the film) all the images undeniably form part of the everyday life of Paris. It is in their selection that we enter into the vision of the pregnant woman. Some are disturbing in themselves, some because of the 'montage of associations' which the film sets up: Varda exploits to the full the effect of comparing the human body to other organic forms, especially food, with the consequent concrete expression of unconscious anxieties. The gutted melon, or a cabbage with a smaller cabbage growing in its centre, become symbols, while remaining everyday objects of a vegetable market. Where Varda

3 'of the feeling for nature', 'of pregnancy', 'of cravings', 'certain people', 'of drunkenness'.
4 'all these, the old, the one-eyed and the tramp-women, all were once babies, new-born babies, often loved, who had their stomachs tickled and their bottoms talced'.

constructs symbols – an egg inside a broken electric-light bulb, for example – these may be read as the logical extension into fantasy of the process of vision which the film is documenting.

L'Opéra-Mouffe is a specifically feminine exploration of the process of subjective or symbolic vision, the conversion of the everyday world into metaphors for feelings which, in some cases, are resistant to verbal explanation. Varda wrote:

> J'étais contente d'avoir transmis cette émotion particulière à ma grossesse: un retour aux instincts (peur d'éventration, attention et sensibilité décuplées, autoprotection) ... Contemporaine pour faire la respiration du petit chien, oui, mais primitive autant que se peut pour vibrer avec les sensations nouvelles. Et leur trouver une forme de cinéma, entre la vérité d'un Cartier-Bresson et les images de rêveries du cinéma dit marginal.[5] (Varda 1994: 115)

L'Opéra-Mouffe was a project destined for the 'cinéma dit marginal', made for an exhibition of avant-garde cinema. This context, unusual in Varda's work, allowed her to explore her personal preoccupations very freely. As we shall see, the exploration influenced the larger-scale work which followed it.

Cléo de 5 à 7 (1961)

Cléo was Varda's first venture into the relatively mainstream cinema, under the aegis of the Nouvelle Vague and specifically of Georges de Beauregard, producer of *A bout de souffle*. It recounts, in 90 minutes of film, 90 minutes of the life of the beautiful Cléo Victoire, a relatively successful pop singer (a 1960s' Vanessa Paradis), during which she awaits the results of a medical test for

5 'I was pleased to have transmitted the particular emotion of my pregnancy. A return to instincts (fear of evisceration, a tenfold increase in sensitivity and attention, self-preservation) ... I was contemporary enough to do breathing exercises, yes, but as primitive as can be when it came to vibrating to new sensations. And to have found a cinematic form for them, between the truth-to-life of Cartier-Bresson and the dream-imagery of the so-called marginal cinema.'

Henri Cartier-Bresson was a well-known still photographer working in Paris in Realist mode in the 1930s and 1940s.

cancer. The film begins with a visit to a fortune-teller, who by confirming dramatic changes in Cléo's life crystallises her fears. The first half of the film follows Cléo and her secretary Angèle home from the fortune-teller's to her lavish flat/studio. In the second half, after abruptly breaking off a rehearsal when she realises for the first time the painful significance of the lyrics she is given, Cléo goes out into Paris again, to visit a friend and explore the Parc Montsouris. Here she meets a soldier at the end of his leave from the Algerian war and strikes up a conversation with him; he accompanies her to the hospital for the test results.

Sandy Flitterman-Lewis (1996: 268–84) particularly has clarified in great detail the mechanism of the film and the way in which it explores the problem of female identity. Clearly, the Cléo of the first part of the film sees herself through the eyes of others, and allows this to determine who she is: she identifies herself with her appearance to such an extent that, looking in the fortune-teller's mirror, she can proclaim that 'Being ugly, that's death'. As she is clearly beautiful, the definition permits her temporarily to deny death, but it is manifestly unsatisfactory. In order to reassure herself of her existence she is obliged to check her appearance at regular intervals, either in one of the many mirrors which surround her or by using other people as her mirror. The problem, already apparent, is that her illness is both very real and quite invisible – a fact which both reassures and annoys her. Although she declares to her friend Dorothée that she is glad that her cancer 'doesn't show', she is still obliged to take account of this part of her subjectivity that most of her entourage are quite oblivious of. Even her lover does not take her illness seriously. Her knowledge of its existence therefore obliges her to see herself differently, to take account of her own awareness. None of the people around her really know her if they are unaware of something so fundamental. The thought drives her to assert her identity, complaining of the way her managers treat her as a doll unable to think for herself. In the second part of the film, instead of expecting others to look at her, she looks at her surroundings, and her meetings with Dorothée and Antoine contain a genuine exchange.

The contrast between the two passages through Paris, in terms of both what is filmed and how it is filmed, illustrates this progress. On her way back to her flat, Cléo makes two pauses; once to sit with Angèle in the café where they meet, once to buy a hat. As Cléo walks to the café, the camera follows her, at a distance and from a slightly high angle, keeping her strictly in the centre of the frame. In the first sequences, Cléo is (as Flitterman-Lewis has pointed out) almost always surrounded by mirrors. These not only keep her own image constantly before her eyes; they also prevent her from seeing beyond them. As she tries on hats, she is seen through a maze of reflections, of mirrors glimpsed through the shop-window. As the camera, outside the window, moves around to keep her in frame, reflections of the life of the street are reflected on to Cléo. This is an excellent visual description of her awareness of that world – it has no substance in her life, other images are nothing but passing shadows over the all-important image of herself. This, of course, is not only how she sees her world, but how she imagines herself to be seen by others. The camera, in the first half of the film, goes along with this, scarcely losing sight of her for an instant.

In the second part of the film, on the contrary, the street is seen 'through Cléo's eyes' in two ways. First, the position of the camera in relation to the sights of Paris often corresponds to Cléo's position – the classic cinematic way of establishing point-of-view. Shots of her walking are much briefer, interspersed with images which correspond to what she sees, and she is frequently decentred. Also, as in *L'Opéra-Mouffe*, the images themselves have a point of reference to Cléo's condition. The street showmen who entertain crowds by swallowing frogs or pushing hooks into their flesh become images of the body's fragility or of its invasion by alien, vaguely sinister objects and pain. They frighten Cléo; knowing what is preoccupying her, we lend them similar associations. Other images of the street reflect, by their selection, that their observer is preoccupied with death. This part of *Cléo* clearly owes much to the ideas of *L'Opéra-Mouffe*, with which it contrasts directly. The observer of *L'Opéra-Mouffe* was preoccupied with birth, Cléo with death (although both preoccupations have a similar bodily location). And yet, while the images of *L'Opéra-Mouffe* are disturbing (transposed to *Cléo*, they would be truly nightmarish), the Parisian sequences in *Cléo* are much less so. The process of observation is a liberation for Cléo, and even the alarming symbol-images have a positive function, helping her to make sense of what is happening to her in her own terms rather than through someone else's inadequate eyes. Besides, they (as with those of *L'Opéra-Mouffe*) are interspersed with observation of people, and in this respect the selection, and the significance, of those observed is quite different in *Cléo*, although the first sequence of 'people-watching' is very similarly titled in both films ('quelques-uns' in *L'Opéra-Mouffe* becomes 'quelques autres' ('certain others')).

Cléo's first real awareness of others invades her in the Café du Dôme, a well-known meeting-place of the Left Bank chattering classes. The camera follows her (again, mostly at her eye-level, but keeping her in view) as she wanders round the vast café, listening to snippets of conversations before rapidly swallowing the drink she has ordered. The conversations are at once serious and trivial, as café conversations tend to be. At the bar they talk about politics, in a corner they discuss Sartre, a woman complains of the music. These are not the battered tramps of *L'Opéra-Mouffe*, but well-integrated, relaxed people. Their function in this film is not to be associated with Cléo's obsession, but on the contrary to distract her from it.

The one thing that is not discussed, indeed barely glanced at, is Cléo; and she does not seem particularly disappointed not to encounter herself among the observations she is making. Indeed she takes precautions not to be observed, putting on a pair of dark glasses to avoid any chance of recognition. While the sights of Paris provide her with a new set of images of herself, darker, more complex images than the 'visage de poupée' (doll's face) which has begun to irritate her, but images capable of reflecting what is really going on within her, the people that she encounters allow her to forget herself in other subjectivities, to look at alternative lives. It is this realisation which will make her encounters with Dorothée and Antoine so much more rewarding than those with

Angèle and the taxi-driver in the first part of the film (which they somewhat resemble).

Thus Cléo changes from object to be looked at to subject who looks and interprets what she looks at – from woman seen to woman seeing. This is very fundamental for Varda (who after all has based her whole life on her status as a woman seeing); although Cléo is afraid that she is going to die, paradoxically her fear makes her come truly to life, taking control of the elements of her own life by reacting authentically to them. In the second half of the film, Cléo (through the camera) is able to integrate the outside world into her consciousness, to begin with certainly as an extension of her consciousness of herself, but, by the time she meets Antoine, she is ready to turn her gaze entirely outward and find respite from herself in all the multifarious details of life which so fascinate Antoine. Her change of attitude is indicated in her attitude to Antoine. Previously, she says, she would have ignored him or thought him a nuisance (that is, seen him only in relation to the expectations he might have of her); now, she allows herself to be interested by him irrespective of his interest in her.

The film's progress is marked by two major sequences, visually and in tone apart from the rest, in which Cléo performs her own songs. These sequences mark turning-points in Cléo's career and also moments of climax in Cléo's perception of herself, since in performing she is representing herself, giving a version of her own identity to an audience real or imaginary. In both these cases, the audience is imaginary within the film-world (although while Cléo is rehearsing the audience is projected to be real some day): however, of course the performances are set up for the benefit of the film's spectators, and the mise-en-scène reflects this.

The performance of the song 'Sans toi' in Cléo's flat is the moment which decides Cléo that her current self-definition is not only inadequate but a deadly trap. The image changes as it progresses. As she starts to sing the surroundings are realistic, in the sense that however artificial the environment of Cléo's flat may be, we recognise that it is a credible place for this woman to live, and that it makes perfect narrative sense that she should be there. She is actually less aware of her audience at the beginning of a rehearsal (when she is preparing for a finished performance) than when she is receiving José or even when talking to Angèle. However, as 'Sans toi' takes off, and as Cléo begins to hear what she is singing, the image changes, until Cléo stands before a dark background as if in an actual performance: she is no longer seen within her surroundings but brilliantly lit against the dark, like a singer on stage (plate 6). Ironically this move from rehearsal to performance means that the audience has disappeared, and Cléo is performing for herself (and us). Cléo really 'sees' herself as spectacle, and this moment is presented to the film audience as a mise-en-scène set apart from the realistic progress of the story.

This is a sophisticated method of marking Cléo's change from object to subject, which approaches a problem inevitable in cinema representation, and especially representation of women. To the cinema audience, even when Cléo becomes herself an observer, she is still there to be observed and therefore an object; the best we can do to mark the change is to observe outside objects as well, through her eyes. In order to observe Cléo herself through Cléo's own eyes (as soon as she stops looking at herself as an outsider, a beautiful object), some other strategy is needed, and Varda opts for a moment of theatre.

The second such moment occurs in the Parc Montsouris, as Cléo, quite alone, goes down a flight of steps as if performing on a glamorous stage, singing one of her songs which calls attention to her outside appearance. Although the environment in this case does not change, the effect is of a number in a musical comedy (such as the films of Varda's husband Demy). The performance has no audience, it is on one level for Cléo herself, on another for the camera. Cléo is announcing, to herself, the artificiality of her singer's image – which she seems to be enjoying, but in an almost detached way. The film audience receives this as a startling contrast to the Cléo we have been watching for some time. It is a return to the earlier glamorous image, but we no longer feel that this is the 'real' Cléo. The first song marked the moment where Cléo feels the urgent need to get away from the constructed image which seems to be all she is: the second marks a return to it from the confident knowledge that she does indeed have a personal, subjective identity apart from it.

Varda has recently toyed with the idea of an American remake of *Cléo*, directed by herself, with AIDS substituted for cancer and starring Madonna. By 1997, nothing had yet come of this project, but it would be fascinating to see what differences the new situation would bring to the treatment of the subject. Madonna embodies already in her public image many of the contradictions which *Cléo* explores. She is herself, like Cléo but unlike Corinne Marchand who plays her, a star with a highly constructed public image; but, unlike Cléo, she has considerable control over her image (at least apparently), and has never hesitated to present herself as desiring as well as desirable. Clearly, the combination of Varda, Madonna and *Cléo* would not be a simple remake ... but what it would be can only be guessed at.

Réponse de femmes (1975)

In 1975, Varda's involvement with the feminist movement had reached a turning-point. She had been occasionally involved in political activity on women's issues since the 1950s, but, recalling this, she comments 'je ne militais en rien' ('I was no militant') (Varda 1994: 107). That issues of female identity interested her and played a part in her work we have already seen, but the specific question of *how* to be involved in a movement does not surface until the 1970s.

This was of course a particularly active time for political expression of women's awareness and indeed for political expression in France generally. The upheavals of 1968 had left much of the intelligentsia of France eager to engage in social struggle. There was a general feeling among creative artists that their talents *should* be used to some sort of political end. In the film world this feeling was fostered by all the main cinematic magazines, and modes of social protest were at the centre of discussion in all fields.

During May 1968 itself Varda and Demy were in California

and had therefore missed the excitement in France. The atmosphere of the period had its effect, however, and of the films which Varda made in California, *Lions' Love* juxtaposes its stars' private lives with distant – but not irrelevant – public events (a dialectic exchange of influence between public and private was another major theme of discussion in post-68 intellectual France), while *Black Panthers* investigates the conduct of a political movement. Of *Black Panthers*, Varda has said: 'Il me semblait capter quand je les filmais une prise en charge d'eux-mêmes qui avait une belle équivalence en les Femmes découvrant qu'elles pouvaient elles-mêmes penser la théorie et organiser l'action sans le secours des anciens penseurs'[6] (Varda 1994: 95).

On her return from America, Varda had also been somewhat withdrawn from film-making because of the birth of her second child. Her only feature-film during the early part of the decade was *Daguerréotypes*, which Varda formulated in terms of 'women's creativity', as we have seen. Françoise Audé (1981: 140), quoting Varda's summary of her experience in 1975 (Varda 1975: 50), records that it was during her stay in America that Varda 'discovered' the intellectual and militant feminist movement through English and American authors. Her contact with American feminism gave her a more sophisticated basis of theory, and in the feverish atmosphere of the late 1960s the issue became more urgent. 'J'ai beaucoup appris sur moi-même et sur le féminisme grâce aux "femmes du mouvement", les américaines radicales, ou théoriciennes, puis les françaises d'après mai 68',[7] she observed in 1975 (Varda 1975: 46). During the 1970s she became practically involved in the forceful movement for the legalisation of abortion in France, which took off in 1971 with a declaration, published in the leftish magazine *Le Nouvel Observateur*, by 343 women (Varda included) that they had had an

6 'I felt that when I filmed them I was capturing a process of taking responsibility for themselves which was a good equivalent of Women discovering that they could think out theory for themselves and organise action without the help of the old thinkers.'

7 'I learnt a lot about myself and about feminism thanks to the "women in the movement", the American radicals, or theorists, then the French women after May 68.'

abortion and were thus technically criminals. She took part in the Mouvement pour la Légalisation de l'Avortement et de la Contraception (MLAC), which organised trips to Amsterdam like that where Pomme in *L'Une chante, l'autre pas* meets her lover Darius. The MLAC campaign was extremely high-profile throughout the 1970s.

It was in this context that in 1975 Varda was contacted to make an 8-minute film for Antenne 2 around the subject 'Qu'est-ce qu'être femme?' ('What does it mean to be a woman?'). Varda's decision from the start was to concentrate on the body, rather than on more abstract subjects such as social role. Given the central importance of the woman's relationship to her body in *L'Opéra-Mouffe* and *Cléo*, this seems to be a factor which coherently links Varda's feminist thinking across two decades and her American experience. *Réponse de femmes* features a group of very different women, speaking to camera, in succession or as a group, about their experience of inhabiting a female body: 'être femme, c'est être née avec un sexe féminin ... être femme, c'est vivre dans un corps de femme'.[8]

It presents itself as a militant statement, introduced by a hand-written title 'Ciné-tract'. *Cinétracts* was the name given to short films made during and after the 'events' of 1968, constructed as political analyses of the situations or events which they showed. The original *cinétracts* were usually made for a militant audience and could not expect a television showing; there is a contradiction here since *Réponse de femmes* was made for TV, and while the film does not mention this explicitly, it underlies much of what is said and shown (or not shown). In fact, *Réponse de femmes* is very much concerned with how women's bodies can be seen, in what circumstances and why, and the relevance that this has for the problem of being a woman.

Much of the problem of 'being a woman', as described in *Réponse de femmes*, stems from the imposition of ways of looking which turn the female body into an object or even a package of

8 'to be a woman is to be born with female genitals ... to be a woman is to live in a woman's body'.

different objects. The speakers attack the way in which their female wholeness is reduced to a number of 'sexy bits', or to a generic perfect figure of woman which encompasses all women and allows neither for ageing nor for difference. What is at stake is not that women should not be looked at, but that they should be looked at on their own terms and as individuals, women and not Woman. Thus *Réponse de femmes* makes aggressive use of nudity, among its protagonists of all ages and shapes. This voluntary, and unglamourised, nakedness is used to denounce the contradiction implicit in a visual culture which uses naked women to sell cars but also tells women 'sois pudique, montre pas ton cul' ('Be modest, don't show your ass') – when Antenne 2 queried certain of the images, Varda made effective use of this, announcing and denouncing the censorship with an intertitle.

Réponse de femmes raises contradictions of its own. The women refuse to recognise themselves in male-imposed generalities especially with regard to the *use* of their bodies (is Woman made to be a mother? The film's answer is, no, but some women are, some aren't), but they are implicated by such generalities, and when one individual woman's body is used to illustrate that stereotype, that woman becomes representative of each one of them. Thus in the words of the baker's wife – a woman who plays an active role, in a different context, in *Daguerréotypes*: 'Je trouve que c'est absurde de voir toujours les femmes nues tout le temps, alors j'aime dire, mais alors, c'est moi qu'on affiche.'⁹ Equally there is a contradiction between the revolt which all the women feel faced with the commercialisation of their own bodies and a desire to show themselves which equates to a desire for recognition.

In its short available time, *Réponse de femmes* inevitably does not go much beyond a statement of the issues which it has chosen to highlight, and many of these are, certainly from the 1990s, rather obvious. Nonetheless its themes are recognisable both in Varda's earlier films and in those which are to come, and the feature-films often offer sophisticated workings through these rather rapidly stated problems. Thus the desire for pregnancy

9 'I think it's absurd always to see naked women all the time, so I like to say, but, that's me posted up there.'

unrecuperated by social discourses about Woman's Duty of
Motherhood appears in *L'Opéra-Mouffe* and *L'Une chante, l'autre
pas* – perhaps also, discreetly, in *Jane B.. Cléo* is concerned with
the conflict between the individual woman and the generic image
of Desirable Woman, made to be looked at, into which society has
transformed Cléo while requiring her to suppress her
individuality. Cléo has her equivalent in *Réponse de femmes*, one
woman who does conform to the glamorous stereotype, joined in
solidarity with the others. The ambivalent relationship to this
stereotype (which Varda is not so naïve as to suggest is an
unpleasant experience for a woman who conforms to it) reappears
in *Jane B.*, and even slips into *Sans toit ni loi*. The problems of
constructing female identity outside a fixing male gaze ('Mais
comment être femme en dehors de l'opinion masculine?' ('But
how to be a woman outside male opinion?') says one of the group
in *Réponse* at one point) is much more searchingly explored in
Sans toit ni loi. In brief, despite its title, *Réponse de femmes* is
important not so much for its answers as for its questions, which
it puts plainly and challengingly. For approaches to answers there
must be more time, and perhaps a less directly militant approach.
Varda is very aware of the uses of fiction as a way of conjugating
many different voices and angles. This is one of the ways in which
she is most close to the novelist Nathalie Sarraute, whom she
much admires and to whom she dedicated *Sans toit ni loi*. A
cinétract is almost by definition univocal: it is a militant film made
to impose an argument. It is to the credit of *Réponse de femmes* that
its principal argument is that society needs to think about the
question.

Réponse is, by its own admission, directed at a male audience;
the women address themselves directly several times to a society
which is identified with its male half, 'messieurs les pères, les
maris, les amants, les patrons, les mecs et les copains'.[10] The only
possible position for a woman spectator of the film is to cross over
and stand, as it were, in front of the camera – the group's
discourse is so absolutely rooted in the biological fact of the female

10 'you gentlemen – fathers, husbands, lovers, bosses, blokes and friends'. The
form of address is difficult to translate satisfactorily.

body that not to join with it would be to deny one's femininity. This is not to say that it does not allow room for difference, but its main challenge seems to be directed only at Men – in the strictly biological sense. In the longer films (and especially *Sans toit ni loi*) Varda poses questions about the gaze and its relation to female identity which are much more subtle, and which implicate the female spectator quite as much as the male. But the seeds of the problem are here.

L'Une chante, l'autre pas (1976)

L'Une chante, l'autre pas, unlike *L'Opéra-Mouffe* and *Cléo*, springs from an enquiry not only into what it means to be a woman but what it means to be a feminist. It is strongly – perhaps uniquely – concerned with political expression and political action. In this, as we have seen above, it is a product of its time and of Varda's concerns at that time. However, it is a fiction film and not a *cinétract*: it does allow for different voices and a number of attitudes to what it shows, although the variety is certainly not as great as in later films.

By 1976, the MLAC had won its battle for legal abortion, and the women's movement could with some justification feel a sense of achievement. *L'Une chante, l'autre pas* is indeed an extremely optimistic film. Its two heroines, Pomme and Suzanne, good friends by postcard correspondence, pursue their separate developments into fulfilment through the agency, one way or another, of the dynamic social climate of the period. Suzanne, the one who doesn't sing, has furthest to go: at the film's opening she is 22, a downtrodden mother of two living with a photographer too preoccupied with his own unhappiness to support her emotionally. He commits suicide, and she returns to her dreadful peasant family who practically ostracise her. With support from her female workmates and from a local organisation she manages to fight her way to financial independence (out of desperation), moves to the Côte d'Azur with her children and finally marries her colleague, a middle-aged doctor. Pomme, the one who sings, a rebellious schoolgirl in the first sequences where she helps Suzanne to obtain an abortion, becomes a successful protest singer and performance artist, always preoccupied with women's problems. After a career setback she briefly moves to Iran with her Iranian boyfriend Darius, gets married there but rejects the repressive traditions which even the apparently liberated Darius drifts back to, and returns to France and to her old life, pregnant with her second child but self-sufficient.

Compared with *L'Opéra-Mouffe*, *Cléo* and *Sans toit ni loi*, *L'Une chante, l'autre pas* is a straightforward film. It is largely concerned with watching its protagonists, whose doings are narrated, sometimes by Varda in voice-over, sometimes by themselves in the postcards they exchange. The time structure, although not quite as limpid as it appears at first glance, is relatively traditional – the start of the girls' friendship in 1962 is followed by their reunion ten years later. Two flashbacks fill us in on their lives in the meantime, and after that the film alternates between them across the next four years, using their occasional postcards as crossing-points. Sometimes the episodes are filmed as fairly traditional narration, sometimes – when the time-scale is greater and the events less precise, for example during Pomme's stay in Iran – the voice-overs take on the task of narration leaving the image to evoke significant glimpses. There is a good deal of performance, especially associated with Pomme, who is the vehicle for most of the reflection on female identity which the film undertakes.

These two parallel lives are presented with a different quality. The sequences concerned with Suzanne are associated with dull colours – grey or earth-brown – until she moves to the coast, thereafter with a naturalistic appearance and colour-scheme; the images are largely self-explanatory and narrative, with voice-overs only to introduce the incidents (except in the Soissons episode). Where there is a voice-over, it tends to be Suzanne's and not Varda's. And although Suzanne is not unreflective, her reflection is largely linked to action and to particular cases, her own or others'. She finds her place in the women's movement as a family planning adviser, working with individual women on practical problems. What is interesting about Suzanne to the audience is what she *does* with her situation – what is important about Pomme is more often what she *is* or presents herself as being.

Illustrative images accompanied by narrative voice-over tend to be associated with Pomme, and occasionally her life is narrated by the external authorial voice, Varda. A good deal of the sequences devoted to Pomme are in fact not of her life but of her performance, a performance in which she takes on the anonymous role of spokeswoman for the Female Condition. Performance sequences are naturally highly coloured, but even when not in performance the images associated with Pomme are brighter, and the filming more consciously stylised when Pomme's story is in progress. We shall return to this.

Pomme's role of spokeswoman develops during the film. Although her lyrics declare from the outset that she speaks for all women, in the earlier sequences she is not immune from the temptation to perform her own individuality and create a personal image on the same principle as – although qualitatively different from – Cléo Victoire. Pomme in fact is a complement and development of Cléo in that both must address (or the audience must address while watching them) the question, raised also by *Réponse de femmes*, of how a woman whose vocation is to be looked at affects the situation of all women. Cléo allows herself to represent Woman as her male managers want her to be; Pomme on the contrary takes responsibility for herself and, at least in principle, provides a positive model which her female audience will gain by identifying with. She also uses her position in front of an audience to challenge that audience, leading discussions after the performance. If it could sometimes be argued that Pomme's mode of action comes close to claiming, not that this is what Women can be, but that this is what Woman is (especially perhaps in her celebrations of pregnancy) the presence of critical spectators in one of the later performance scenes represents an indication that if performance is to be used as political action, it must involve its intended audience actively and creatively.

Throughout the film Pomme challenges her audience with her interpretation of what it means to be a woman. The film offers an early sequence which can stand as a defining moment, that at which it becomes necessary for Pomme to ask questions about her identity. Here the film presents an Image of Woman to the audience and at the same time to Pomme, who we as yet know very little about and so are inclined to accept as 'one of us', another audience. This image is then, traumatically, detached from and denied to Pomme. Suzanne's photographer husband Jérôme makes his career from photographing women in their 'truth'. He explains his method to Pomme, who has come in to inspect his exhibition (here she like us is a viewer): uncovering 'truth' to him means continuing the photo session until his subjects get tired and drop their guard. On the face of it it seems a logical procedure – strip away the pose (or performance) and reality will appear. However, from the start doubts are sown. Pomme instantly notices the homogeneity of Jérôme's portraits – all the subjects seem worn down and sad. The 'true' image of all these women seems to be that of victim. Jérôme asks Pomme to pose for him. The session is not a success: at the end Jérôme announces with a touch of irritation that he can't 'get through' to Pomme, despite having resorted to literal nakedness as well as to the psychological stripping which he usually practises. Pomme the schoolgirl experiences this rejection as a crisis of identity – 'It feels as if I'm not a real woman' she tells Jérôme, who hastens to reassure her, clumsily, that this is not at all what he means. With typical resilience Pomme soon apparently forgets the incident, but in fact it stands at the root of her search for a more satisfactory 'truth'.

If it was not sufficiently clear already, Jérôme's session with Pomme reveals to us that his unmasking exercise has a strong element of bullying. What he is doing is not unmasking reality, but replacing one image (the pose, created by the woman) with another, which he has created. Pomme is unable to abandon her self-consciousness (although she tries), and retains a control over her own image which Jérôme cannot accept. The episode functions as a prologue for the gradual construction of a female-centred woman's identity which both Pomme and Suzanne engage in once Jérôme is out of the way.

Denunciation of a male-constructed image of woman as victim

was not new by 1976, but Varda has introduced a certain subtlety by ensuring that the image-maker Jérôme is far from a brash manipulator. His belief that he is unmasking the reality of his sitters appears to be genuine. Although weak, he is a likeable character, and the position of helpless victim he 'reveals' in the women corresponds quite closely to his own passive attitude to life. Nonetheless, he is incapable of accepting the 'revelation' of Pomme when she does not correspond to his preconceived notion of what she should reveal. He blames her for not being herself when the problem is that she is not what he wants, but he does so innocently and without malice. Pomme equally accepts the criticism, temporarily, with a certain innocence and without resentment. The whole episode illustrates neatly the process of formation of a male-defined female identity which does not imply any conscious desire for domination on one side or subordination on the other. Jérôme's nature is such that he might well consider the natural condition of all human beings to be that of victim: nonetheless when behind a camera he becomes an active and even aggressive force, creating the victim he desires – the structure of the image during the photo session encourages the (easy) analogy between the intrusion of the camera into her private existence and the violent intrusion of rape.

Pomme overcomes her initiatory doubt about her identity in large measure through her performance. It is this apparently which gives her the self-confidence which comes much more slowly to Suzanne. Through her performance she is able to choose and to construct the image she projects according to her own priorities. She experiments with various images, including the non-image represented by the wearing of the veil in Iran. The film portrays this as a voluntary step: it does not appear to be much more than another performance, and at the first hint that this may be a role capable of trapping her, Pomme leaves it and returns to France.

The Iranian episode attracted much criticism at the time, largely because Varda attempted no political analysis of a dubious regime, and to some extent accepts a picture-postcard image. The latter image is of course highly appropriate to the narrative structure of the film (at this point the story is being carried on by means of postcard correspondance), and it is perhaps unfair to attack the film for not exploring wide political issues which would be peripheral to the main theme. That the Iranian women are literally invisible (and when Pomme 'performs' one of them, she too becomes invisible) is a fairer criticism. In fact the film is interested in the development of feminist consciousness in two *French* women, and one wonders why it was necessary to send Pomme to Iran at all. Certainly the veil represents the nearest feasible approach to the extreme term of invisibility – a necessary counterpart to any examination of how women are seen. It is an experience that Pomme initially finds liberating, and finally rejects, but it is not clear whether the disadvantages of her situation are directly connected to the absence of the gaze. The case could be made: in Iran Pomme can be seen only in the domestic space. In the street she is simply a shape similar to a crowd of other shapes; she is not noticed, and this, perhaps, deprives her not only of an image but also of a voice. However, the connection is never directly made, and Suzanne in France, very little concerned with her image and indeed even allergic to an audience (see her reaction to the showy clothes Pomme brings her from Iran), nonetheless succeeds in gaining and keeping independence and a certain influence.

Otherwise, Pomme discovers in Iran that her liberal, feminist man has the potential to be a domestic tyrant, despite his own best intentions, under the pressure of the surrounding culture. But setting this revelation in Iran reduces the force of the argument with relation to France, which is implicitly found not guilty of encouraging a similar process.

One thing which the episode does do, apart from emphasising Pomme's view of life as a succession of roles, is to increase further the distance between Pomme and Suzanne, not only literally but in terms of decor and of film style. We have already seen that the filming of the Pomme episodes is richer, more varied in style and more highly coloured than that of the Suzanne episodes. Even the actress, Valérie Mairesse, with her flame-red hair, is brighter. There may be another problem here which the film does not wholly address: the class difference between the two women, though evident, is largely taken as given. This is despite the fact that Varda has said that inequalities of class in the female condition were perhaps the most important issue of the women's movement to her at the time that the film was made, and it may be that the questions one is tempted to pose were in fact intended to be left unresolved. But it is actually quite easy to put the difference between Suzanne and Pomme down to factors of personality – the outgoing woman can sing and perform her identity, discovers it quickly and helps others to find theirs in a bright and fun-loving way; the quiet inward-looking one finds her own feet the hard way, leads a low-key life and travels very little. The film's title encourages this interpretation. However, though neither are of particularly wealthy backgrounds, the cultural baggage associated with Pomme's family (lycée, music training with a choir and at least a semblance of family conversation, however frustrating) is a dramatic contrast with Suzanne's home in Soissons where a typewriter is an alien intrusion. (If Suzanne is banished to the barn to practise typing this is not, of course, explicitly because her family reject writing as alien, but the image is powerful.)

Looked at from this distance, *L'Une chante, l'autre pas* is not the most successful of Varda's films, but at the time of its making it was influential and it remains almost unique as a commercial French film concerned with the militant aspects of the women's movement. The women's private stories are totally dependent on the public aspects of the movement; their political activity forms them and they also help to form the movement. The reunion of the two women, which takes place during the (reconstructed) demonstration outside the courtroom of the Bobigny trial,[11] is really the point of origin of the whole narrative and the centre of

11 The Bobigny trial, in 1972, of four women accused of procuring an abortion for the daughter of one of them. They were found guilty but fined 8 francs, and the result was seen as a victory. The case, taken by the famous barrister Gisèle Halimi, highlighted the ways in which the current law penalised working-class women, and the class issue was one reason why Halimi's line differed from that of the MLF (Mouvement pour la Libération des Femmes) and MLAC, more oriented to gender issues pure and simple. Varda's subsequent statements (at Edinburgh Film Festival, 1996, personal communication) about the importance of class align her to some extent with Halimi. (See Duchen 1986: 53–5.)

gravity of the film. Although the demo is a reconstruction, the barrister Gisèle Halimi who won the real case really appears on the courtroom steps, and the demonstrators were not paid extras but were taking part out of a certain commitment to the case and the cause.

The idyllic final scene provides a very optimistic closure: Suzanne's daughter Marie's future seems to be assured and in the family reunion the public space of street demonstrations or performance is forgotten. However, it is made clear that this is a temporary, although renewable, Utopia: the group meets up from time to time but the other spaces, places and activities of the film are not abolished. The role of past political action in the construction of this brief fulfilment is also underlined: if these women are comfortable with the identity they have constructed for themselves and project to others, they have achieved this against heavy odds and with the collaboration of groups and organisation, perhaps also of the spirit of a period. Such participation of society in the establishment of a satisfactory way of defining oneself as woman will not appear again in Varda's work, although the questioning remains.

Sans toit ni loi (1985)

The first important consideration in discussing *Sans toit ni loi* is that the approach to the subject of image-forming has changed dramatically, and become extremely complex. Is Mona a woman seen? Yes, presumably, since the film is constructed around various witnesses' interpretations of her – and yet, who really sees Mona? There is no character in the film of whom it can safely be said that they *understand* Mona, or even that they construct a full and rounded image of her. Those with definite impressions tend to be those who have seen her for the shortest time (like the peasant women who decide she is a free spirit). The longer any witness is in Mona's company, the more likely they are to be puzzled or simply dismissive. Most people, and the spectator with them, are left with nothing more than a question mark.

So is she a woman seeing? Is the failure of every attempt to construct her as an object the result of the overpowering importance of her subjectivity? From the spectator's point of view, not really. We are given no hint of Mona's subjectivity: this is one of the main ways in which the film's concerns seem quite divergent from those of *Cléo*, despite Varda's parallelism. She certainly looks, but it is very hard to say what she sees: a total contrast to those previous films (*La Pointe Courte*, *L'Opéra-Mouffe*, *Cléo*, *Documenteur*) which make a point of ensuring that we understand exactly how the outside world enters the protagonist's consciousness and mutates in consequence. What she thinks of the other characters is particularly unreadable, and if we wish to find out we are obliged to read the external signs much as they would be: we are thus invited to share the witnesses' subjectivity, if anybody's. When we come to the question, surely vital to any extended enquiry into construction of identity, is Mona a woman who sees herself, the answer is a resounding No. There are no mirrors in Mona's world – or, if there are, they reflect other things. Sometimes she stands behind them, as in the shot of her opening the caravan window on the goatherd's land. She talks about herself only with enormous reluctance, and says as little as possible. When asked to sum up her life, and perhaps to sum up herself, she says simply 'Je bouge' (I move). The suggestion that she might pose for pornographic photos – which would fix some sort of visible image of her – is met with brief amusement, as if the idea is too ridiculous to contemplate. She does not even reject it, it is unthinkable from the start.

What we have in *Sans toit ni loi* is a large number of varied, subjective witnesses, all directing their gaze at one shifting central point, Mona. Of Mona herself we learn very little, except that she remains outside all the social structures which surround her, and that her insistence on continual movement ultimately leads to total detachment, and death. The film investigates not Mona herself but the traces she has left in others, and, if we are prepared to listen carefully, this is announced even in the introductory speech.

Sans toit ni loi begins with the discovery of Mona's corpse in a ditch. It is a tough introduction, the pictures are indefinite and grim but not at all sensational. The actual shots of the corpse have the kind of realism which we associate with news footage. Intercut shots of red stains being cleaned from a phone-booth suggest blood and violence, but the police assessment that there is no foul play rules this out. As an introduction to the film this sequence provides a warning of the frustrations to come. The elements of a mystery are put in place, expectations of a detective enquiry may be raised, but no, there is no murder ... it takes perhaps a second of adjustment to this before we realise that the mystery is no less, quite the reverse. The bizarre red stains are unexplained, and for the audience they may function as a false clue, analogous to the Rosebud of *Citizen Kane* to which *Sans toit ni loi* has been compared. Already, expectations about the subject of the film have had to be readjusted. Readjustment of expectations is a continual requirement of *Sans toit ni loi*; the spectator has continually to change preconceived ideas which spring up in the face of incomplete evidence, and we also watch as a series of different people form *their* expectations of Mona and cope with their destruction.

After the first sequence, the main body of the film will consist of a combination of flashbacks of Mona's life and interviews with witnesses, arriving in the end at the point at which we started. This reconstruction is announced by the voice-over of a female narrator. As she speaks, the image of Mona's body zipped into a body-bag fades into a stretch of sand with a single line across it, whence the camera rises to show a beach with, at a very great distance, a naked Mona coming out from a swim.

The narrator 'announces' the film thus:

Personne ne réclama le corps: il passa du fossé à la fosse commune. Cette morte de mort naturelle ne laissait pas de traces. Je me demande qui pensait encore à elle parmi ceux qui l'avaient connue petite. Mais les gens qu'elle avait rencontrés récemment se souvenaient d'elle. Ces témoins m'ont permis de raconter ces dernières semaines de son dernier hiver. Elle les avait impressionnés. Ils parlaient d'elle sans savoir qu'elle était morte. Je n'ai pas cru bon de le leur dire, ni qu'elle s'appelait Mona

Bergeron. Moi-même je sais peu de choses d'elle, mais il me semble qu'elle venait de la mer.[12]

The narrator's speech is of prime importance to *Sans toit ni loi*. Like much else in the film, it is more complex than it seems at first glance. The immediate impression received is that the film-maker is here announcing her intention to enquire into the life of the dead woman: 'raconter les dernières semaines de son dernier hiver'. Given that this is a fiction film, this introduction allows an impression of documentary destined to make the audience more committed to the illusion.

This is borne out by information available about the film outside the cinema. Average first-time spectators know that the film-maker is a woman, they have seen the posters for the film with the living Mona glaring out to camera. They may have read a summary which described the film as being 'about a vagabond woman in the South of France' – the English title of the film, *Vagabonde*, provides much of that summary in one word. They may even know that Mona was partly inspired by a homeless woman named Settina whom Varda had met – this information was fairly widely available – and that the original project had been a more general work on the life of the young rural homeless.

However, at a second look the narrator's identity and intention are both more complex. We shall return to her identity later: here it is the intentions that are of interest. Practically everything she says betrays that her centre of interest is more in the traces that Mona has left than in her life where it is unrecorded. For clearly the statement that Mona 'left no traces' is quite untrue. If the narrator wonders how many of Mona's long-ago acquaintances

12 'No-one claimed the body: it went from the ditch to the common grave. This woman, dead of natural causes, left no traces. I wonder who still thought about her among those who had known her as a child. But the people she had met recently remembered her. These witnesses have allowed me to tell the story of the last weeks of her last winter. She had made an impression on them. They talked about her without knowing that she was dead. I thought it best not to tell them, or that she was called Mona Bergeron. I know little about her myself, but it seems to me that she came from the sea.'

still think about her, she seems in no doubt that some do. Very certainly, Mona is remembered by those who have met her recently, and here she has left not only a trace but a strong trace, an 'impression'. The narrator makes clear that these impressions are all that she has to go on. So the story she tells will not be Mona's story, but an amalgamated story of all the 'impressions' that Mona has left. That we do not immediately think about this probably reflects how common a procedure it is in a documentary reconstruction, it does not even appear to be dangerous. *Sans toit ni loi* will demonstrate that it is. The demonstration begins even here, since at the end of her introduction the narrator allows herself an impression of her own. It is unlikely to be an accurate one, but it is intriguing, romantic, tempting – and borne out by the image briefly. The warning has been given – if we hear it – that every incident in *Sans toit ni loi* is filtered through a subjectivity.

I would contend that there are in broad terms two different ways of seeing Mona, and that these two ways are – roughly – gendered. Mona herself, female but conforming to no female stereotypes, is by definition difficult to place. Susan Hayward has suggested that all the witnesses look on her from a patriarchal perspective. 'Male discourses (whether uttered by men or women)' are used to try to assign her to a simple slot, but 'she defies identification, will not be made other' (Hayward 1990: 286).

Undoubtedly all the witnesses are impressed by Mona according to their own ideals and desires, but I do think that different kinds of desire are involved, and that there are thus different ways of seeing evoked. The two main ways of imprinting Mona on the mind, as it were, bear a close resemblance to the two ways in which Edgar Morin, in 1960, found that fans related to stars – ways which he relates inseparably to gender: 'This identification functions in two directions: the first is the amorous projection-identification addressed to a partner of the opposite sex ... The second, more widespread today, is an identification with an alter ego' (Morin 1960: 95).

It is relatively easy to divide most of the witnesses (except Mme Landier, of whom more later) into one or the other type. The division does not quite follow a neat male/female split, but it is nonetheless reasonable to refer to it as gendered. Exceptions are rare in any case. A rapidly-drawn up list would, I think, give: 'male' gaze – seeing Mona as a possible sexual partner, companion or in any other sense entering into a relationship with the witness (Paolo, David, Assoun, Jean-Pierre, the station pimp, the lorry-driver, the garage-owner, the foreman, the 'wild man of the woods', the timberyard manager, Tante Lydie, the goatherd's wife – and a number of other casual encounters in cafés and garages); 'female' gaze – seeing Mona as a reflection, revised and probably but not necessarily corrected, of the witness (the young countrywoman at the pump, the old countrywoman, Yolande, the foreman's wife, Eliane, the prostitute).

The goatherd shows a combination of the two reactions, but the female version is probably predominant.

It can be seen from the above that the male gaze, which seeks to relate to Mona or to have Mona relate to it, is the more common – although, from the point of view of the problem of the woman seen and a film about her, probably not the more interesting. Obviously the list includes a good deal of variety. To the timberyard manager or the foreman Mona means very little in any case, she is nothing but a casual worker or a curiosity. The other men in the list all see her as either a sexual or at least a romantic companion, in most cases a desirable one at the outset (Jean-Pierre being the only one repulsed). Of the two women, the goatherd's wife seems to have little impression of Mona, but what she has might be as worker or casual friend. Tante Lydie is more interesting. She clearly does not identify with Mona, but finds companionship with her, and apparently – exceptionally – she is never disappointed in her. However, Tante Lydie's status as witness must be doubtful – her powers of perception are very fluid (she is supposed to be almost blind), and her reactions after the event remain unknown. Among those listed as constructing their Mona-image in the 'female' way, there is more variation in initial reaction. The first three women mentioned – and the goatherd – start out with a Mona they are pleased to identify with, the latter three reject the identification from the start and find her more or less threatening.

As has been noted Mona escapes all attempts to construct her as an Other; she escapes equally attempts to construct her as a self-image. All the impressions which Mona leaves in the people she meets are marks of attempts to take over her identity, take possession of her and construct her according to the pattern the witness prefers. (The original title of the film was *A saisir*). If this pattern depends on a relationship with her (as the 'male' construction of her does), the attempt is doomed from the start. If she stays, she will sooner or later fall outside the ideal image; as soon as she leaves, there is no longer any relationship. Where the witness desires a very temporary interaction, she ensures that he does not even get that, or not in the way he expects. Once she falls short of the ideal, all members of this group lose interest, and therefore they will never 'see' her reliably. Most of them consider that Mona has rejected *them*, rather than the image they had of her. It seems that the only viable form for this kind of image of Mona, given her refusal to accept to be anyone's other, is one that rejects her from the start. Jean-Pierre will not be disappointed in her, or proved wrong; he has chosen, in a sense, the safest option, but it is not one which is very rewarding for him. He is fascinated even while – literally – taking refuge from involvement; he at once wants to look at Mona and refuses to look at her. The result gives neither understanding of Mona nor much self-understanding, since he will not confront the emotions she arouses.

The 'female' approach to Mona, quite as much as the male, begins with an ideal image, and it is quite as likely to reject Mona – possibly with even more virulence – when this image falls apart. The 'female' approach and the reasons for its frequent failure have considerable implications for the representation of women by women in the cinema. It might seem to be an alternative to a manipulative, 'patriarchal', image of 'woman as other'. In *Sans toit ni loi* it is seen to be equally exploitative, equally distorting, as is the 'male discourse', even though essentially different, and one is left to ask whether it is ever possible to escape from patterns of representation which project one's own desires on to the object represented. The question applies not only to the characters, but to film-maker and audience too.

At first sight of Mona, the two countrywomen and Yolande have in common the very rapid formation of an extremely positive image, an image formed entirely on the basis of a comparison. They look at Mona in order to see their own lives as if in a mirror. For the foreman's wife the process is somewhat similar, but she fears the reflection she sees and creates a negative image. The goatherd is initially more wary, but his very reticence springs from a similar process of comparison with his own life, Mona presenting him, however, with an image of himself that he has rejected, and which he is uncertain whether he desires or fears. To all these people, Mona functions as a very selective mirror, for they see in her, at least at a brief glance, what they wish to see. This sort of construction may be compared to the Lacanian description of the mirror-phase in its two defining characteristics: idealisation and simplification. Mona tends to represent a single, simplified concept which the women perceive as lacking to them: they construct her as 'themselves plus this vital thing'.

For the two countrywomen, the vital thing is freedom, and since they only glimpse Mona briefly, they retain this image of her which allows them to express their dissatisfaction with their own lives. Freedom is indeed widely perceived as Mona's defining characteristic, although it is not universally desired – the foreman's wife, for example, fears it, along with Mona's dirt, because along with it goes the loss of the ability to attract men and win a husband, the destiny which she presumably embraced and which she aspires to for her daughter. The ambiguous reaction of the goatherd to Mona's freedom stems from conflicting feelings of attraction and repulsion towards 'Mona as himself free'. On the one hand, freedom is the aspect of Mona which he relates to and desires in himself, congratulating her on having avoided the ties which he has accepted. Although he feels that a life on the road leads inevitably to self-destruction, an opinion which is borne out by Mona's subsequent fate, he seems still obscurely to desire it: his definition of freedom is considerably more subtle than that of the two peasant women, and relates to Mona's indifference to her own fate – freedom from fear rather than from physical ties. On the other hand, he makes some effort to draw Mona into the kind of life that he has chosen, offering her land and help to work it, attempting to lure her away from that very freedom which he apparently admired. Desiring Mona's insouciance and the life she has chosen, he also seeks to confirm the rightness of his own choice by persuading her to change her mind and settle down. The 'intolerance' which Flitterman-Lewis criticises in him ('he imposes his own conception of "alternative" on everybody else'; 1996: 291) probably stems from his own implication in Mona's choices. It is not 'everybody else' that he wants to change, but specifically Mona who has come to represent 'himself without the ties of family and animals', a desire which he wishes to suppress. After Mona's departure, he links his disappointment in her to her lack of political motivation, fixing on the major difference between himself and Mona which allows him to deny any identification with her; but while she was in his household, 'exchanging philosophies', politics were not an issue. If it is difficult to avoid the conclusion that this ex-academic also wants a pupil, and may also be disappointed at her failure to relate to him in the way that he hoped she might, and that he thus represents a combination of the 'male' and the 'female' approach, his disappointment in her way of relating to him finds expression, in the latter part of the film, in a damning criticism of what she *is*, and he finally rejects not only Mona but that part of himself which she had initially represented for him.

Yolande sees in Mona and David not freedom – which does not attract her – but an image, revised and corrected, of her own unsatisfactory relationship with Paolo: a couple entirely satisfied in each other. Yolande's first experience is a glance rather than a gaze, and literally at a 'frozen' image, since she has had to glance twice to be sure that the couple were not dead. The gaze comes afterwards; as Yolande talks about the couple she has found, she gazes into the distance, her eyes fixed on the mental image she has formed. At the real couple she looks only very briefly, and what she sees, explicitly, is the image of what she and Paolo ought, in her view, to be, presented to her as if in a mirror. The momentary idyll of the relationship with David is even more illusory, in fact, than Mona's freedom – and the audience suspects this, I think, even before their story is told. But its function for Yolande is immense.

It is clear that the specular relationship, while generating apparently positive feelings towards Mona, necessitates no inter-action at all: Mona, having once been glanced at, becomes irrelevant to the progress of the formation of the image. Mona the beloved becomes so real to Yolande that she tells Paolo 'Je connais un couple qui fait tout ensemble ... Tu ne les connais pas'.[13] She has evidently invented a great deal more than the little that she saw. She really does 'connaître ce couple', but they are not Mona and David: they are the image, realised in her mind – for perhaps the first time clearly – of what she would like to be. This is a very clear example of how little the 'female strategy' of relating to Mona has to do with Mona herself. The 'male gaze' at least implies some interaction, a recognition of her alterity even if this is aggressive. Such images contain their disavowal in their very existence, since they automatically project Mona *and* the gazer. An image based on the kind of specular reverie which Yolande indulges in is not only very unreliable indeed as a means of understanding the object of the gaze, but also it tends to be self-satisfied; that is, it does not need to be verified with reference to the *real* Mona to become firmly fixed and grounded in its holder.

It is of great value to that holder, however. The brief glimpse of Mona has provided Yolande with the possibility of articulating her desire, at least to herself. She still cannot communicate her feelings to Paolo, who does not share them, but at least, in providing her with an alternative self-image, Mona has enabled Yolande to locate her dissatisfaction and to begin to express it. Thus Yolande has reached a better understanding of herself through her glance. But as a means of reaching an understanding of *Mona*, it is utterly inadequate. Yolande's Mona-fiction is simultaneously Yolande and not-Yolande; she is certainly not Mona. Obviously this attitude cannot build a relationship between two individuals: Mona has aspects which are similar neither to what Yolande is nor to what she desires to be, and they will eventually come into the open.

13 'I know a couple who do everything together ... You don't know them.'

When Yolande meets Mona again, the image formed from a combination of glance and desire is confronted with the need for a longer-held gaze, and interaction with the object of the glance. The fact that Mona does not conform to the Mona-construction which Yolande has created is not initially negative. The self-knowledge which Yolande has gained from comparing herself with her invented Mona is irreversible, and Yolande does *not* reject Mona because she does not correspond to this idealised image which was really of Yolande herself. Rather, her reaction is sympathetic. Her previous 'identification' with Mona has been an entirely positive experience for her, and she therefore sees Mona positively. As the part of her Mona-fiction which is specifically not-Yolande – that which Yolande lacks – falls away, Yolande is left with the assumption that Mona is as herself, with the same lack felt in the same way. Since Yolande has located her dissatisfaction as the need for love, the situation must seem ideal to her. Yolande, disappointed by Paolo, can lavish affection on Mona, while the latter, similarly disappointed in David, will return the favour towards her benefactress.

Yolande's readjustment to the new reality thus reinforces her identification with Mona. She takes on board Mona's solitude, but interprets it according to her own experience and values, and equates it with loneliness. Similarly she accepts Mona's comfortless existence, but assumes immediately that Mona must desire to escape it – as Yolande herself would. There is none of the aggressivity with which the 'male' gaze greets the discovery that Mona is 'different' from its expectations. Precisely because the construction of her as a desired object implies some interaction with her as between two different individuals, the image formed by the 'male' approach includes some conception of that interaction which can be disappointed. Yolande has never imagined herself with Mona until now. The readjustment which she is forced to make does imply some projection of Mona as an 'other' to interact with, as companion and as protégée, but the projected other is as herself.

In inviting Mona to stay with her, Yolande thus refictionalises her as a companion who will, in some ways, be a mirror-image of herself, herself projected on to another. She imagines this new, 'real' Mona to have similar reactions and values to herself. However, she also assumes that Mona will submit to some extent to her control, as a mirror-image would move only as she moves. Apart from the projection on to the stranger of the docility of her own character ('Yolande est serviable ...' ('Yolande's obliging ...')), Yolande has lived for some time with an imaginary Mona whom she has practically invented, the 'couple' that she told Paolo she knew being a fiction of which she is the author and over which she has complete control. She has thus been conditioned to consider Mona as her own creation – and she reacts with violent hostility when that creation acts independently of her.

All the witnesses in the film can be seen as authors of their respective narrations and to some extent 'authors' of Mona. The 'female' approach to Mona, which depends on identification, inevitably implies this: Mona represents a part of the self rather as Mme Bovary represented a part of Flaubert. The analogy between Yolande's relationship to Mona and the relationship of author and creation is, however, clearer than with some of the minor characters. The film plays on this ambiguous relationship, externalising it. Mona, once in interaction with Yolande, does in some ways become a projection of her. She expresses interest in Paolo: later, she dons Yolande's apron and takes her place with Madame Lydie. Yolande has previously claimed not to exist for Lydie as an individual: she believes herself to be 'only an apron and a duster' for this woman who can scarcely see. In that case, Mona and Yolande should be exactly equivalent and substitutable for the old lady: but, of course, Yolande is wrong in believing herself to be completely anonymous to Lydie, and Mona is far from a perfect copy. Her mirror-image of Yolande is a distorting mirror, and Yolande soon perceives that her situation and her very identity are in danger. Into her Mona-fiction Yolande has really invested her self-image – so that it is herself that she sees communicating with Lydie in a way that she has never before been able to do and evoking ideas of desire in Paolo. As she realises this, there also comes the realisation that Mona is not part of herself, but really an-other, in whose pleasures and achievements Yolande can have no part. If Paolo makes up to Mona, he moves away from Yolande. Mona is a rival. Realising, too late, that she cannot cope with the undisciplined alter ego that she has taken in, she throws her out unceremoniously.

Thus the 'female' approach to understanding Mona results in a rejection of her, just as inevitably as does the more superficial male approach. The realisation of Mona's otherness, her failure to conform to the subject's desires, is eventually even more traumatic. Mona's refusal to conform to Yolande's image of her becomes a crisis in Yolande's own identity, as if a part of her own personality had revolted against her.

We have seen that the process of identification, which characterises Yolande and the other 'female' characters discussed, can be equated with a kind of 'authorship' of Mona. It is an attempt at presenting rather than representing her: and it fails because Yolande assumes Mona to be a subset of herself rather than an independent other. The questions raised by the previous discussion lead inevitably into consideration of the relationship between Mona and the author of the film.

So who is the author of the film? Well, Varda, of course; but the author exists within the text, somewhat more ambiguously, in the form of the narrator. The immediate reaction to the narrator's intervention is probably to assume that she is Varda, but all we can say for certain about this voice is that it belongs to a woman. It is in fact Varda's voice, and we may suspect this, but it is important to stress that the narrator is *not* Varda. At most, we may identify her as 'the Film-maker', a persona adopted by Varda who will not further intrude into the diegetic space, whose function is to change our perception of the narrative from presentation of fiction to representation of reality. The narrator presents the film as a documentary exercise, involving techniques of research (interviews with witnesses) to reconstruct real past events. This is her only intervention in the film, and the temporal logic of the flashback sequences eliminates her even from sequences which present themselves visually as filmed interviews.

The identification of the narrator with 'the Film-maker/Varda' is not in fact inevitable. The narrator, after all, does not even mention that her narration is to be a film. There is I believe a case for attributing the status of narrator – and even, more interestingly, the status of author – to one of the characters, Mme Landier. First, because the un-named narrator is implicated in the fiction by her establishment of Mona as a real woman who has lived and whose life can be investigated. She is thus *already* a character in the film, and we have the option of assuming this to be her only appearance or of admitting the possibility of others. From what little we know of the narrator's identity and connection to Mona, Mme Landier is 'eligible'. The narrator is an educated woman with an interest in Mona and the means to make a film about her: the vast majority of the film's characters have few means and little education. The tone of the narrator's introduction corresponds quite well both to the nature of Mme Landier's relation to Mona (curiosity both about Mona and about the nature of her own reaction to her, suggestions of a maternal role) and to her way of relating to other people in her projects (the witnesses help the narrator, but she is in charge: Mme Landier defines her role in the plane-tree campaign in very similar terms).

Such correspondences are of little weight on their own. However, Mme Landier has other characteristics which set her relation to Mona apart from that of the other witnesses, even such important ones as Yolande. She does not appear until about halfway through the film, but her appearance marks a change in the nature of the film, most clearly in the complexity of the flashbacks. Mme Landier's framing narrative contains some quite dramatic shifts in time and space, while up until her appearance the main events have been in acceptable chronological order. These shifts are potentially very significant and I will return to them.

Of course, just as Mme Landier is the only character in the film whose education and position permit of her being the narrator, she is also the only character who corresponds in any way, socially, to Varda herself. The correspondence is quite close: there is even a physical resemblance created through hairstyle and manner of dress. More importantly, for anyone who has read the background to the film, the encounter of Mme Landier and Mona parallels the encounter of Varda and Settina which inspired the film in its final form, although the association of Mme Landier and Mona does not last so long or take on such significance as Varda's/Settina's.

Mme Landier's attitude to Mona veers somewhat uneasily between that of friend and a caring 'dame patronnesse': she is not sure herself what her role should be. Neither is the audience: it is hard to insert Mme Landier into the neat categories of 'male' or 'female' desire which we have discussed above. The only thing which she seems to expect of Mona – at least in her presence – is answers to her questions: in this she is disappointed, but Mona's failure to oblige her curiosity does not lead to rejection; on the contrary. As the sequences of them together progress, it becomes more and more clear that Mme Landier is constructing Mona as a mystery ('genre sauvage et sale' ('the wild dirty sort')). Her descriptions of Mona to other people emphasise Mona's 'otherness', particularly her smell. When introducing her to Jean-Pierre, she seems to present Mona as a source of entertainment: 'elle m'amuse' ('she amuses me'), 'vous voulez la voir?' ('do you want to see her?'); and she encourages Jean-Pierre to study Mona 'as if she were in a specimen glass' (Hayward 1990: 286). All this suggests that Mme Landier has constructed Mona for herself as a sort of freak, something suitable for exhibition. (It is hardly necessary to point out that the act of filming Mona is a way of exhibiting her, to provide a kind of entertainment for a putative audience.)

Mme Landier is not always patronising, however. Describing how she became accustomed to Mona's presence, she explains it by saying 'elle était bien dans la voiture' ('she was happy in the car'), with a touch of surprise, as if Mona were a wild animal whom Mme Landier does not expect to appreciate human company. While the implications are still to set Mona outside the community of humanity, there is a hint that her presence confers a sense of privilege on Mme Landier with whom she has deigned to stay a while. From this to the figure of Aphrodite coming from the sea, with which the narrator opens the film, there is a very short distance. Freak to be exhibited or demi-goddess: in either case Mona becomes a construction of the mind, a fit screen on which to project fears and desires, and no longer ascribed a human existence, comparable to that of her observer, at all. As we have argued, Mona functions as a projection-screen for desires for most of the characters, but most take her as being the true embodiment of the said fears and desires. Mme Landier is certainly the only character who could be said to have the detachment necessary to construct a Mona separate from herself, the only one who seems aware that it is her reaction to Mona which it is important to understand and not Mona herself. That privileged viewpoint corresponds to Varda's, and perhaps to the narrator's. It is not necessarily unbiased: to construct Mona as an archetype – Aphrodite or 'wild woman' – is to expect her to be something which, if she is a human being, she cannot be, just as much as Yolande's projection of her as another, better-off Yolande was. But it is an authorial viewpoint in that it gives importance to reactions to Mona, reactions which can be described and analysed: it does not depend on interaction with Mona who is seen as absolutely separate, not of the same species and so neither an alter ego nor a possible companion on equal terms. This is a frustrating position which requires a certain effort to maintain. The care with which Mme Landier washes herself as she describes Mona's dirt immediately suggests that she is washing off any contamination by Mona, any invasion of her personality by this alien one. Her alarm at the realisation that she was not repelled by Mona seems again to be an effort at establishing a necessary distance against her own will.

Further argument for the equation of Mme Landier, narrator and author comes in the complex time structure of the episodes involving her.[14] In summary, Mme Landier's encounter with Mona is the only such meeting where we are not given a straightforward account of the incident from meeting to parting. The scene of their separation is not shown until Mme Landier, after her near-electrocution, is forced to think back over how she has dealt with Mona, and before the electrocution scene we have watched several minor adventures which happen to Mona after she has left Mme Landier. However, Varda has structured the film

14 For a detailed discussion of this, see Smith 1996.

very cleverly so that the viewer does not notice that the end of the Mme Landier episode has been missed out, and we have no reason to believe that it is in any way significant until Mme Landier evokes it herself. When she does, it is with some signs of panic: she begs Jean-Pierre to find Mona, describes the place where they parted, and adds 'C'est si dangereux dans les bois' ('It's so dangerous in the woods'), suggesting that she imagines something terrible happening to Mona. It is worth noting that this fear is a result of an experience which has first taken place while Mme Landier was looking in a mirror, and which secondly might be expected to give her images of her own life (according to the cliché, which she mentions, of 'one's whole life passing before one' at a moment of crisis). Confronted, doubly, with images of herself, Mme Landier responds by a mental image of Mona. We are immediately transported into the scene which she remembers (the separation), which continues, after Mme Landier has gone, into an evocative, but vague and half-hidden, image of Mona's rape in the woods. Thus only after Mme Landier's expression of fear for Mona do we see the incident which proves her fear justified, and it comes as a surprise since nothing in what we have seen of Mona after she has left Mme Landier has led us to suspect it, even though it is a perfectly credible part of the narrative. The rape is a unique incident in the film for several reasons – it is the only instance of part of an episode being withheld and then shown in a later flashback, it is unusual in its poetic and shadowy filming, such that we never see the rapist's face clearly but experience him only as a menacing presence, and it is the only major incident in the film which falls completely outside the documentary logic announced by the narrator. There is no witness who could be interviewed to help reconstruct this part of Mona's life. All these factors combine to create a question over the sequence. Was Mona really raped in the woods? Or could this be a projection of Mme Landier's imagination, played out on the screen? It seems coherent with Mme Landier's ambivalence towards Mona that she should imagine her subjected to violence. She needs to rid herself of what she fears in Mona, unable to accept what she represents (the wildness, the dirt) as integral to her own structure of being; at the same time she is extremely reluctant to lose what she desires in her and feels guilt at her own destructive urges.

Of course this question itself is paradoxical. If we decide that the rape really happened, it is still a product of Varda's imagination – or the question must be reframed at one remove: how many of the film's incidents are imagined by Varda, how many are genuine parts of Settina's experience? In any case the reality is already many times removed from the event on the screen. In the complex structure of illusion which is a film, it makes no sense to ask whether any incident is real or imagined, but the fleeting impression that the film may be created by the fantasies of one of the characters, rather than a comfortably invisible author, is nonetheless disconcerting and even subversive. If Mme Landier can take on the position of author, not only of 'her' Mona (which we can check against the reality of 'our' Mona), but of Varda's Mona, with the people she meets and all her world, the impression which emerges is that the narrative is generating itself. One of the constructions, or Mona-fictions, which are, theoretically, all equivalent in their inadequacy as a way of representing a 'real' woman, has become identified with that woman herself, and the status of any pre-existing reality is thereby entirely denied.

Thus we return to the first problem, the various constructions of Mona. We have seen that 'male' and 'female' strategies alike are unsatisfactory as a way of knowing her; both fall down when the witness has to interact with a 'real' Mona who does not correspond to his or her assumptions. The differences arise only in the degree to which Mona is rejected when the assumptions fail. All these strategies seem to be, to some extent, failed attempts to establish authorship of Mona. Each person's Mona is their own creation, but each comes up against a reality over which they have no control. The only character who does manage to achieve a relationship with Mona which does not fall apart against reality is Mme Landier, but her position is ambiguous. Either Mona is a spectacle to 'amuse' her (and in observing she seems to adopt the documentarist's ideal position, perfectly objective, abandoning all control), or, in the later sequence just analysed, Mona may be a blank screen on which Mme Landier can project what she chooses to resolve her own interior contradictions, in which case Mme Landier has entire control. The options thus presented are those of spectator or author. When Mme Landier tries to get back in contact with Mona in order to engage with her on a more human level, she fails: it is inconceivable that she could succeed. The absolute condition for any extended frequentation of Mona is the absence of Mona herself, either because she is dead or because she never existed outside the author's mind in the first place.

All this inevitably leads, in a way that the earlier films do not, to questions in the spectators' minds about our own role. The challenge to ways of seeing posed by *Sans toit ni loi* is universal (unlike the challenge in *Réponse de femmes*, for example, which was addressed to men alone). It is open to us to approach Mona through either the 'male' or the 'female' strategy, despite the obvious fact that we will never be required, or indeed able, to interact with her in reality. The 'male' strategy would consist in judging Mona according to her reactions to others (implicitly, identifying with those she meets). This tends to lead to a very negative reaction to her, since she is systematically offhand to everybody and notoriously smelly, but one might also imagine that one could cope with that – the film does allow of potentially more rewarding attempts at relating to her (Assoun or Mme Landier).

The 'female' strategy seems to offer a more fruitful approach to Mona for the spectator, if only because it is independent of interaction and therefore does not require the impossible from the start. However, as we have seen, the 'female' strategy in the film is only satisfactory where the viewer has been restricted to a glimpse of Mona. The film imposes a long and concentrated gaze which allows ample time for disillusion. One friend has told me that she lost interest in the film after the goatherd episode, because sympathy failed when Mona turned down that offer. The episodes of Yolande and, indeed, of the goatherd, indicate that reading Mona as a mirror of oneself is fatal to any understanding of her. Acceptance of only parts of her implies rejection of other parts and, finally, of the whole.

The other possibilities remaining seem to be the two open to Mme Landier; absolute detachment or absolute authorial control. I have never yet encountered anyone who claims to have achieved absolute detachment with regard to Mona; and it is hard to feel that the result would be rewarding if one could. Authorial control, however, is not as impossible as one might think. The film spectator is in the enviable position of not having to inter-relate with Mona, since she is, eventually, nothing but an image – albeit an image not under our control. Once the film is over we can forget or minimise the inconvenient aspects of the image, and thus take control of the film in memory and become the authors of our own Mona if we so wish. Flitterman-Lewis (1996: 306) has observed that the film's structure seems calculated to involve the spectator: 'we become absorbed in the observational process ourselves, constructing our own fictions of Mona, as well as of the people she meets ... The film gives us, its spectators, the same status as its fictive characters', that is, the status of witnesses, who can recount our encounter with Mona after the film is over, and fictionalise through our interpretations: but also, if we so wish, the status of author, free to fantasise further episodes and even – once out of the cinema – alternative endings. In according this last freedom *also* to one of the film's fictive characters, Varda leaves the text absolutely open: there is no final authorial version if the author is herself fictional. In this way the film's structure becomes truly subversive.

As a narrative strategy this is extremely fruitful for the viewer-turned-creator, but if we are discussing ways of seeing, and indeed of representing on screen, a supposedly real woman, it is quite unsatisfactory because as a strategy it is absolutely manipulative and bearing no necessary relation to its subject. *Jane B.*, two years later, was to illustrate the temptations and the problems of using this approach to a woman with an extra-filmic existence and her own opinions. It only works in *Sans toit ni loi* because Mona apparently has no self-image, and because she is dead before the narrator permits herself to reconstruct her.

If all ways of seeing Mona fail to produce a reliable image, they nonetheless provide some benefit for those who produce them, and I have tried to link the effect of Mona on different characters with that which she has on the audience. However, it seems that the conclusion to be drawn from *Sans toit ni loi* is that representation is always impossible: that the only rewarding strategy is some form of presentation, of authorship, which if it is to be successful must subordinate Mona's identity to the desires of the 'author'. The fiction which Varda has created out of the life of her real model Settina is another example of this. Although certainly Mona avoids all reduction to other people's interpretations in the film ('Mona's independence from a fixed identity is an assertion of her *altérité* (her otherness)' (Hayward 1990: 286)), that avoidance does not mean she is presented in her own right as a subject. In the end, her otherness makes her subjectivity irrelevant: she serves as a mirror for those who look at her to see their own desires, or indeed as a screen for the author(s) to project what they/we choose.

Jane B. par Agnès V. (1987)

Such problems recur two years later when, in *Jane B.*, Varda, this time in her own person, turns to the film-portrait of Jane Birkin, who is undeniably a real woman, well known to the audience. The pessimistic conclusion for the future of representation which *Sans toit ni loi* seems to impose does not augur well for the possibilities here: all the more, because Jane Birkin as starlet, pin-up and actress is as it were professionally the blank screen for projecting desires, which Mona proves to be. Unlike Mona she is not oblivious to the expectations of others, and has occasionally allowed some external authorship of her image, but also, again unlike Mona, she has subjectivity. Jane Birkin is a woman who sees herself, and Varda uses this in order to construct a new strategy of representing the feminine. In brief, this consists of admitting from the start her own involvement, without hiding that Jane as Varda sees her will to some extent be the Jane that Varda would like to see. At the same time, and also from the start, the film establishes that Jane Birkin also has ideas about how Jane

Birkin should be. In fact, the relation between Birkin and her persona is not unlike the specular 'female' relationship between some characters in *Sans toit ni loi* and Mona, but since the identity is relatively real there really is a possibility of control.

The difficult relationship between subject and camera is posed very explicitly from the start. In an early, semi-introductory sequence Jane and Varda meet in a café to discuss the film. The conversation turns upon the function of the camera, and, equally, upon who is looking at whom. The two women attempt different metaphors for the process of filming – can the camera act as a mirror? Allowing for the disturbing presence of another person looking through the camera's eye, does it then become a distorting mirror, and what does that imply for the relationship between Jane and her image? Or could the process be better compared to portraiture, a procedure which allows for the presence of a mediating third party?

The conjunction of portrait and mirror gives an image which combines the seen and the see-er, where the painter sees himself painting what he sees, and appears in the image in the act of transforming it to paint. It is a conceit well known in baroque portraits,[15] and sure enough baroque portraits play a very important role in *Jane B*. Although the pictures selected by the film are not ones in which mirrors feature, the art-historical reference is certainly not forgotten.

Another combination of painting and mirror-image is proposed by Varda when she tells Jane, 'C'est comme si j'allais filmer ton auto-portrait' ('It's as if I was going to film your self-portrait'). As she says this, the camera travels around a picture of Jane in front of a mirror. The mirror frames in succession Jane's face – at which point we do have an image of the structure of the self-portrait – the camera with the cameraman beside it and finally Varda's face (plate 8). The mirror used is an old-fashioned one with a frame which could recall the frame of a painting or, alternatively, of the mirrors which appear in paintings such as

---

15 E.g. Van Eyck's *Arnolfini Marriage* (National Gallery, London); Velasquez, *Las Meninas* (Prado, Madrid).

those in note 15. The shot creates dynamically the same effect as such paintings – from the simple image of the mirror, which involves only one person, we turn to the process of creating a film and the personality of the creator of it. The latter two stages are reached separately. The appearance of the camera and the cameraman is startling, because it suggests that Jane's image will be mediated by two people, one of whom is a man. But Varda's voice-over describes the camera as 'un petit peu moi' (me in a way) and the picture turns rapidly to her face in the mirror as she declares her willingness to be seen in the frame. This is a very important summary of the approach the film will take. It will be a portrait in which the painter is visible. It may also aspire to the status of mirror, but neither Varda nor Birkin are duped. Two shots later Jane stands in front of a distorting mirror, and says: 'Moi si j'accepte qu'un peintre ou un cinéaste fait mon portrait ... oui je veux bien me déformer ... mais c'est comme avec toi. L'important c'est l'œil derrière la caméra, la personne derrière la brosse à peinture. Je m'en fous un peu de ce que tu fais avec moi, du moment que je sens que tu m'aimes un peu.'[16]

As she says 'oui je veux bien me déformer' she turns to the mirror, and the camera concentrates on the reflection which grows unnaturally long, splits and vanishes completely. The words could be an interjected response to an unheard request from Varda, but they fit into the logic of the sentence. Jane is willing to lend herself to the exercise but she knows that the image which comes out will be 'distorted'. If we believe the picture rather than the sound-track, she may even disappear altogether leaving only the surface of the mirror visible. Neither is she prepared to accept the idea that the film can be her 'self-portrait' made by someone else. The most she hopes for is that the woman who creates her image will be sympathetic to her and see her positively. We have already seen in relation to *Sans toit ni loi* what this implies. The options open to Varda are, apparently, to create Jane

16 'If I accept that a painter or a film-maker does my portrait ... yes I'm very willing to distort myself ... but it's like with you. The important thing is the eye behind the camera, the person behind the paintbrush. I don't really much care what you do with me, as long as I feel that you love me a little.'

as someone she desires to know, or as someone she desires to be, or as a phantasm without any personal humanity at all.

In fact the film finds a strategy which consists in experimenting with all the above possibilities. In doing this it uses Jane's adaptability as an actress, and remains faithful to the structure of the portrait where the painter is visible. To think about these portraits is soon to realise that they are both mirror-images and self-portraits, but of the painter not the sitter. The succession of different characters which Varda turns Jane into are thus, avowedly, revealing of Varda and her expectations of Jane rather than of Birkin who is taking on her professional role of blank screen, also avowedly. For example, after the striking Laurel and Hardy sketch, we cut to Jane's reactions to the role, and we learn that it is not her idea of herself, that she was doubtful that she could carry it off, but that she is more than willing to try. Varda described the genesis of the Laurel and Hardy sketch to Françoise Audé (Varda 1988: 3): 'quelqu'un m'a parlé de l'accent de Jane deux jours avant l'arrivée de la neige. J'ai répondu qu'elle a l'accent de Laurel dans les versions françaises de Laurel et Hardy et immédiatement j'ai eu l'idée de lui faire jouer Laurel'.[17]

The idea arose as a result of a conversation between Varda and someone else, Jane being no more than a manipulable doll whom Varda can use to represent who she likes. But the doll has opinions on Varda's idea of her. When asked to dress up as a Spanish dancer, she makes as if to perform a flamenco, but not for long. Having taken her bow and returned to the stage, she denounces the costume and all it represents. She then replaces Varda's construction with her own choice of image. This is the other side of the film's plan to circumvent the inevitable traps of representation. Jane too has ideas of herself, costumes she would like to try, desires she would like to project on to the screen.

In fact, several of the projections of Jane are ones she has chosen herself. She is never entirely free in her self-representation, since she is not behind the camera – however, Varda is also

17 'someone mentioned Jane's accent to me two days before the snow arrived. I replied that she had an accent like Laurel's in the French versions of Laurel and Hardy and immediately I had the idea of getting her to play Laurel.'

dependent on Jane for the detailed realisation of *her* fantasies.
Both women are present in all the sketches, so if Jane becomes the
image of the film-maker's fantasy it is with her agreement and co-
operation, and therefore to some extent on her own terms (unlike,
for example, Mona's function in Yolande's head). And thus
sometimes, Varda accepts Jane's requests and re-creates her
according to *her* desires. Here we come closer to the self-portrait; it
is as if the sitter has her own mirror and can guide the painter's
hand. In the episode under discussion Jane takes this process
particularly far. Carried along by the revolt against the Spanish
dancer role, 'so far from me', she demands to be filmed in T-shirt
and jeans, 'barefoot in the garden', and claims that this sequence
represents her real self, 'transparente'. It is Varda's turn to
criticise the image, reminding Jane and the audience that the
trappings of stardom are also a part of her life and a part she
values. She sums up the paradox thus: 'T'es originale et en même
temps, tu voudrais avoir une apparence anonyme. Ton rêve, c'est
d'être une inconnue célèbre.'[18]

Which may be true, but the wary spectator will hear the decided
tone here, and be aware that from criticising Jane for defining
herself too easily, the film-maker is slipping towards another
definition of her own. The first sentence simply points out a
contradiction in Jane's own previous self-definitions. The second,
apparently, tells her what she wants. The warning is given – what
follows has little relation to Jane's life or her self-image. Indeed
Jane is assumed not to have heard of 'L'Inconnue de la Seine'[19] to
whom Varda compares her.

At this moment, photographing Jane's face in the position of
the famous death-mask, Varda requires the actress to *act* the blank
screen. Of the 'Inconnue', Varda says 'On ne savait rien d'elle, et
certainement, à cause de ça, tout le monde pouvait fantasmer sur

18 'You're original and, at the same time, you want to look anonymous. Your
   dream is to be a famous unknown.'
19 The 'Inconnue de la Seine'. In the 1930s a young woman was found drowned in
   the Seine. A plaster-cast was made of her face, which wore a slight smile, and
   copies of this mask became immensely popular, although no-one knew who the
   young woman was. Varda tells the story to Jane in the film.

elle'.²⁰ And, finally, 'je me demande si le seul vrai portrait n'est pas le masque mortuaire'.²¹ Everything Varda says denies the validity of the Inconnue as a portrait. Nothing is known about the subject, everybody sees it differently, and even its appearance is manipulable: the person who takes the cast can 'make' it smile. If it manages to remain intriguing, this is precisely because of the contrast between the infinite possibilities which can be imagined and the limited reality which, surely, must *be* behind it somewhere. It is the portrait it is possible to make of Mona, but only after her death or her reduction to fiction. It is not possible of Jane, who has her preferences and counters the film-maker's interpretation of her with her own. But, as we have seen with regard to Mona, it is perhaps the ultimate temptation for the author/creator/film-maker. And so at last Varda admits: 'au fond tu t'offres à l'imagination de chacun. C'est peut-être ça qui m'a fasciné, qui m'a donné envie de faire ce film. Parce que je peux t'habiter avec mes rêveries – des histoires de mythologie, des souvenirs de cinéma, des choses que j'ai dans la tête.'²²

The authorial attitude *par excellence* is posed here only as one interpretation among others. Varda claims authorship of Jane in the title of the film, but within the film she challenges this. In the above sequence, the image cuts to Jane in her Spanish dancer costume, which we already know that Jane violently detests: so Varda cannot install all her daydreams unopposed in Jane. At least within the parameters of this film she cannot, because they are in the same space – even if very rarely in the same image, they are both within the film's space on equal terms – and must interact, as the characters in *Sans toit ni loi* had at some stage to interact with Mona. To expect absolute authorial control is in that case to fail in understanding, and *Jane B.* cannot stop there. So when Jane claims that the most important element in a role is 'not the

20 'Nothing was known about her, and certainly because of that everyone could fantasise about her.'
21 'I wonder if the only real portrait isn't a death-mask.'
22 'basically you give yourself to everyone's imagination. Perhaps it's that which fascinated me, which made me want to make this film. Because I can install my daydreams in you – stories from mythology, movie memories, things I have in my head.'

costume but the partner', Varda suggests that *she* choose that most important element next time. Her response ('Marlon Brando') complicates matters further, suggesting that representing on this level is not just a matter of subjectivities. Economic constraints can counter both Varda's and Jane's desires, and to that extent authorship in a film is shown to be a fiction. Varda, exponent throughout her career of the claims of *cinécriture* and of the importance of a personal vision, here reminds the viewer of the limits her vision is subject to.

In discussing these last two films we have moved from consideration of gender issues to authorship in general. In *Jane B.* in fact the issue is almost entirely the possibilities of woman representing woman. The male gaze is apparently absent, or subordinate; the cameraman is 'part of Varda', the men who appear are only supports for fantasy. Contrast is provided by the archive documents which show us Jane seen by Serge Gainsbourg: almost parodies of the exploitative soft-porn photo at first glance, they are nonetheless not dismissed. Jane looks at them and speaks of them with mild amusement, some nostalgia, a faint tone of guilt which she seems to feel is expected of her; but she does not deny the image which they give of her, because at the time she accepted and even desired it.

Clearly, Varda's approach to the filming of femininity has grown increasingly complex over the years, reflecting both her developing understanding of the ramifications of the problem, and probably a growing sophistication in the debate on gender and representation generally. There are common threads, however: the relation between female perception and female body – the body inhabited and the bodies displayed, whether one likes it or not, for comparison – is studied in all these films except perhaps *Sans toit ni loi*. The problem of how to present a woman to be seen unexploitatively, inevitable to a feminist female filmmaker, is tackled through various permutations of the theme of self-image, from the projection of the self on to outside objects (*L'Opéra-Mouffe*), to a kind of self-construction which, taking as given that desire inevitably distorts any image constructed, allows at least that it should be the desire of the person portrayed, or, perhaps more profitably, the crossed and conflicting desires of the person portrayed and the portrayer, and perhaps of others too.

References

Audé, Françoise (1981) *Ciné-modèles, cinéma d'elles*, Lausanne, L'Age d'homme

Duchen, Claire (1986) *Feminism in France: From May '68 to Mitterrand*, London, Routledge & Kegan Paul

Flitterman-Lewis, Sandy (1996) *To Desire Differently*, New York, Columbia UP

Hayward, Susan (1990) 'Beyond the gaze and into *femme-filmécriture*: Agnès Varda's *Sans toit ni loi*' in S. Hayward and G. Vincendeau (eds), *French Film, Texts and Contexts*, London, Routledge, pp. 285–96

Morin, Edgar (1960) *The Stars*, tr. Richard Howard, New York, Grove Press

Smith, Alison (1996) 'Strategies of representation in *Sans toit ni loi*', *Nottingham French Studies*, 35: 2, autumn, pp. 84–96

Varda, Agnès (1961) 'Agnès Varda', interview with Jean Michaud and Raymond Bellour, *Cinéma 61*, no. 60, October, 1961, pp. 4–20

Varda, Agnès (1974) 'Autour et alentour de *Daguerréotypes*', *Cinéma 75*, no. 204, December, pp. 39–53

Varda, Agnès (1988) 'Conversation avec Agnès Varda', interview with Françoise Audé, *Positif*, no. 325, March, pp. 2–5

Varda, Agnès (1994) *Varda par Agnès*, Paris, Cahiers du cinéma

5

Time and memory

The importance of time and memory is something which has always existed in Varda's work, but which has come to the fore much more visibly in her films from the 1970s onwards. Her treatment of the past, and the memories, of her protagonists, has developed throughout her work while retaining its importance, and in the 1990s she has been almost exclusively concerned with our sometimes troubled relations with our personal, and our shared, past. Memory and its unreliable but deeply evocative power, and acceptable ways to deal with memory without relapsing into nostalgia, are preoccupations which have characterised Varda's most recent films.

In *Varda par Agnès*, Varda uses Marot's famous poem 'Plus ne suis ce que j'ai été' as an important part of the introduction.[1] She

1 Plus ne suis ce que j'ai été
  Et ne le saurais jamais être
  Mon beau printemps et mon été
  Ont fait le saut par la fenêtre.
  Amour, tu as été mon maître:
  Je t'ai servi sur tous les dieux.
  O si je pouvais deux fois naître
  Comme je te servirais mieux!

  (I am no longer what I was
  And never can be so again
  My fine spring and summer
  Have jumped out of the window
  Love, you have been my master:

TIME AND MEMORY   143

observes that 'ce poème tout baigné de la nostalgie du temps passé, perdu ou mal employé, désigne des sensations à ne pas sous-estimer'² (Varda 1994: 6). She refers to the book itself as 'Contes de la Mémoire Vague après la Vie'.³ However, under the title 'Mémoire' in her alphabetical first 'chapter', she claims to have very little and 'des mauvais rapports avec elle' (Varda 1994: 24) (bad relations with it).

An interest in memory is obviously to be expected in someone whose preoccupation with representation has always centred on the inevitability of personal, subjective perception, since the process of memory involves personalising the images of the past. Varda's 1990s films, however, have been specifically concerned not only with memory but with commemoration – that is the celebration of the past in a public arena. In the case of *Jacquot de Nantes,* both private memory and public are concerned, since the film itself is designed to bring before the public images created from records of a private past. *Les Demoiselles ont eu 25 ans* and *L'Univers de Jacques Demy* give a more central place to public recollection: *Les Demoiselles* is a record of a community event, designed around elements of the past but using these to create something new in the present. *Les 100 et 1 nuits,* similarly, dramatises the tensions between memories of the past and creation in the present and for the future: the history of cinema as remembered by 'M. Cinéma' is finally only valuable if it can be used, without dilapidation, as material for a film of the future. *L'Univers* deals with the life of Demy, as does *Jacquot de Nantes,* but it is much more concerned with Demy's influence, his effect on others, than is *Jacquot* which concentrates on his own memory. All these explicitly commemorative films are therefore concerned with the purpose of evoking

---

I served you above all the gods.

Oh if I could be born twice

How much better I would serve you!)

2 'This poem bathed in nostalgia for past time, wasted or badly used, describes feelings that should not be underestimated.'

3 'Tales of a Hazy Memory after Life': a play on the French title of a famous film by the Japanese director Kenzo Mizoguchi: *Contes de la lune vague après la pluie* ('Tales of a hazy moon after rain', usually known in English by its Japanese title *Ugetsu Monogatari*).

the past, and its relationship with the present, especially inasmuch as it can provoke creative action. Such creation is clearly based on an interpretation of the past, and thus we return to the reprocessing, through subjectivity, of past experience into something immediately relevant, but in the later films the process is collective as well as individual.

Many of Varda's films before the 1990s have in fact dealt with the communal presence of the past without being explicitly commemorative. Throughout her work Varda has maintained an ambiguous but never indifferent relationship to traditional values and traditional ways. This chapter will deal with the ways in which both personal and social past act on the protagonists of Varda's worlds, the ways in which she evokes them and the significance she finally lends them.

Of course tradition and memory are inseparably linked. Already in *La Pointe Courte* both are present and interact. Part of the film's effect is obtained from the resonance of images of the fishing-village in the memory of the young man, and at the same time, for the spectator, in a more general visual 'memory'. The geography of the village and the objects it contains seem likely to have been unchanged for centuries. Very few of the images of *La Pointe Courte* would be easy to date: the forms of boats, houses, nets, or washing owe nothing to modernity, while the props of twentieth-century life are conspicuously absent (no cars, no engines, no machinery other than the most primitive: the train is seen only as a passing presence, as remote as it was made to appear in images of the Old West). This is true not only in La Pointe Courte, but in the images of Sète at the moment of the *joutes* – itself a word with medieval connotations, describing a festival which is clearly presented as recurring year on year from an (unspecified) past. The film captures a moment of minor crisis related specifically to the intrusion of modern problems into this unchanging world. Varda's treatment of her fishing community's drama is significantly different in message from *La Pointe Courte*'s coincidental twin, Visconti's *La Terra Trema*, which presents a similar village at a moment of crisis. The threat in Visconti's film is of exploitation, and his fishermen seek solidarity in order to combat it. In *La Pointe Courte* the threat comes from an unexplained 'restriction' on fishing in contaminated water. Official regulation carries with it connotations of modernity interfering with 'what has always been', and the inspector represents an unwelcome exteriority. The village bands together to defend its traditions and its autonomy; the threat which regulation poses to the fishermen's livelihood is dealt with, but the larger question of the source of the undescribed pollution is not touched on. It is the inspectors, not the polluted water, which the village rejects.

The village rituals are presented in *La Pointe Courte* as an extremely strong force of social cohesion, although the couple, engrossed in their personal dramas, are separate from them and draw no strength from them. The persistence of the traditional alongside the modern continues as a theme in Varda's work, but it very soon ceases to be so positive; the communal past brings strength, but also oppression and stagnation. By the time of *Sans toit ni loi* the traditional celebration has become a source not of reinforcement but of terror, bringing death to the outsider and establishing even within the community a sense of power based on fear. As Susan Hayward has pointed out, the wine festival is a patriarchal rite. Peasant life, at least in its un-reconstructed form (the hippie goatherd opens other possibilities) breeds frustration; the farm-women who speak yearningly of Mona's freedom indicate this, and they echo the chilling farm-family of *L'Une chante, l'autre pas*, the most negative picture of traditional French life anywhere in Varda's films. Even La Pointe Courte may seem not so much 'timeless' as anachronistic; in the fast-changing France of the 1950s, the village seems like a survival, an island where time may have stopped.

However, this effect is not unambiguous. From her earliest interviews Varda reveals a certain attachment to the past. 'Je souffre quand le modernisme va contre les sentiments profonds', she says in 1961, on the subject of *L'Opéra-Mouffe*, 'Les amours libres vont vers une désacralisation de l'amour. Vous pouvez avoir une vie libre et éprouver l'amour comme votre grand-mère. Il y a une mythologie nouvelle qui ne convient pas à tout le monde. Je ne vois pas pourquoi on n'aurait que les images de son progrès social' (Varda 1961: 12).[4] These are surprising views in a film-maker with links to the avant-garde, in 1961. Later films emphasise frequently the importance of tradition to identity (especially communal identity) even while emphasising the importance of moving beyond 'immobile' past values. For example, in *Daguerréotypes*, the community of the rue Daguerre is marked as belonging to the past; this leads to 'immobilism' but it is also a major source of its fascination, and Varda is well aware of this, as the long, loving travelling shots over the jars and phials of the Chardon Bleu, all filmed in sepia colours, make clear. The evocation of the youth of the protagonists in various provincial villages (by interview, never visually) is uniformly affectionate, and in recalling it everyone is shown gazing out beyond the camera in the expression associated with the recall of an interior, desired image. Varda practically assures this by the question she asks: 'How did you meet your husband/wife?'

And if the community's apolitical apathy, and its lack of dreams, are criticised in the sound-track and in the statements which Varda made at the time, the tightness of its unity and its attachment to the objects of its various trades frequently appear attractive. At the moment when she was regretting to *Cinéma 75* that the film called forth no self-criticism on the part of its subjects, Varda said, rather ruefully: 'Je serai tentée d'y voir la preuve que dans le cinéma, le son atteint les gens bien moins que l'image'[5] (Varda 1975: 44). This is a tacit admission that the image does not reflect the sound-track's criticisms. Indeed, the associations of Mystag's fantastic tricks with the daily chores of the characters imply that these characters do dream, and if, as they say in interview, they tend to dream about work, then this raises the evocative power of the work rather than devalorising the dreams. The association of the baker's old-fashioned oven with a

4 'I suffer when modernism goes against deep feelings. Free love moves towards a desacralisation of love. You can have a free life and feel love like your grandmother did. There is a new mythology which doesn't suit everyone. I don't see why we should have only images of social progress.'
5 'I'd be tempted to see this as proof that, in the cinema, the sound reaches people much less than the image does.'

description of fire-eating makes it magical and powerful in a way which is itself rooted in the past, as Mystag at this point is explaining the traditional origins of fire-eating. And though the community may be immobile, it is not (unlike that of *Sans toit ni loi*), hostile; it has indeed a strong power of absorption, integrating those of different backgrounds into a common comfortable, slightly nostalgic calm. Witness the interviews with the Tunisian grocers, late arrivals (1971 whereas most of the shopkeepers have been in place since at least the 1950s) from a truly 'exotic' location, and already absolutely parallel with everyone else, accepted by the community and also accepting of its values, united by a common nostalgia for a provincial past and daily interactions with others in a semi-provincial Paris. The daguerreotypes certainly illustrate their subjects' immobility, but it is an immobility which goes along with a calm assurance: they all gaze firmly at the camera, standing beside the tools of their respective trades with pride (as in old photographs, frequently). Old photographs have a considerable positive power, and while the cinema can call them into question it has also frequently used them to affirm the worth of the past.[6] Here their value is ambiguous; Varda is not denying the truth of the content of the images – neither their stillness nor their pride. She is questioning only the possibility of such stillness as a viable response to today's world, and the film leaves a sense that, however far from urgent concerns it may be, it is not all that unviable: these people may not have exciting lives but they are apparently contented.

In *Sans toit ni loi* there is much less sympathy for the traditional past, and no recourse to the 'vintage chic' of old photographs. The countryside through which Mona wanders is filled with survivals of an older world. Old or new, structures are run-down and ramshackle; it sometimes seems that the past in *Sans toit ni loi* is taking over the present. The new is everywhere threatened with obsolescence and decay. René Prédal has described Mona as 'amen[ant] avec elle l'inquiétant retour de la crasse'(Prédal 1991: 25) ('bringing with her the disquieting return of filth').

6 On this subject see Raphael Samuel, 'Dreamscapes', in *Theatres of Memory*, London, Verso, 1994, 350–63: esp. 350–1.

This allots to her a role which could be seen as a counter-memory, if we accept Wendy Everett's description of the function of memory as the past envisaged in the present: 'We do not remember in the past tense, but in a flash of past as present; temporal categories are not discrete, our memories are part of the way we see and experience the present' (Everett 1996: 106–7). *Sans toit ni loi* contradictorily envisages a present already past and gathering dust. Mona who travels through the film may be seen to be carrying this obsolescence with her. She is herself a survival of the past, and it is thus that Varda describes her: 'Vers 84, les journaux parlaient beaucoup des *nouveaux pauvres* ... Au mot *nouveaux pauvres* j'associais toujours *anciens pauvres*, ceux qui depuis la nuit des temps jusqu'à aujourd'hui, mendiants ou pas, se traînent dans les villes ou sillonnent la campagne'[7] (Varda 1994: 166). Mona carries the influence of this bitter tradition into every corner of the film. Within *Sans toit ni loi* there are also those who seek out the past of collective memory and attempt to merge it with the present. The goatherd and his family, who have returned voluntarily to a traditional way of life and refuse all 'modern' trappings, while being as 'contemporary' as anyone else in the film in the sense that this very return is an expression of post-68 social readjustment, perhaps embody a different way of relating to the inescapable collective past in this film where on the whole the relics of old times are hostile and decaying.

In *Jane B. par Agnès V.* the collective past reappears, in the form of the various 'stock' images through which both Varda and Jane act out their perceptions of Jane Birkin's problematic identity. These often have a perfectly locatable 'retro' setting and work to remind us of the extent to which our ways of forming images of a person are dependent on pre-formed images from the collective memory. The film taps the Renaissance (the paintings), the 1920s (Laurel and Hardy), the nineteenth century (Calamity Jane), ancient Greece and some strange amalgamations of period. The

---

7 'Around 84, the newspapers were talking a lot about the *new poor* ... The words *new poor* always made me think of the *old poor*, those who from time immemorial until today, beggars or not, have hung around the towns or roamed across the countryside.'

photographs from Jane's starlet days in the 1960s, a part of her personal past, play an intriguingly double role, in that they are almost as universally recognisable as the 'mythical' figures Jane plays. Birkin was really – among others – the face of an era. They are set – briefly – against the present-day, individual Birkin, who does not criticise or reject them but sees them with amused detachment, because she has moved on from there. The pictures still exist as a collective image of the time, but they no longer have much relevance to their subject except inasmuch as they recall purely personal relationships.

In the films of the 1990s the relationship to the past is the central premise of the film. In films such as *Jacquot de Nantes* the whole film turns from the present to explore and to re-create the past. Collective and personal memory are inseparable in such a context: what we are dealing with is an image of the past as the past, not its preservation in the present. Certainly in re-creating the image Varda makes use of a number of signs of the period which have similar associations for a large number of people, and which thus could be called a 'collective' memory (Charles Trenet's hit song 'Boum', or the World War II posters, are examples). Such signs validate the reconstruction by linking it to the memories of a portion of her audience and more generally to a 'traditional' image of what wartime France looked and sounded like – the black-and-white film also plays a part in this. The film's success depends on the audience having the cultural baggage necessary to pick up these signs, and to that extent it is concerned with the survival of the past into the present in a collective sense. But *Jacquot de Nantes* mediates this through the problems of dealing with individual memories.

Les Demoiselles ont eu 25 ans, however, is obliged to face the conjunction of personal and collective memory, since the event which different people recall in different ways has also become a part of the history of a community. Again, Varda approaches this largely through a combination of personal memories – the event is relatively recent and has not yet become part of tradition – but if the film seems apparently inevitably to be enshrined as tradition eventually this is to be seen as an unreserved triumph and a source not of immobilism but of movement. The vintage postcards at the start of the film valorise the idea of history from the start. Within the town, the old is used now as a springboard for the new: the Arsenal restored has become a cultural centre and the film is the inspiration for a carnival. *Les Demoiselles ont eu 25 ans* approaches the problem of communal commemoration that should not become simply a regression, and finds everywhere in Rochefort indications that on the contrary the past is a spur to creativity.

The presence of a subjective and personal past is, in the early films, largely at second-hand. Although in *La Pointe Courte* the influence of the young man's memories of his village is vital to the theme, the film itself does not take on the task of evoking them. We take them on trust, linking what he says about his roots with the glimpses of the place in the present which we are accorded as he shows it to his wife. Certainly some of the shots of *L'Opéra-Mouffe* are flashbacks of past experience, taking their place alongside present impressions to compose the subjective world of the pregnant woman; these, however, although they make clear that the past is integral to perception of the present, place it only as one quite minor element in the overall subjectivity of the woman. The idea of reconstruction of the past as a fundamental task of the film does not yet appear. *La Pointe Courte*, *Cléo de 5 à 7* and *Le Bonheur* are recounted over a cohesive period of chronological time, which may be described as objective – the events are presented in the order in which, to a detached outside observer, they would have appeared to have taken place.

With *L'Une chante, l'autre pas*, we begin to observe a different process: events are recounted largely by an outside observer, but the outside observer takes on the modes of narration of her characters. Thus certain episodes are recounted in flashback, as Pomme and Suzanne remember them after they are reunited. These flashbacks are accompanied by the narrating voice-over of the protagonist, who thus takes charge of this part of her own past. Indeed, the film's construction as an exchange of letters leads to a construction in flashback even when the film no longer claims to be reconstructing the past of the characters. By introducing this very slight gap between the time of the action and the time of narration (between the events and the writing of the letter), Varda allows for a process of selection and reconstruction which converts the raw 'events' into the character's perception of them. In order to achieve subjectivity, the film-maker has recourse to memory.

It is from the beginning of the 1980s that Varda's films begin to engage centrally with the problem of memory. Perhaps the movement begins with *Documenteur* which takes as its theme 'comment filmer l'amour après, en l'absence du sujet du désir, comment filmer le manque'[8] (Dubroux 1982: 48). Obviously the overwhelming power of memory and nostalgia will be, at least, a force to be reckoned with in overcoming this, but Varda's decision regarding the film was to avoid going by way of memory-images. In fact, *Documenteur* contains only three 'memory-images', although they are effectively the same image recurring three times and thus insistent. Shots of a naked man, then of a couple making love: 'interrompent la narration et cassent le rythme lent des séquences. Ce sont des *flash-backs*, images subjectives donnant forme aux pensées qui submergent Emilie de temps à autre. ... la douleur de l'absence fait surgir du passé les moments de plénitude'[9] (Tigoulet 1991: 59–60). Otherwise Varda concentrates on images from Emilie's *present*. The flashbacks are necessary in order to understand the substance, and even more the physical intensity, of Emilie's sense of loss: their insistent close scanning of the naked bodies is similar in its overwheling intimacy to the filming of Demy in *Jacquot de Nantes*. But they are few and brief, and otherwise the film uses images which Emilie, according to the familiar pattern of Varda's earlier films, selects and interprets through her over-riding preoccupation. That is to say, of course, that Varda selects the images, and through Emilie's voice-over and

8 'how to film love afterwards, in the absence of the subject of desire [sic], how to film a lack'.
9 'interrupt the narration and break the slow rhythm of the sequences. These are *flash-backs*, subjective images giving form to the thoughts which submerge Emilie from time to time. ... the pain of absence evokes these moments of plenitude from the past.'

the flashbacks enables the spectator to enter into Emilie's world-view to the point where we adopt the appropriate interpretation. It is the procedure of *L'Opéra-Mouffe* or of *Cléo de 5 à 7*, but here adopted in order to elucidate the operation of memory. It is through the past, or rather, the present absence of the past, that Emilie perceives and interprets the presence of the present. Thus *Documenteur* is a film not so much about memory as about a pervasive past without which the present cannot be comprehended; the past is, as it were, the glass through which Emilie sees. To an outside observer it might be said to distort her view, or at least to prevent her from gaining a complete picture of her surroundings, as we said in Chapter 3: hence the *Documenteur* 'ment'.[10] We are made to understand the presence of this distorting, or interpretative, glass, but the film is most interested in the way in which it affects what is seen through it. It illustrates a memory which is, in any case, still an active force on the present and has not yet been relegated to a separate set of images: to include more flashbacks would, paradoxically, have separated Emilie further from her lost love by dividing the film into clearly defined timelines (as later films may often be divided).

Ulysse (1982) is the first of Varda's films to take the theme of memory and passing time and to use it as the centre of an exploration of the work of image-making. *Ulysse* is constructed around a still photograph – a moment of frozen time, taken in 1954. The photo shows a beach; in the background are a man and small boy, both naked: the man looks at the sea, the boy towards the camera. In the foreground is a dead goat (plate 7). The film begins with a reflection on the picture and what it meant at the time, to the photographer and to its two protagonists. Varda recalls the taking of the picture, in words which accentuate mainly her consciousness of its formal possibilities: 'une chèvre morte c'était un sujet en or, un 'sujet de composition' comme j'aimais

10 'ment' = 'lies'. Do*cumenteur* is another untranslatable title, meaning both 'documentary-maker' and 'docu-liar'. This time Varda did not initiate the word-play (fairly widespread in the late 1960s and 1970s when the purposes and possibilities of documentary were everywhere in question), but its appeal to her should be clear given her preoccupation with subjective vision.

les faire à l'époque. Natures mortes, ou Paysages avec figures comme disaient les peintres anciens: des figures c'est-à-dire des personnages nus dans la nature.'[11] The photographer's memory, clearly linked to this picture and no other, nonetheless at first renders the people in the photo almost anonymous, 'figures in a landscape'. However, with the next breath she identifies them; they become personal, and the film moves from a discussion of the image as formal composition to an enquiry into subjective memory, a photograph being an undeniable proof of a past moment. How will this 'objective' proof compare with the recollections of the people in the photo?

Thus Varda conducts a series of interviews, first with the man in the photo, then with the little boy who has now grown into a man, then with Bienvenida, the boy's mother, to whom the film is dedicated. At the start of each interview Varda shows the photograph to her interlocutor. She asks them if they remember the occasion, as she does: their reactions make it clear that the apparently 'frozen', objective moment takes on very different aspects when it is approached from the angle of others concerned with it. For the adult man in the picture, Fouli Elia, the general situation surrounding the making of the picture remains clear, but the occasion on which the photograph was taken escapes him. He remembers the little boy, he also remembers his embarrassment when asked to pose naked, but not specifically on this occasion. Varda shows him other images of himself twenty-eight years previously, naked and clothed, and he experiences the same reaction several times, one which he himself finds remarkable: he remembers the clothes he is wearing ... 'on se souvient des habits, et on ne se souvient pas de qui on était' ('we remember our clothes, but not who we were'), he says. Apparently, when he is unclothed, there is little to latch on to other than a sense of embarrassment.

It is perhaps in order to respond to this particular quirk of memory that Varda shoots the interview with him, once again, naked, and also gives him a handful of stones from the beach. If

---

11 'a dead goat was a jewel of a subject; a "sujet de composition", as I liked them at the time. Still life, or figures in a landscape as the old painters said: the figures being the people naked outdoors.'

this is an attempt to reconstruct the physical conditions of that day on the beach, it fails to the extent that it does not elicit total recall on his part. But the concept of a physical, rather than visual or intellectual memory, remains a theme of the film, and recurs in the second interview, with the little boy Ulysse, now a bookseller in Paris. At first sight of the picture, Ulysse denies all recollection of it, although Varda points out that, at the time, the photograph had impressed him so much that he had made a drawing based on it. He recognises the drawing from having 'vu à la porte intérieure d'un placard de ton bureau' (seen it inside the cupboard in your office), but still claims no memory of the scene. However, when he is later asked whether he remembers having a painful hip – during the interview with his mother it has been established that he had a hip problem at the time – he has no hesitation. 'Ah bon', says Varda, 'tu te souviens de ton corps, de ta douleur' ('you remember your body, your pain'), 'Du corps et de la douleur, c'est exact, oui' ('My body and the pain, precisely, yes'). This, coupled with Varda's procedures with Elia, evokes one aspect of the functioning of memory closely linked to its subjectivity: it is a profoundly personal process which passes through the entirety of each person's experience.

Bienvenida's reaction to the photograph springs similarly from a deeply personal relation to the past, which connects the picture primarily with her little son's illness and hence makes of this 'neutral' memory a painful one. Unlike Ulysse and apparently Elia, she does recall the actual moment of the photograph, but its associations mean that it is 'not her favourite photograph' of her son.

These interviews are interspersed with frequent returns to the photograph which initiated the process. It is fragmented and isolated details of it are shown in close-up, a procedure which not only serves to 'focus' on the element currently most relevant, but also underlines once again the frustrating incompleteness of a photo as a concrete visual memory. No matter how much one detail of the picture is blown up, it reveals no more about its subject than at the start (unlike the famous photo in Antonioni's 1966 film *Blow Up*, there are no hidden details). A process of enlargement to close-up would usually, in a cinematic context, correspond to an advance of the viewpoint into the scene, and a real approach to the object of the gaze, but here there is no such thing. The photo's grainy surface merely becomes apparent, like a barrier to any entry into the image. The camera also digresses on to other photographs of the protagonists, sometimes shown to them in the course of the interviews, sometimes used as illustration to Varda's own recollections. These too are visual fragments of the past which seem incomplete in themselves – at best they act as illustrations to the explanations offered by the sound-track. By the end of *Ulysse*, Varda seems to have established that a photograph alone does not in fact hold a concrete, objective memory; as a key to the past it can only function in conjunction with the consciousness of the people involved. The image is, objectively, 'how it was', but – apart from the fact that it is very constructed: Elia would clearly not have stripped naked in the normal course of events – it does not correspond closely to anything in the minds of the people concerned in it. It was not really a significant moment for them, although it does provide a possible route into their personal pasts, through other occasions which it evokes without showing them.

Having established that this 'moment of the past' is, in fact, in its present existence in the minds of the protagonists, a proteiform thing, Varda then proceeds to the final 'protagonist', that is the goat. Not, of course, the original goat of the photograph, long since dust and existing now only insofar as the image of it exists. However, Varda says, she prefers not to talk about 'the image of a goat'. That this is not the first goat to become an image is illustrated by a series of famous goats from art, literature or mythology. Images of all these are shown, before Varda introduces 'a goat, a goat, any old goat'. In fact an ordinary white goat, very much alive, which considers the photo briefly before taking a bite out of it. The reviewer for *Cahiers du cinéma* observed: 'une chèvre venge sa défunte congénère en bouffant la photo' (Chevrie 1984: X) ('a goat avenges its deceased relative by scoffing the photo'). Varda prefaces the scene with a question, 'how does it see its own image as a goat?'

Clearly, a goat has no interest in its own representation. But the goat eating its own image is also a living and very present animal devouring an image of a dead, past one, and as such may also be seen as the present cannibalising the past and annihilating it. (In the context of allusively meaningful artistic images, to which we have just been introduced, I think the interpretation is fair.) The memory of a past moment and a 'deceased relative' is of no relevance except as nourishment for present life, as far as the goat is concerned. It is an attitude which bears some affinity to that of the men, although they cannot adopt it so easily. Elia, finally, admits confusion: 'Je ne sais pas. C'est que je ne veux pas me souvenir: mais si on ne se souvient pas, on est mal parti. Oh je ne sais pas ... je dis ça comme ça, est-ce que je sais moi?'[12] Ulysse, more straightforward, refuses all memory – and something in his manner suggests that it is an active refusal, however good his faith may be.

And then, of course, the goat is not merely eating a memory but also a representation; its snack forms part of the arsenal of 'images of goats' which not only represent them but give them added shades of meaning in the process. Ironically, the goat eating the image of the goat becomes itself an image of a goat, with all the potential significance which we have just touched upon. Apparently, there is no escape from the process of becoming an image, and thus 'beginning to mean something', except in an 'animal imaginary', which Varda touches on in a comment which ends with an untranslatable pun: 'imaginaire' becoming 'imanginaire' (*manger* = to eat), 'a self-predatory imaginary'. The goat knows nothing of images, it simply destroys them, but for the human 'imaginary' it's not so simple, representations and interpretations come to us naturally and inevitably. Similarly the goat is unconcerned with the past, but no matter how much they want to avoid it, the human protagonists are obliged to contend with memory.

In its last sequence, the film reaches out beyond the image it started with. Other images from 1954 are produced, this time

12 'I don't know. I don't want to remember. But if you don't remember, it's a bad start. Oh I don't know ... I'm just saying that, what do I know?'

unconnected with Varda – newsreel images of the fall of Dien
Bien Phu (the most remarkable event of May 1954).[13] There are
also some portraits of well-known figures, this time taken by
Varda, from the same period. These images surround the first
with 'its time', showing the aspects of May 1954 which will be
remembered in a general sense, in history, but Varda comments
that she doesn't remember them at all, and that she had to check
what happened in the world in that year. The photograph itself
gives no sign of them, 'j'aurais pu la faire dimanche dernier' ('I
could have taken it last Sunday'). It seems in no sense determined
by the historical context in which it was taken, and Varda's final
interpretation emphasises all the ways in which the picture could
be seen as 'symbolic', taken out of context – she suggests the child
torn between father and mother, or the three ages of life, as
possible themes. 'Mythologies vous me faîtes rêver' ('Mythologies
you make me dream'). With the mention of mythology, Varda
moves not only to Greek myth but also towards Barthes and his
description of the myth as signification outside time and history.
Thus, starting from precise social context (the people actually
involved, who remember the period but have lost the memory of
the moment of the photograph, so that it does not for them
represent that part of their lives, or only incidentally and very
imperfectly), she moves to a wider historical perspective (but not
even she can remember much about that, and the photo offers no
clues) and comes to rest, finally, in the timeless. The picture could
belong to 1954 or to 1989, it could show Ulysse and Elia or any
other man and boy, it provides an image which can be adjusted to
fit an illustration of 'humanity' in general – 'the child between
father and mother'. Even its title does not drag it back to its social
context.

In the end, the image is ambiguous. The mythological
interpretation is not *the* ultimate explanation for the picture, it can
never, in fact, be timeless. Inevitably boy, man and dead goat
existed somewhere and the nature of photography forces

13 The French defeat of Vietnamese forces at the stronghold of Dien Bien Phu
signalled France's withdrawal from colonial interest in Indo-China.

awareness of that – this is not Ulysses but someone else. 'The real hero is Ulysse', but which? As memory, as symbolic image, a still photograph is necessarily incomplete, which doesn't prevent the interrogation of it from being both fascinating and revealing.

Sans toit ni loi is concerned with memory to the extent that it is entirely a flashback or rather a montage of flashbacks, which rely for their content on the memories of a large number of witnesses. *Sans toit ni loi* is thus a montage of memories, but this is a simplification of its actual structure. Sandy Flitterman-Lewis, in her discussion of the film, speaks of the use of direct and indirect address by the witnesses (Flitterman-Lewis 1996: 304–5) (In indirect address, the witness speaks to someone within the diegesis, although the information given contributes to the overall discourse/ narration on Mona provided for the audience; in direct address, the witness – apparently – addresses the camera and therefore the audience directly.) One would assume that, as in *L'Une chante, l'autre pas* or in the classic documentary which *Sans toit ni loi* mimes, episodes of direct address take place in the 'present' of the film's making, and the memories they call up are thus evoked in *that* present. In *Sans toit ni loi* this is not the case. Several 'interviews' clearly take place after the event certainly, but before Mona's death which is the point at which the process of recon-struction is set off – or so it is claimed in the voice-over at the beginning. To take an example, when David sums up his acquaintance with Mona, his head is bandaged, indicating that it is not long after he was slugged during the burglary.

What are we to make of this? If we adopt the fiction of a documentary-investigation announced by Varda's voice-over, this interview is out of place. The act of recollection takes place, not after Mona's death and several weeks after her separation from David, but at a moment when their co-habitation is much nearer. The same can be said of Yolande's dreamy evocation of the couple she has found, cited by Flitterman-Lewis as direct address (although it is a very indirect form of direct address: Yolande's discourse seems directed inward, to herself, rather than to the camera). Yolande is framed in front of Tante Lydie's elaborate dresser; she is therefore clearly still in Lydie's employ, but she has left this position before Mona's death and therefore before any investigation could take place.

In a sense, this procedure, while throwing into doubt the trustworthiness of the investigation (see Chapter 4), also eliminates the problem of memory as such. Subjective though the various constructions of Mona that we are offered may be, they are not subject to the additional distortion of a long time period between perception and interpretation. Not only do Varda's witnesses in *Sans toit ni loi* not know that Mona is dead, a condition which is set out in the introduction, they are allowed very little time to incorporate her into the pattern of their own lives. Interviews, like indirect witness, speak of the immediate past, and reactions to Mona are thus presented 'raw'. (In the case of Yolande above, this is the only way in which the film can insert this particular perception of Mona, which is absolutely vital to understanding what she means to Yolande but which does not survive Mona's reappearance in the servant's life.) Despite the flashback structure, the problem of *Sans toit ni loi* is one of perception rather than memory.

Jane B. par Agnès V. and its partner *Kung-Fu Master* leave the problem of memory largely to one side, but *Jane B.* at least is notable for its subtle manipulation of time. Certainly part of Jane Birkin's construction of herself passes through her memories of childhood, but construction, reconstruction or manipulation of the past are less central than the setting in motion of a number of alternative presents.

However, the film is apparently very much concerned with time and its passing; this is inscribed from the first images, where Jane, inserted into the position of a character in a painting, talks of her feelings on reaching her thirtieth birthday. At the end of the film the finished product will be offered, in voice-over above the credits, as a birthday present to Jane on her fortieth birthday (a procedure which will be considered in more detail in the next chapter). This gives the film an apparent time-frame of ten years. Of course this does not correspond to the actual time of the diegesis. As far as *Jane B.* can be said to have a time-frame, it is that of the making of the film, which we know from interviews took place intermittently over about a year and a half. However, it is far from obvious: although we do start with the beginning of the film-making (the preliminaries in a café) and end with the gift of the finished product, the order of the sequences as the film takes off follow a thematic not a chronological logic. Seasons change in response to subject, interpolated episodes often have a clearly defined season (winter for Laurel and Hardy, autumn for the Léaud episode) which need not be that shown in the conversation where they are announced – if indeed they are. In fact it is very hard to get one's temporal bearings at all in *Jane B*. The 'time-travel' among historical archetypes involved in the sketches increase the sense of a film which incorporates an infinitely expandable period of time. The ten-year framework, much longer than the time actually covered in terms of Jane's life (except in photographs) but considerably less than the total of periods evoked, helps to stabilise the whole in the viewer's mind.

With the advent of the 1990s, it seems that memory has returned to Agnès Varda's work and become its guiding principle and theme. The only major feature-film she has made so far in the 1990s, *Jacquot de Nantes*, is deeply concerned with it. Although *Jacquot* is officially a tribute to Jacques Demy, its engagement with memory is not that of a commemorative film, it is not so much *in* Demy's memory as *about* his memory, that is the way in which his relationship to his own past was converted into films which bear no outward sign of being 'autobiographical' or concerned with the past life of their maker. Varda's film stands as the explicitly autobiographical film that Demy himself never made, and the complex transfer of memory which presided over its making is also the subject of the film. The making of *Jacquot* involved the translation into images of the descriptions which Demy gave to Varda verbally of his childhood. It may be assumed that the selection of episodes represents a synthesis of Demy's and Varda's subjectivities, Demy selecting what seemed to him most significant, but Varda being responsible for the narrative structure which makes the film explicitly an evocation of the formation of Demy the film-maker. Personal memories are all directly relevant to the corpus of his films; when they are not directly connected to his growing passion for cinema, they are chosen because they subsequently found their way into his fiction.

Jacquot de Nantes, in other words, is concerned with memory mediated, the transformation of personal memories into something communicable. The film explores the ways in which the past can be passed on, represented satisfactorily to others who have not shared it. What Varda returns to Demy (for there is no doubt that Demy is the film's first destined audience as well as its primary object, and Varda is proposing to give him this structured account of his life) will be a reconstruction of the past which sets out to be genuinely evocative.

How this can be done has already proved problematic. *Ulysse* found that an apparently unaltered 'relic' of the past, even though it has arrived directly from it, cannot in fact reproduce the past. It may indeed function as a sign of the period, obliging Elia, Ulysse and Bienvenida to think about a holiday which they would otherwise have forgotten, but it neither substitutes for their memories nor adequately expresses the experience of that past moment for any one of them – scarcely even for Varda. In *Jacquot*, the past is evoked, with more success, through reproduction, reconstitution, in another context and at another time. Clearly, the substitution of moving for still images bears some relation to the more satisfactory evocation which is achieved (cf. Everett 1996: 107); however, it is tempting to suggest that the process of reconstruction itself, which adapts the experience of the past to the needs of a present (the moment of creation), provides a means of remembering as powerful as any 'authentic' relic of the past, even of moving images.

Jacquot could broadly be said to consist of three series of images, which intertwine and interrelate. These series, for convenience and in the context which we are here discussing, may be represented as 'time-lines', although this is more complicated than it seems; there are two relevant times for each series, the time of the story and the time of the narration, and neither is altogether straightforward.

The first series (A) is 'present tense' both in its creation and in its representation. It is concerned with the presence of Demy before the camera, in 1990. In majority it consists of shots of Jacques Demy's body in very intimate close-up. In connection with these gentle tracking-shots over the fragile (and fragmented) body of a dying man, the *Cahiers* critics, probably inevitably, recalled Cocteau's famous description of cinema as 'death at work'. However, impending death is never directly mentioned, although it is inscribed from the beginning in Demy's position, lying on a beach and sifting its sand through his fingers, a long-established and readily accessible image-symbol. The camera-movement, which amounts to caresses, creates nonetheless a tender intimacy which insists more on the fact that he is still, for the present, alive and (therefore) able and indeed inclined to remember the past.

The second series (B) consists of black-and-white sequences representing Demy's childhood in Nantes, during and just after the war. These are reconstitutions of Demy's memories, made by Varda in 1990, although the choice of black-and-white relates them to the cinema of the period. There is indeed a great deal of reference to cinema, since the story concentrates on Jacques's passion for moving pictures – although the films themselves (which would be 'authentic' parts of the past which is evoked) are not quoted. It is within series B (and only series B) that *Jacquot* has a narrative. The structuring and explanation of that narrative does not come only, or even primarily, from the pictures; a voice-over provides its context, authenticates its source, and justifies the choice of episodes by relating them to Demy's future destiny. In the first part of the film the voice is Varda's, and the narration is in the third person and somewhat distanced, as if 'Jacquot' was the hero of a children's novel or even a fairy story. Further into the film, Demy's voice, in the first person, begins to take over the narration, until finally, with the production in a series A image of the camera which plays a key role in the final stages of the story of series B, the two time-lines meet, albeit over a considerable distance of unrepresented time. The camera, like the photograph in *Ulysse*, is a physical remnant of the past. Its importance, and its singularity in the structure of Jacquot, are extreme. Up to the moment when Demy produces this camera in his study in the series A shots, every part of series B has been construed as reproduction or substitute, a created image based on an insubstantial memory-image in Demy's mind itself translated into another image in Varda's. The camera, however, is memory incarnated, the actual object which existed at the time when the past was present, integrated into a re-formation of the same events, the same organisation of space and time. It is qualitatively different from every other element in series B, simply by virtue of this, and it becomes the anchor, the guarantee of authenticity, as well as of continuity between past and present.

No doubt the effect which the camera has is increased by the insistence on corporeality which pervades series A. The tactile reality which the extreme close-ups of Demy's body evoke is belied by series B: we know very well that the body which represents Jacques in these scenes is not the same body (it's not even the same body throughout series B, and the change of actor is noticeable as more than an aging process) (plate 9). Demy's physical identity is so important to series A that we can never entirely forget this. But the camera *is*, physically, the same, in series A, in series B and in the authentic past of the real Jacques's childhood. It belongs both to past and present, unchanged. The power of this permanence of objects has rarely been so successfully illustrated.

Series B is the structuring skeleton of the film, but it exists only in relation to series A which calls it forth. Demy's presence requires no justification – he simply exists; the representation of his childhood in series B, however, does need an explanation, or at least explanations are offered. The film is a crafted object created from raw materials Demy provided, as a gift for him – more will be said about this context in Chapter 6 – and the B-series is that part of the film which involves the most work on memory and transfer of memory, the real meeting of the inputs of Demy and Varda. The choice of biography/autobiography as the content of the gift is justified, on the one hand, by Demy's assessment of childhood as 'a treasure', on the other, by the significance of this childhood past to the development of the creative adult.

This last point provides the justification for the third series (C), a number of extracts from Demy's films. These are inserted in series B whenever the narrative reaches a point which corresponds to an episode in a film. Obviously, whether they are in colour or black and white depends on the decision made by Demy at the time of filming, so in order to make transitions clear, Varda adopts a 'direction-sign', a pointing hand. In the time-structure of the film series C is a complicating element. The time of narration is the past, but an intermediate past, a point somewhere between the ending of the narrative period represented by series B and 1990. On one level, the time of the story is a parallel, unconnected fantasy-time, since the sequences are taken from fiction films which have no declared relationship to Jacques's own life. However, they find their place in *Jacquot* by virtue of their status as transformed re-creations of Jacques's own childhood. Thus the time of the story has been changed in the course of their transfer from Demy's films to Varda's. Just as series B is explained by series A both in its existence (the desire of the film-maker, represented in series A by the camera, to give a gift to Demy) and in its form (Jacques Demy at the end of his life is also the producer of the images of series B, by means of his verbal descriptions which the film-maker must translate), so the existence of series C can be explained by reference to the content of series B, both in its existence (it is during his childhood that Demy's desire to make films forms in him) and in its form (Demy's visual and narrative imagination draw directly on his own experience).

The three series of images which constitute *Jacquot* thus arise out of each other through relationships based on memory. It is the memory of the protagonist of series A which produces the content of series B. It is the process of remembering the events portrayed in series B which is responsible for the content of series C. There is also a complicating element, in that the content of series B is also to be explained by series C. Where the visual rhyme between an episode of series B and one of series C is particularly exact, the reason is not only Demy's use of his past to create his films, but also Varda's use of Demy's own films to re-create his past. In one sense, since the conversion of the memory of an event into a spectacle, as apparently illustrated in the transition from series B to series C, is a way to actualise the past, to bring it into existence in the present – the present, that is, of the creation of the spectacle – it would seem that both series of images are authenticated by these matches, their respective parts of fantasy being minimised by the conjunction between the *authentic* memory (in C) and the realist context of B. (A similar function is performed by the camera, visual evidence linking series B to series A.) On the other hand, the argument of the influence of Jacques's childhood on his creativity is overdetermined, if not circular: Varda shows that Peau d'Ane's baking is based on how Jacques saw his mother cook, by using the scene in *Peau d'âne* as the model for her reconstruction of the Demy kitchen. Certainly we can assume that Demy authenticated this equation, but one might suspect that at the time when he made *Peau d'âne* other factors, such as childhood memories of the nursery poem she sings, came into play. The transformation of memory into film inevitably involves some practical distortion, and where Varda recontextualises passages of Demy's films, repackaging them as authentic memory, the audience becomes intensely aware that her versions integrated into series B show, not necessarily the authentic past, but the past as it has become for Demy and Varda, mediated not only by memory but by previous representations of it.

The act of remembering in *Jacquot* is inseparable from the act of creation. The order of these acts is the inverse of that portrayed in *Ulysse* (here the memory comes first, the creation of images afterwards) and, while the latter concluded at an impasse, *Jacquot* seems to have discovered a dynamic relationship between visual artefact and memory. The still image of *Ulysse*, despite its authenticity, provided no help to the memory and, worse, no desire for memory in the minds of the people concerned. On the other hand, *Jacquot* argues that memory may prove a very successful material for the creation of effective visual images which purport to satisfy quite other desires – for escapism, fantasy, transformation of the world, or enchantment of the spectator for example. Jacques's development as a film-maker is defined throughout the film in terms of his desire to explore not his own subjectivity but his relationship with an audience (see

Chapter 6). Varda's film recycles the images in order to evoke the real past, subverting their function or revealing their origins.

Despite its avoidance of film quotes, *Jacquot* does offer a direct relationship of the past it evokes to the past of cinematic creation. The fairly long-established cinematic tradition of filming the *flash-back* (memory) in black-and-white, which as we have observed the film respects, relates to the era of black-and-white film in which the story is set, but here it also refers, I think, to the Nouvelle Vague which presided over the early careers of both Varda and Demy. Truffaut's *Les 400 coups* must be the definitive film of cinema-obsessed childhood, and series B of *Jacquot* shares with it not only that basic theme but its freedom of camera-movement and angle and even the occasional incident, for example the united family outing to a movie. The reference provides another level of evocation of the past and reference to Demy's memory, since the atmosphere in the cinema industry during the Nouvelle Vague, and the personalities which animated the movement, were an integral part of his and Varda's experience during their early filming years.

There are a few cases, however, where the flashbacks of series B appear in colour. These are mostly related to performance and spectacle, and will be considered in relation to this subject in the next chapter, but it is worth noting here that this too is respectful of cinematic tradition in the early days of colour film (the period with which *Jacquot* series B is most concerned), when the expensive colour processes were most frequently used for spectacular (and theatrical) effects. Thus it was not only Jacques, but the cinema of the period, which tended to see spectacle, and especially musical spectacle, in colour and the rest of the world in shades of grey, and this choice in the film suggests that cinematic conventions influence perception of the world and perhaps memory – at least in the case of a screen-struck child.

Since *Jacquot*, Varda has made two other films concerned with Demy's work. The first, *Les Demoiselles ont eu 25 ans*, again interlaces strands of different provenance, resulting in a plait of time-lines. Two of the three strands correspond fairly closely to the A and C of *Jacquot*: the present-in-the-present represented by footage in Rochefort in 1992, and the past-in-parallel of the fantasy world of the film. The last strand here consists of footage of the shoot taken at the time, some by Varda and some by André Delvaux. These images from the past, according to the pattern we have traced in *Ulysse* and *Jacquot*, might be expected to be a less effective means of evoking that past than reconstruction according to already processed memories. However, Varda's images were already mediated at the time according to her own perceptions: she chose them, and, unlike the photograph in *Ulysse*, chose them according to personal not formal criteria. She points out that they are thus rendered evocative for her in ways that an official documentary of the shoot would not be: 'personne d'autre n'aurait filmé en longueur mon chéri mettant son pullover d'une façon qui n'appartenait qu'à lui'.[14] Delvaux's black-and-white images command less screen-time, although their value as a record is not in doubt.

Unlike in *Jacquot*, the present series is not simply descriptive/contemplative – it bears a narrative or a series of narratives, linked by their starting point in the eruption of the past into the present life of the small town. The moment of the film-shoot permanently marked Rochefort, and therefore this particular past has always to some extent been present; part of the point of the film is to take note of this. The rest of the narrative of the commemoration is concerned partly with moments of reunion, partly with the process of preparing for a celebration, an entirely present-tense activity which is contrasted with the work involved in producing a film – again, the production of spectacle is a central theme. The process of remembering is thus an active one, and the film takes pains to avoid melancholy, although, as Catherine Deneuve points out, the task is not always easy. The film recalls not only an event (which can quite easily be converted into creative energy) but the director and one of the stars, and the central point of *Les Demoiselles* is the inscription of these personal memories into the

14 'no-one else would have filmed at length my beloved putting on his jumper in a way that belonged to him alone'.

collective one with the naming of two streets after them,. This involves a decisive *act* – swinging a champagne bottle – which in both cases is fixed by the film in a still image.

The third film about Demy, *L'Univers de Jacques Demy*, follows an old pattern of Varda's in approaching its subject from as many different angles as she can find, mixing memories of the man and of his films with statements of his importance, through his films, as an influence. The very procedure adopted indicates that Varda envisages memory as an active process; the past is something which has an active role in the present and which can be put to creative use as inspiration, not something to be nostalgically desired. *Jacquot* allows somewhat more place to such contemplative desire, through the figure of Demy who is presented as remembering, now, without needing to make use of his memories in the present. However, it is made clear, first that his memories have all through his life served him as a creative base and, secondly, that if he is now indulging in quiet recollection, this in itself will be a creative process since it is now inspiring in Varda the work of reconstruction.

Varda's latest film to date (1997), *Les 100 et 1 nuits*, is also concerned with commemoration, since it was made for the centenary of cinema. Again, the attitude taken is resolutely hostile to nostalgia – the past enters the present of a symbolic 'old man' who has supposedly experienced the whole history of cinema at first hand. It enters in a distinctly substantial sense, sometimes inconveniently. The film is first and foremost a celebration of cinema's present: its protagonists are a group of young people who dream of making a film and who are prepared to persuade M. Cinéma to part with his fortune to allow them to make it. The leading lights of French (and even world) cinema flit in and out of M. Cinéma's mansion as he tries to recover his memory, but memory is not an unadulterated good. Luis Buñuel, in the form of a cow, tells M. Cinéma that commemorations are dangerous, 'Vive l'oubli!' (Long live forgetting), to which even M. Cinéma, the embodiment of the past, responds that in the absence of memory he uses imagination. In the final sequence Buñuel has the last word as M. Cinéma's voice-off states, over footage of a commemoration ceremony: 'Je suis content de n'être pas avec eux. Moi je suis comme Buñuel – A bas les commémorations, vive l'anarchie. A bas les discours, vive le désir'.[15] The commemoration ceremony gives place to Buñuel's *L'Age d'or*, a film from the past which champions the present exactly as the voice-off says. Thus the commemorative film becomes an affirmation of present and future potential. A steadfast refusal of regret is a constant in Varda's most recent films, and the determination to turn an even potentially devastating process of grieving into life-affirming creation is perhaps what Varda means when she claims to have a 'bad relationship with memory'.

References

Chevrie, Marc (1984) 'Tu n'as rien vu à Saint-Aubin', *Cahiers du Cinéma*, no. 358, April, p. X

Dubroux, Danièle (1982) 'Un auteur face à Hollywood', *Cahiers du Cinéma*, no. 331, January, p. 48

Everett, Wendy (1996) 'Timetravel and European film', in Wendy Everett (ed.), *European Identity in Cinema*, Exeter, Intellect Books

Flitterman-Lewis, Sandy (1996) *To Desire Differently*, New York, Columbia UP

Prédal, René (1991) 'Agnès Varda: une œuvre en marge du cinéma français', in *Etudes Cinématographiques: Agnès Varda*, Paris, Lettres modernes, pp. 13–40

Samuel, Raphael (1994) *Theatres of Memory*, London, Verso

Tigoulet, Marie-Claude (1991) 'Voyage en pays féminin', in *Etudes Cinématographiques: Agnès Varda*, Paris, Lettres modernes, pp. 57–70

Varda, Agnès (1961) 'Agnès Varda', interview with Jean Michaud and Raymond Bellour, *Cinéma 61*, no. 60, October, pp. 4–20

Varda, Agnès, 'Autour et alentour de Daguerréotypes', *Cinéma 75*, no. 204, December, pp. 39–53

Varda, Agnès (1994) *Varda par Agnès*, Paris, Cahiers du cinéma

15 'I'm glad I'm not with them. I'm like Buñuel – Down with commemoration, long live anarchy; down with speeches, long live desire.'

6

Performance, audience and actors

Elle relie toujours les documents bruts à ses histoires articulées, avec ses réponses affectives ou rationnelles. Ce va-et-vient continuel entre le monde objectif et sa subjectivité, la perméabilité entre l'extérieur et l'intérieur sont les premières caractéristiques de sa 'cinécriture'.[1] (Birò 1991: 51)

Throughout the preceding analyses of Varda's films, this oscillation between objectivity and subjectivity has been a major and recurring theme. The early procedure of *L'Opéra-Mouffe* and *Cléo* involves the objective world being (re-)constructed through the eyes of a protagonist whose interpretation the film-maker ensures that we adopt. The identification of the protagonist of *L'Opéra-Mouffe* with Varda herself is peripheral to this process, as she exists as an unrecognisable figure in the film. Varda's own subjectivity, therefore, is less important to the reception of these films than that of her characters: it is the Pregnant Woman or Cléo who is reading the world. Cléo represents a more complex case to the extent that we are witnesses to the development of her subjectivity, but the films nonetheless, while clearly centring on the interpretation of, or the acquisition of meaning by, real experience, do not explicitly announce themselves as artefacts made from transformed reality. No doubt the process of transformation is

---

1 'She always links the raw documentary footage to her constructed stories, with her emotional or rational responses. This continual coming and going between the objective world and her subjectivity, the permeability between the outside and the inside are the main characteristics of her "cinécriture".'

more to the fore in the documentaries, where the only subjectivity available is the film-maker's own. In *O saisons, ô châteaux*, or *Du côté de la côte*, Varda has treated the object of her enquiry in a very individual way, which allows for the intrusion of fantasy. The fantasy is inserted by Varda's own imagination, but it finds its spark in another, collective, fantasy, which in the case of *Du côté de la côte* (original title *L'Eden-toc*) becomes the subject of the film. Imagination is vital to Varda's early documentaries not simply because there is no perception divorced from all subjectivity, but because the subjects of the documentaries are themselves highly artificial, created with the aim of appealing to the imagination. The châteaux of the Loire, the Mediterranean coast, as later the caryatids of Paris or the mural paintings of Los Angeles, are already creations with a large part of subjective fantasy, to which Varda's own imagination adds its interpretation or critique.

The transformation of experience has a further dimension. Beyond the transformation of an objective look into a subjective interpretation, the film – any film – requires that the subjective experience then be transformed into a structured presentation, or rather representation, a spectacle. Not only does Varda link the 'document brut' (raw documentary footage) to 'ses réponses affectives ou rationnelles' (emotional and rational responses), but also to a 'histoire articulée' (constructed story), a presentable form which will allow the audience to see it differently. It is essential to Varda's work, as René Prédal (1991: 29) has pointed out, that this transformation takes place on the observed world; it is also essential that it be constantly questioned, to avoid the kind of easy clichés whose manifest failure is the subject of *Le Bonheur*.

In 1975, in *Daguerréotypes*, we are presented with an extended metaphor for the central process of transforming the everyday. Varda herself does not appear in *Daguerréotypes*, though she has a place in its world, established by the voice-over which identifies itself in the last few minutes. It locates Varda within the space of the rue Daguerre; although we never see her in the interiors of the shops we are *told* that she uses them every day – and we see many other customers, illustrating the position which Varda would hold in the street when she does her daily shopping. The absent woman of the voice-over is thus someone who belongs *in* this reality – in a sense, ought to be in the image.

But it is not only Varda's voice-over which frames the construction of *Daguerréotypes* or asserts a claim to the status of creator. There is also the conjuror, Mystag, a professional creator of spectacle. If, once the film proper begins, the sound-track presents and frames it with the authoritative voice of a neighbour, client and friend of the protagonists, the credit sequence belongs to Mystag. In his conjuror's garb, before a backdrop of the Eiffel Tower, in a dramatic pose, he announces the show to come. At this point he has no location in the narrative, no name, background or reason for existence. He connotes fairground fantasy. The conjuror possesses a power of transformation which presents itself as magic while relying on the spectator's complicity and suspension of disbelief, and it is this attitude to the forthcoming film which his appearance as announcer of the credits seems to require. After the credit sequence, we are allowed for quite some time to forget the existence of Mystag. Nonetheless, the expectations which he raised do not quite die; the charge of mystery which is probably intrinsic to the Chardon Bleu is all the more visible because we have been sensitised to look for magic.

Eventually, Mystag returns to the film, integrated into the narrative, named and located, watched by the camera in his preparations for his work as are the other protagonists. However, he remains set apart. He is an 'outsider', although admittedly not from far away. The voice-over has a little gentle fun at the expense of the film's – and implicitly the protagonists' – very tight spatial limits: 'un homme venu d'ailleurs ... du 20ème, en fait',[2] but when the community is defined by a daily network of transactions and contacts distance is irrelevant to remoteness. Mystag, unlike the unseen film-maker, has no daily position in the rue Daguerre. Like the film-maker, however, he is a creator of spectacle, a spectacle which he presents to the same public for which *Daguerréotypes* is in the first instance destined, that is the

2 'a man from Elsewhere – the 20th arrondissement, actually'. The distance between rue Daguerre in the 14th and the 20th arrondissement might be about two miles, across the Seine.

inhabitants of the rue Daguerre to whom Varda dedicated the film. We shall return later in more detail to the question of the designated public for Varda's films, and the complications this raises for the position of the ordinary cinema audience. *Daguerréotypes* is the first film where Varda explicitly offers the completed work to those who are featured in it, giving her version of their lives back to them.

The second part of *Daguerréotypes* is structured round Mystag's show. His role is so important, and possesses such obvious parallels with that of the film-maker, that it is worth analysing in detail his presence in *Daguerréotypes*, the way in which he relates his spectacle to his audience, and the way in which the film presents him, his public, and the relationship between them.

When the forthcoming show is first announced, by the voice-over, its role in the life of the community is instantly evoked. Mystag will be a catalyst – of 'les demi-frayeurs et les rires à blanc' ('half-fears and uncharged laughter') – but his role is contradictory: he disturbs and reassures, awakens while at the same time 'il va endormir un monde déjà immobile' ('he will send an already immobile world to sleep'). This last is an allusion to his practice of hypnosis but also to the 'reassurance' which his show provides by valorising its audience's lives. The voice-over's summary, focusing on broad psychological effects, invests Mystag with genuine powers. The image on the other hand at this point publicises his banality. We see him making up. An unremarkable middle-aged man in ordinary clothes, rather tired-looking despite his professional smile, his face in close-up stands out not at all from those of his audience (unlike the dramatically expressionist poster in the café window, with which we are invited to compare him).

These shots are interspersed with others showing the arrival of the audience, and during the start of the show the camera concentrates on the audience while Mystag takes over the role of voice-over. Mystag's spiel further underlines his filmic function. He announces that he is an 'illusionist' (thus asking the audience to *see* rather than to believe, encouraging a measure of critical distance) and evokes science-fiction as a model for what he is doing. He adopts, in short, the position of the early fairground cinema of Georges Méliès – also a conjuror by training – although Mystag works with solid objects. It is in the choice of objects that the secret of his act lies, as well as its importance for Varda, but his cinematic preamble increases the audience's (the cinema audience's) awareness of a link between him and Varda.

The following sequences are a sophisticated work of cinematic montage (the domain of the illusionist, according to the theories of the Nouvelle Vague). Mystag's gestures are shown in close-up – but with strategic cutting so that the cinema audience receives the illusion perfectly, as the audience at the stage show never could. They are juxtaposed to the daily gestures of the tradesmen whom we have already met. Thus, in the first such incident, we see Mystag preparing some bowls of rice, while intercut images show the grocers also dealing in rice. The rice in the conjuror's bowls changes first to water, then to wine – of course, the means of transformation is hidden by the ellipsis, in good Méliès tradition – there are quick cuts to transactions in wines in the grocer's shop, and then a longer sequence where the camera remains close to a customer. As soon as she takes her leave the voice of Mystag is heard once again and we return to the show. For his next trick, he takes a small handful of banknotes, ruffles through them, and twice doubles the number. This too is shown in close-up, interspersed with close-ups of several different hands counting money on counters and over cash registers.

Mystag's props are thus also the props of the daily life of his audience. However, in his hands they behave in extraordinary ways, ways which, if they were to be extended into daily life, would completely change the meaning of the objects in question for their owners. Clearly, these tricks work on the audience to some extent through wish-fulfilment – most obvious in the case of the multiplying money. The Mystag act is here, however, functioning on a more permanent level than mere momentary fantasy. The apparent acquisition of unexpected powers by familiar objects can have the effect of changing the way in which those objects are seen even in their banal daytime form. This process becomes clearer with the following sequence. Here Mystag is warming up the audience for his fire-eating act with description, placing what he is about to do in an exotic setting: 'les fakirs qui jouent avec le feu, qui par exemple mangent le feu' (fakirs who play with fire, who eat fire for example). The words are clearly intended to provoke an image, in the absence of anything spectacular on stage for the moment. The camera, meanwhile, cuts to the baker's shop, the people coming in for bread and the baker poking in his oven. Instead of the exotic world of fakirs we have the rue Daguerre, but the description of the fakir's trade seems not inappropriate to the baker. This is a very clear example of the transformation of experience, the baker being briefly seen as unfamiliar, powerful and, indeed, magical.

It is not, of course, entirely clear to whom Varda is attributing these subjective connections. Is this new vision of the baker shared by the baker's neighbours, or indeed by the baker himself (not the most imaginative of men, as the film will subsequently reveal)? Up to this point, the audience reaction has not been shown, although we have heard applause. However, the subsequent Mystag scenes do include shots of the audience, and finally involvement of audience members in the act, and these episodes tend to attribute the connections to the spectators themselves. Thus when the audience is involved on the stage, the chosen victim is usually in some way appropriate to the act – it is the butcher's wife who volunteers to have a finger chopped off, for example, after some demonstration of what Mystag can apparently do to himself with the tools of the butcher's trade and emerge unscathed.

The Mystag act is interrupted by two long sequences or series, one in which the elderly couples of the rue Daguerre relate how they met, another which relates to dreams. The second of these particularly seems to be provoked by the Mystag act, specifically to the start of his hypnotism session. Unsurprisingly, those susceptible to dreams prove also to be those susceptible to hypnosis. At the end of this sequence, almost the last in the film, Mystag announces to his audience 'je vais tous vous endormir' (I'm going to send you all to sleep). This precedes the series of shots of false daguerreotypes, where everyone has clearly been instructed to remain absolutely still, not even blinking. After this series as the image returns to the street, Varda's voice-over comes back to take over the narration and control of the film in its closing moments.

Varda's spectacle and Mystag's are embedded in each other, and they carry both similarities and oppositions. The principal similarity which interests us here is that both attempt to approach the same local audience by means of a transformation of the familiar, a transformation which involves investing it with meanings which are created by the new context in which it is seen, and which differ from, or are added to, its most obvious function. The difference of course is that Varda's film is only nominally directed at the street-inhabitants; in fact, she is 'presenting' them to a much larger audience. There is little encouragement in the film to identify with the characters, they form a circle too tightly closed to allow the cinema spectator to enter. Mystag's strategy does involve identification, as soon as he involves the audience itself in his act; the soon-to-be-hypnotised hairdresser exchanges chat and laughter with his watching friends, and the importance of the audience to the camera's interpretation of the act increases greatly. In a sense, what Mystag does to his guinea-pig he does to all the community, exercising his power over them and also revealing to them unsuspected sides of their own nature.

The film too may have this effect on the local audience, but this is never revealed to the film spectator who, deprived of any real entry into the community, tends to see the protagonists as objects, like the banknotes and the bowls of rice. Varda surrounds them with a text, spoken and visual, which concentrates on their difference. They are in many cases artisans (therefore with a knowledge *different* from the spectators), provincials (separate from Paris), concerned only with their commerce and their households. In the case of the Chardon Bleu couple the construction goes further, and they are moulded into a mystery by virtue of their stock-in-trade, of their age, and of Marcelle's incommunicability (never explained) and her irresistible and mysterious attraction to Outside and Elsewhere. The Chardon Bleu is the most extreme example of Varda's ability to situate her subjects in a parallel world while never allowing us to forget that they look and behave like an ordinary old couple – and if they look and behave ordinarily, then they *are* ordinary, but at the same time extraordinary. Thus the film heightens the tension, as it were, attached to the people, and the things, which the camera sees.

A transformation of experience, then, but through a process of alienation. The film works through emphasising that its protagonists are both ordinary and extraordinary, but it is the experience of meeting them that it transforms, rarely their *own* experience – and when it does this, for example in the case of the baker's furnace, it is through the medium of Mystag. In *Daguerréotypes* it seems that the primary audience is still the general one, and Varda, despite her claimed 'insider' status, is approaching the rue Daguerre with an outsider's eye. However, through the Mystag show, she reveals the mechanisms of a more intimate transformation, one which she will return to later, and especially in the 'vicarious autobiography' of her husband, *Jacquot de Nantes.*

We have already discussed *Jacquot* in the previous chapter in the context of its treatment of memory and the uses of the past. Here we shall be concerned with the way in which the film treats the question of spectacle and performance, and its relation to direct experience.

Jacquot is a film obsessed with spectacle. From the credit sequence we are introduced into a theatrical world, albeit one which is turned on its head. The film begins with the final curtain of a play which we have missed. As the young Jacques insists that they may begin again, the credits roll over a shot of the shuttered stage. These are the full credits, the list of assistant make-up artists and catering crews which have been relegated to the end of films since the early 1960s. Thus *Jacquot* announces its temporal situation; it proposes to replay a life which is indeed very nearly at an end. At the same time it presents that life as a performance, to begin and end with the raising and lowering of a red curtain over a Guignol stage.

The content of the film is entirely consistent with that introductory image. It is no exaggeration to say that every incident in Jacques's early childhood is somehow connected with acting or with putting on a show. The first shot in series B is a prolonged travelling shot across the front of Demy's parents' garage, which finally cuts after the appearance in the opposite upstairs window of the girl next door who performs a little dance, framed in the window, before closing the shutters on the performance which we understand has been principally for Jacques's benefit but also for ours. Although the other activities of the garage in this opening shot are not performances as such, the camera catches them in subsidiary frames, formed of doors or partition walls, which presents the people involved as if on stages. The device of subsidiary frames is consistent throughout series B of *Jacquot* – doors, windows, mirrors and, most frequently as a pervasive visual refrain, the broad arch of the garage entry opening on to the street, through which Jacques can watch the passers-by as if on a cinema screen. Thus constructed, even the most everyday activities seem to be put on show and directed at a spectator, and there is often an internal spectator available, most frequently Jacques. Hence the displacement from Jacques as watcher of life-as-a-show (his mother framed in the window as she bakes a cake or sets a customer's hair) to these same activities presented in entirely spectacular guise in extracts from Demy's later films is presented as entirely logical and predictable.

In the selection of episodes made for series B, the majority of the sequences do actually involve a greater or lesser measure of conscious acting and/or of disguise. Discounting, for the moment, the large part allotted to performances of the official variety – puppet theatre, operetta and finally cinema – we may call attention to the following examples. Jacques and his brother create a model garage and car delivery service which they set up in the stairwell. This involves acting but also arrangement of moving props – Jacques's first spectacles will be as much concerned with creation of decors as with performing.

Jacques imitates the singers at an operetta, first spontaneously, for his father, later on a constructed stage with rudimentary costume.

Jacques and his brother say their prayers as their mother watches. Although not strictly a performance, this little scene, framed in the door-jambs like so many others, takes place for an audience (the mother) who has requested it and who is appropriately appreciative (and rewards them accordingly). The mother's comment 'ils sont épatants les petits gars' (aren't the little lads great) assesses the actors rather than the action ...

Jacques plays with a clearly home-made model car at the moment when his aunt from Rio arrives. The aunt is presented as a natural performer of her own life, with self-conscious costume and gesture as well as a fund of graphically told anecdotes. She is compared with the singer in the restaurant where the family go for dinner. The singer is a professional performer; she incarnates a porcelain shepherdess, with the use of some of the same props (wide-brimmed hat) and gestures which Jacques's aunt uses to act out her sophisticated femininity. The last shot in this sequence is of a doll dressed and arranged on a bed as if to reproduce the appearance of the singer, but perhaps also of the aunt – who appears in an intercalated sequence of a film as a Hollywood *femme fatale*, a synthesis of the tough side of the middle-aged sophisticated aunt and the constructed seductiveness of the shepherdess-singer.

Inspired by the puppet theatre or wanting to prolong the magical experience, Jacques sets up a puppet theatre at home. This constitutes a thread rather than a sequence of the film; first attempts, failures and new departures are chronicled, interspersed with other sequences, until the theatre is complete and its first performance takes place before an audience not quite as appreciative as the impresario would have chosen. This is really the first important step in Jacques's career and the episode is enormously important in understanding the film's conception of the function of spectacle and what role is expected of its audience. We will return to it.

The carnival procession passes twice in the film, on both occasions framed in the opening of the garage courtyard. In the first sequence, in Jacques's early childhood, the emphasis is on the fantasy which explodes into real life through the strange masks worn by the participants. The sequence is placed between two others which illustrate the effect on the Nantes children's lives of another kind of fantasy, that of Disney and *Snow White and the Seven Dwarfs*. In the second appearance of the carnival, after the war in Jacques's adolescence, the relation between protagonist and event has subtly changed. He is now a participant (although not a masked one) and the sequence reveals that the masquerade is itself a pretence. Jacques is seen unmasking his girlfriend: the mask/disguise is no disguise but only an excuse for a brief moment of liberty – this sequence being inserted at a moment in the film where freedom of action is in short supply, creation of spectacle – Jacques's main desire – having been forbidden or relegated to the hidden space of the attic by his father. It is noticeable that, although the desired freedom provided by the carnival is apparently mainly sexual, it is not this that poses a problem for Jacques nor is it of more than subsidiary importance in the film. There are no barriers to his meeting his girlfriend, but she eventually comes to represent another obstacle in the way of his ambition to create; at which point she leaves the film, unlamented. The real forbidden treasure of the carnival is the opportunity to participate in fantasy.

Reine, the little girl next door, whose dance provides the first striking announcement that the film will be concerned with spectacle in everyday life, continues to play this role. Much more concerned than Jacques, apparently, with entering the fantasy world of the films, she is marked out by her playmate as a future star largely because she has so marked herself out. As children they plan to go into partnership, and Jacques's early daydream of putting a ballerina on stage resurfaces in the subject of his first attempt at animation. But the young woman's perception of spectacle soon diverges from Jacques's. She sees the world of the movie stars as a fantasy world, but one which she will be able to enter by powers of seduction – not so far removed from Jacques's own perception of the power of spectacle, which depends on seducing an audience. However, Reine works to perform her own identity, to seduce by her person rather than by a constructed performance. Although the foreseeable result is a return to the everyday world apparently divorced from the glamour of the stage, Varda does not depict Reine as renouncing performance. In her last appearance Jacques watches an argument between Reine and her mother: the mother would prefer that Reine hide her pregnancy but Reine has no objection to an audience, she even exaggerates her big belly, especially when she becomes aware that Jacques is watching. Reine for Jacques remains throughout the film a person to be watched, an actress even when her only role is herself, and Jacques remains an appreciative audience, aware that Reine in her turn enjoys, even needs, this confirmation.

The episodes during the war introduce a different kind of performance into the film, but the subject remains central. However, it is several times displaced from the ludic and escapist to the deadly serious – even if still regularly concerned with escape. The small boys in the first months of the war are most fascinated by the idea of a hidden enemy to whom the normal surroundings of their lives would be a pretence. They stare wide-eyed at a poster proclaiming that 'Walls have ears' and enemy spies may be anywhere: they relay stories of German soldiers hiding under nun's habits, and even follow a group of nuns in the street in the hope of catching a glimpse of hairy Wehrmacht legs. The 'phoney war' is thus remembered as a period when the boys are looking for the war under its peaceful disguise -and, by and large, not finding it. The first intrusion of the 'real' war in Jacques's consciousness comes in the form of two French soldiers, who arrive in the garage seeking civilian clothes so that they can escape unrecognised. M. Demy and the garage-hands provide the necessary items with a speed and efficiency which suggests that the operation had been expected and planned for. Later, the presence of the war takes the form of a little princess in hiding with Jacques's neighbours. This episode – apparently idyllic – ends with a brutal unmasking of violence apparently quite unconnected with war and indeed unexplained: the children discover the body of their mysterious neighbour ('la sorcière'), and the camera moves upwards from her face to slide across the various masks which hang on her walls. It is a disturbing image which throws the serenity of the previous episode into doubt: the two are inseparably linked.

The theme of pretence and performance continues throughout the wartime sequences. Rations are hidden in the car's engine, the women hide their bare legs with pencilled seams, the last German soldier of the war is a lost boy pretending to be ferocious. Jacques and his classmates at school act out the bombing raids and the tensions of the war in their games, while the raids themselves are partly spectacle. The descent of a German parachutist – a deadly serious episode of war – becomes a 'film' watched through the frame of a classroom window by a score of excited little boys, before being literally converted into reconstructed entertainment when it becomes the inspiration for Jacques's first attempt at translating experience on to celluloid. Another sense in which the war becomes performance is illustrated by the shot of the bombing of Nantes. This for Jacques in his childhood was a very real episode. By avoiding reconstruction, and restricting herself to the scenes in the air-raid shelter, Varda might have represented it relatively realistically, but she inserts a shot of the burning city which flaunts its studio artificiality and reminds us that all this representation of the war is nothing but performance of experiences long over.

Jacques's childhood as recounted by Varda seems thus to have largely been spent under the sign of representation, performance and disguise of one sort or another. Clearly, this is the result of a subjective assessment of his early experiences, a subjectivity which has not only selected episodes which relate to this theme but which constructs images of other episodes in such a way that they appear as framed spectacle, episodes of a film. In these circumstances the transition from memory to genuine, later, film seems so natural as to be, in some cases, scarcely a transition at all, despite the non-realism of Demy's work. Such sequences are a continual reminder that the B-series constitutes a very processed version of the 'raw material' of Jacques's creativity, but also that within the most basic raw material of experience there is already quite a lot of processing, of representation, going on. This is all the more complex in that the experiences which are represented in Jacques's childhood fantasies are as often as not unknown or known only through other representations. This is most obvious in the children's obsession with reproducing the plays, musicals and films they see – all of which are set in a fantasy-world – but it is also true, for example, in the little boys' eagerness to discover a German spy under a nun's habit. They choose to believe that the familiar reality is *not* real, but that it must mask a 'truth' which they draw from comic-book fantasy. One may assume that they are at least not entirely convinced that there is any such hidden reality – but its possibility enhances the familiar. The result is to underwrite the *realism* of Demy's fantasies. Jacques Demy may seem very remote from the ideals of the cinema of the 1960s, which at least paid lip-service to the idea that the vocation of cinema was to reveal the world as it is; nonetheless, the conjunction of series C with series B in *Jacquot* illustrates the concordance of the spirit of Demy's films with the imaginary constructions of the world which have a very real influence on lives.

Apart from the elements of life-as-performance, of course, a very large part is played in the film by the performances which the children, with or without their parents, attend as spectators. The first of these, the puppet theatre, is used by Varda to open the film, and interspersed with the sequences listed above are representations of puppet shows, operetta and the all-pervading presence of the cinema, which becomes more and more important.

It does not take long for Jacques to progress from totally spellbound spectator of the introductory puppet-show, his eyes glued to the stage even after the curtain has come down, to a more active and enquiring position. Indeed, even at this stage, his first words in the film, 'sometimes the curtain rises again', apart from announcing the film's intention to realise his memory and replay his life, make it clear that despite his wide-eyed gaze he is already taking note of the mechanisms of the spectacle, if only in order to ensure his continued enjoyment of the fantasy. After being taken to see an operetta, he promptly succumbs to his desire to replay the magical experience. In this first example of Jacques as *creator* (or re-creator), the experience of reproducing performance occurs in two stages. The first is totally spontaneous, with very little of the props of performance, but demanded by the desire to satisfy an audience; in this case, to allow his father to share something of the wonders that he has missed. In the second stage, Jacques has procured several of the accessories necessary to set the performance apart, in a privileged, staged world. He has a makeshift stage in the garage, he has acquired a curtain to drape round his shoulders, he is surer of the words and the tune and also adopts the grand manner of the opera company. This restaging, however, appears to satisfy himself alone, there is no sign of an audience. Clearly in Jacques's urge to create there are several factors in play, and these two – the desire to entrance an audience, the desire to create a privileged space set apart from real life, will recur in his subsequent, gradually more successful, attempts.

The next stage in this apprenticeship process is, again, a direct result, and a restaging, of a spectacle which he has seen and enjoyed; in this case the Guignol puppet-plays. This incident is clearly a key stage in Jacques's development and its narrative unfolding takes time and is integrated with other elements of the story of his childhood. Despite its importance, it is an unsatisfactory experiment – as reproduction of the pleasures expected from its model it provides a series of relative failures. The first relate to the re-creation of the performance space, or rather of the performers themselves who, since they are puppets manipulated by Jacques, are props and part of the created magic. Jacques has the – apparently very good – idea of making them out of potatoes, but the potatoes decay and his puppets change their appearance drastically overnight. With this disappointment the subject is temporarily abandoned by the film, a change which expresses Jacques's discouragement as well as anything the character could say or do.

But the puppet-theatre project re-emerges. Again, the first preoccupation is the creation of the space, and it is clear that the form of that space is very important. Not only must there be a stage-frame, but that frame must itself be elaborately decorated. To that end Jacques removes two angel-figures from the cemetery, transplanting them to his own sacred space, the theatre (the theft recalls *Jeux Interdits*, but here the booty serves the child not to represent the death-rituals but to imitate an imitation of life ...) (plate 11). More satisfactory puppets are made, with infinite care, from cardboard, and finally Jacques is able to stage his version of Cinderella before a small and obviously hopeful audience (plate 10). But – although the audience clearly gets pleasure from the show – its reaction does not reproduce the hushed stares which greet the 'professional' Guignol. Jacques's illusion is not perfect enough, the audience is able to be critical: 'C'est pas des étoiles, c'est du sable!' ('That's not stardust, it's sand!'). Again, with this disappointment the film abandons the subject, as if, after that comment, there is nothing worthwhile to be said about the experience.

However, the sequence does not allow us to retain a sense of failure. Just prior to it, a moment when young Jacques tries out a penny-whistle, perhaps in the hope of providing musical accompaniment to his puppet-play, cuts into a sequence from Demy's later film of the Pied Piper, and after the play is over, Jacques attends a new Guignol, *Peau d'âne* – a story which the audience do not need to be reminded became the subject for one of Demy's best-known fantasies. Despite the initial setback, therefore, the sequence is optimistic, adult success frames childhood failure. The childhood experience in this context becomes a moment in the future film-maker's training, and we see it in terms of lessons learned – the perfection of the illusion is necessary in order to keep a fascinated and attentive audience.

The only sense in which this first spectacle of Demy's transforms reality is in its clumsy attempts to make everyday objects appear to be something else – to transform sand into stardust, for example. Recognition, in this case, is a disaster. However, Jacques's next experiment with creation of spectacle illustrates the way in which reality can be transformed in such a way that recognition is, on the contrary, a triumph. The content of *Le Pont de Mauves* (the first film which Jacques creates himself, as opposed to simply projecting) is the account of a direct experience, but it is an experience which Jacques and his friends lived as a spectacle, packed against the classroom window. He is therefore reproducing an experience of spectatorship which he has already had (and which has provided him with a point of view, as well as a guarantee of the suitability of the subject), but although the original was a spectacle, it was not already a representation: the events had their own logic and the objects and places their own reality. Therefore it is Jacques who transforms these events into a primitive story destined only for the spectator, and who is obliged to represent, and transform, events which he can clearly not restage. When his small family audience recognise his rough drawing of the bridge and remark on its likeness, it is a moment of triumph, which Jacques emphasises by pointing out the difficulty of the task of achieving that likeness. This kind of transformation of reality has contributed to the approval of his audience, and the lesson will be learnt, to reappear triumphantly in the last of Jacques's 'films' to appear in *Jacquot* series B, *Attaque nocturne*, which illustrates not only a grasp of the tricks of cinematography but also of the importance of using and manipulating the raw material of 'reality'. *Attaque nocturne* repackages the everyday world of Nantes, and Jacques's drawn version of it is then offered to the audience. Admittedly, *Attaque nocturne* seems mainly to satisfy its creator's desire to *make* film, but nonetheless Jacques cannot gauge his achievement without the aid of an audience, and at every stage of his creative apprenticeship the presentation of the result to an audience is given equal prominence in the film to the creative process. It is through the audience reaction that the spectacle finds its justification, especially when the audience is *a priori* unsympathetic, as is the case with Demy senior as Jacques's mania for film threatens more and more to distract him from getting a 'proper job' and to take him outside his father's domain.

All Jacques's efforts as showman are made for a small, known audience, although his fascination with more public models makes it clear that his family and friends are not really sufficient. The ultimate audience for the young Jacques is represented by the cinema professionals whose approval can open the way to access to a much wider public. Fernand Jean and Christian-Jacque are spectators who do not appear on screen, but whose all-important reaction is recounted by the old Demy of series A. Demy repackages and recycles his childhood, and this conversion of experience into spectacle is, it is implied, even more important, indeed central, to his commercial films – however, the repackaging is not primarily intended to be viewed by those familiar with the original. Indeed his father rejects his film-making, and when Demy tells his own story, he implicates his mother too in this rejection: 'Mes parents n'étaient pas d'accord' ('my parents were against it'), although she is presented on screen as supportive.

When Demy reconstructs his past, then, it is for an indefinite and general audience. Varda's intentions are different – the first recipient of the film *Jacquot*, with all its construction and interweaving of the three strands of images, is Jacques himself. The introductory sequences use this idea in order to establish a firm connection between the child of series B and the old man of series A. The film begins with a shot of Demy on the beach (in fact, it begins with a shot over the sea, something which two of the most famous films of the Nouvelle Vague – and many other films since – have established as almost inevitably an ending). Then the image cuts to a painting of a couple, which the camera runs over as it will later do over Demy's body, as Varda's unmistakable voice announces the intentions of the film in the words of Baudelaire's 'Le Balcon', a poem directed unequivocally at one person -(although, of course, the same ambiguity which attends Varda's films is already present in the poem she uses to introduce it: the intimate private message is intended for publication) for whom it proposes to recall the memory of past happiness. As soon as the poem or rather the selections Varda makes from it are finished, the image cuts to the final curtain of a puppet-play, and we are engaged in the credit sequence described above. The film will fulfil both the promise made through the poem to the man on the beach and the expectations of the child, and this is its primary purpose.

That the general audience is secondary to *Jacquot* is also indicated by the way in which Varda has talked about the film, not only at the time of its appearance, just after Demy's death when the emotional charge was inevitable, but three years later in a text apparently destined to prove that the outside audience *was* in fact important. This article ('Quand j'y pense en 1993', Varda 1994: 206–7) concentrates to start with on a wider audience, in fact a child audience whose interest in the social conditions of Jacquot's time she notes. But the article soon deviates, through one child's question about the possibility of remembering another person's life, into the successes obtained in entering into Jacques's memory and his reactions to her reconstructions. The power of the film for Varda is linked above all to these successes (which she returned to in interview in Glasgow in 1996), with the proof that they provide of a real community of thought and the pleasure that an unexpectedly close correlation between reconstruction and memory gave to Demy. *Jacquot* was 'a film for Jacques'; he was the first audience, and the film did not appear before a wider public until after his death.

Jacquot is perhaps the most concerned with spectacle and representation of all Varda's films. It is not, however, the first to present itself as a transformation of experience destined primarily for an internal audience of the person whose experience is in question. The idea of the film as a gift to its subject, already broached by *Daguerréotypes* and even, long before, by *La Pointe Courte*, replayed every ten years in the village where it was shot, is perhaps brought to its most explicit point in the twin films *Jane B. par Agnès V.* and *Kung-Fu Master*. The gift is a pervading image in *Jane B.* The film ends with birthday wishes from Varda and all the team of the film, offered to Birkin on her fortieth birthday – together, it is implied, with the completed film. The whole film is itself explicitly a gift, and it contains others which reflect on its own status; for example, in the sequence which explores Jane's house. This begins with some shots of Jane in front of a derelict wall, while she evokes her demolished childhood home: the lifelong influence which a house exerts is established. Then comes a long shot of the courtyard of a Parisian building, which Jane enters remarking, as she advances from background to foreground, that 'il paraît que l'on fait un acte décisif quand on a une maison à soi' (Apparently you take a decisive step when you have your own house), an act, as the context makes clear, of detachment from childhood. The house is thus a symbol of autonomy. The next shot shows the house, through the grille of the gate, with an enormous ornamental knot hanging over the door from a crossed ribbon. The camera registers Jane's surprise and emotion: 'ça c'est bien de toi', she says to the off-camera Varda, 'envelopper ma maison comme si c'était un paquet-cadeau'. Varda responds 'Une maison, ce n'est pas un cadeau?'

Jane is dubious: 'Je l'ai payé quand même'.[3]

As a choice of gift the house echoes the later gift of the film. Like the film, it is a reflection of the self of the recipient: not only does it represent independence for Jane, but also the organisation of her present life and the memories of her past; she furnishes the staircase with photographs of all her family as children, herself included. The camera follows her as she enters the house and moves from room to room, and once she is in the house the series of static shots which made up the sequence outside the gate gives way to a long travelling from right to left, outside the windows, following Jane's movement through her suite of ground-floor rooms. Another seminal French woman film-maker, Marguerite Duras, described the relationship of protagonist and house in her 1973 film *Nathalie Granger*: 'une femme qui déambule dans sa maison fait le tour d'elle-même, comme si elle en épousait même le contour, comme si la maison elle-même avait forme de femme (...) Il y a donc une sorte de symbolisme, d'osmose de la femme et de la maison'[4] (Ishaghpour 1982: 233). The quote is in place here, although Birkin – when outside – denies her attachment to the house other than as a refuge for her family: 'le dernier qui claque la porte, eh bien je suivrai, je partirai moi aussi, pour un hôtel'.[5] However it is clear, as soon as she is inside and 'déambulant' before our eyes from room to room, that the house does indeed contain a structured reflection of Birkin's life, and in gift-wrapping the house Varda is making a symbolic present of Jane's life, repackaged.

There is ambiguity and even irony in this gift. Varda is making Jane a 'present' of something which she already owns – or rather, perhaps significantly, part-owns, the other part being under the control of exterior institutions in the shape of the bank – and over which Varda has no rights whatever. The layout of the house/the

3 JB: 'That's just the sort of thing you'd do, wrap up my house like a present!' AV: 'Isn't a house a present?' JB: 'I have paid for it.'
4 'a woman who wanders about her house is exploring herself, as if she herself borrowed its outlines, as if the house itself had the shape of a woman (...) There is thus a sort of symbolism, an osmosis of the house and the woman.' Unfortunately Ishaghpour gives no source.
5 'the last one who slams the door, well I'll follow, I'll leave too – for a hotel'.

intimate organisation of Jane's life is something which is already complete and over which the film-maker has no control, not even that of encouragement. The film respects this in its insistence on remaining outside, filming Jane within her life, but through a window of which, finally, the frame appears in the image to remind the audience of that distance. The camera cannot cross the threshold until Jane invites it, and at this point, we are given two frontal images of the camera to underline the significance of this change of position. Once the invitation has been offered, Varda appears behind the camera: before, when the machine is outside, it is alone, unhumanised. It is paradoxical that the film is able to take possession of Jane sufficiently to offer her its version of herself, while at the same time it is dependent on an invitation/ consent (another kind of gift) in order to enter her house, or her life, in the first place.

The film provides an interior organisation to her life, however, which is not necessarily that which Jane herself would have created. Unlike *Jacquot*, in *Jane B.* Varda is not attempting to give Jane a representation of her past but a composite image of her present. The past appears primarily as a formative influence on the present, on which it has an effect but where it cannot be reconstructed. It is rarely represented in images, only once in moving images, never in images created by Varda. The metaphor for what the film offers would be not as in *Jacquot* the staging of a spectacle, but rather a mirror, and sure enough mirrors play a large part in the imagery of *Jane B.*, as we have seen in Chapter 4.

The ambiguities inherent in the film as gift, illustrated by the sequence of the house as gift, are not unlike those which caused problems when the film was considered as a mirror – how can Jane see the film as a *reflection* of herself when Varda too is facing her, holding or at least commanding the camera? If Varda can offer Jane her own house as a symbolic gift, does that imply that the house is in part Varda's? It is a reminder that the ability to transform the experience of others into film, which Varda has through her training and talent, can only work if she can first take possession of that experience. All the film-gifts offer their recipient a reworked version of something that the recipient has first given to Varda. In *Jane B.* that first moment of gift is shown, in the early sequence when Jane repeats two or three times that she is willing to be Varda's model, to sit for her portrait and so on. It is no mere formality. When she wavers Varda calls her sharply to order – 'Tu as accepté de faire ce film quand même' ('You *did* accept to make this film'). In *Ulysse*, which is dedicated to Ulysse's mother Bienvenida, the reworked and intertwined memories which Varda creates around the fixed fragment of their past is not necessarily reworked in the way Bienvenida would have chosen. She admits that she prefers other pictures of Ulysse, because of the painful memories associated with this one. Nonetheless she is ready to be interviewed, briefly, about this picture. Ulysse's reluctance is much more evident, and yet the film requires from him too the gift of a part of his past (the photo) and of a small amount of time.

It is worth noting that Varda's gifts, when they are not to communities, tend to be to women: Bienvenida, Jane Birkin, Elsa Triolet (in an early documentary), or Nathalie Sarraute for *Sans toit ni loi*. Demy of course is the exception, the exception also in that the giving and receiving involved in *Jacquot* escapes the tensions which exist in other films. Varda never has to ask anything of Demy. His interviews are given spontaneously, and Varda's voice is never heard in them, there are no orienting questions. He shows no reluctance, queries no decisions. Also, Varda is not alone in her transformational talent. Demy has already made artefacts of his experience, and we see portions of this throughout the film. More, the introductory painting represents – presumably – Demy's translation on to canvas of a mutual experience, so that the process of heightening and returning the image of the self really does work in both directions.

If in *Jane B.* the gift is ambiguous, and Varda takes possession of Jane's life in no uncertain terms before wrapping up the images and giving them back to her, *Kung-Fu Master* is constructed, within *Jane B.*, as a gift to Jane much less ambiguous than the portrait, because the idea of it and the desire for it springs from Jane herself. As presented in *Jane B.*, *Kung-Fu Master* starts life as a tentative idea for a sketch to be included in the film. The importance given to it has implications for the other sketches in the film, at once indicating that Jane potentially has a creative power over what is shown, and that actually she rarely uses it. The scenario of *Kung-Fu Master*, even in its brief primitive state, is described by Jane as something exceptional, 'la première chose que j'ai jamais écrite' ('the first thing I've ever written'). It does not find its way into *Jane B.*, being adjudged too complicated; however, breaking off – apparently – the making of the latter film, Varda proposes to turn Jane's scenario into a full-length film. The first idea of the scenario appears to take root while the camera of *Jane B.* watches Jane tentatively explain what she has in mind, while Varda, off-screen, discusses with her what might be done with the idea. *Jane B.* also contains sequences from *Kung-Fu Master*, however, indicating that the shooting of the second film had at least begun, and possibly reached an advanced stage, before the first was completed. *Kung-Fu Master* is thus, temporally, surrounded by, or wrapped in *Jane B.*, and rather than to refer to them as twins one should perhaps think of them as mother-film and offspring – an image which obviously fits the subject.

In form, and seen without the support of *Jane B.*, *Kung-Fu Master* seems to be a fairly straightforward fiction. Jane plays a woman approaching 40 who falls into a kind of love with one of her daughter's schoolfriends, played by Mathieu Demy. The circumstances of its making obviously lend *Kung-Fu Master* added significance, but these are scarcely inscribed in the film. It takes an attentive observer to notice the discreet dedications in a corner of the screen, just as the image is about to take over from the credits (and therefore when the attention is most distracted). Without outside knowledge of Varda's and Birkin's lives it is impossible to know that Mathieu is Varda's son, or that Charlotte and Lou are really Birkin's daughters, or even that they are sisters. Admittedly it would probably be hard to find a film-goer in France who did not at least know the relationship between Jane and Charlotte, but the family ties which are vital to the conception of the film are disguised as much as possible. Inevitably the involvement of the Birkin family is visible, and thus even a perfectly ignorant spectator might deduce that Jane's involvement was greater than a starring role and a rather delayed credit as originator of the story might suggest, if he or she was inclined to do detective work on the credits while watching the first images of the film. There is nothing at the end of the film to alert the audience either: indeed in *Kung-Fu Master* Varda followed the old-fashioned procedure she was later to use with *Jacquot* and ran all credits at the start. Knowing the circumstances in which the film was made it would be possible to feel that it rather minimises Birkin's role; but, of course, *Jane B.*'s existence remedies this.

Kung-Fu Master then is a film-gift which does not contain within it the complications which this status implies. Its dedicatee is apparently no more than an actress in it; but this is a not unusual occurrence, since Varda's actors often have an involvement or an investment in the film-making which makes them more than mere actors. *Kung-Fu Master* is dedicated to Mathieu as well as to Jane. Varda's account of the film's making emphasises that she gave as much importance to his vision as to the actress's, allowing their different attitudes to the subject to co-exist and play off each other. In normal circumstances this would presumably be a potential source of conflict, and the personal input must have been made possible by the family intimacy which seems to have reigned during the shoot, not surprisingly. Mathieu has in fact been a regular player in Varda's films since the age of 5, when he took a starring role in *Documenteur*. In 1995, for *Les 100 et 1 nuits*, he plays an adolescent eager to make a start in the film business.

Varda frequently has her friends and family take part in her films, and chooses to make them for a preliminary audience who are also involved in the film and who, often, lend their experience to Varda's creative talents. Even when the films are not nominally about her own circle (and as we have seen many are), acquaintances will make 'guest appearances' and faces which are not star faces recur in several films; we recognise several of the women from *Daguerréotypes* in *Réponse de femmes*, and the baker appears again in *Jane B.* The old woman who plays Tante Lydie in *Sans toit ni loi* was recruited for an adventurous short film, *7 P., cuis., s. de b... (à saisir*), the previous year. Varda tells a delightful story about the discovery of this woman. *7P* required its protagonist to appear naked. Varda sent a newly recruited assistant to find a volunteer:

> Je crois savoir que la drague fut dure, particulièrement avec les vieilles dures d'oreilles à qui elle devait répéter trois fois en hurlant: 'C'est pour un film. Est-ce que vous accepteriez de poser nue?' Dans l'avenue de la République, elle en aborda une qui, contre toute attente, répondit: 'Si je ne fais pas ça maintenant, quand est-ce que je le ferai?' ... Elle avait 84 ans.[6] (Varda 1994: 157)

Like so many others who have made brief appearances in Varda's films, she remained in occasional touch with the film-maker.

Varda's fiction films are remarkable for their absence of star actors. Although a constant preoccupation with budgets has to be taken into account, there is enough evidence to suggest that the absence is not a result of stars simply not being available. Jane Birkin after all approached Varda to ask to work with her. *Jane B.* contains a list of 'names' in French cinema, *100 et 1 nuits* even more so – but they play only in brief cameos, and in the latter case they mostly play themselves. *Kung-Fu Master* is extremely interesting, in that it contains two national and even international stars, Birkin and Gainsbourg, in roles which are a hair's breadth only from playing themselves. Catherine Deneuve appears very early in Varda's work in the obscure *Créatures*, then reappears ... in *Les Demoiselles ont eu 25 ans*. *Lions' Love* stars Viva, Jim Rado and Jerry Ragni, and it is practically a documentary about them. In other words Varda's interest in major actors is stirred most by their existence as human beings rather than their professional talents; and where the actors are required to take on a role in a more conventional sense, the personal investment which she demands can prove problematic, as Bonnaire's comments on *Sans toit ni loi* indicate.

This attitude gives to the body of Varda's work an unusually

6 'I am sure that the hunt was hard, particularly with old ladies who didn't hear too well and had to have it shouted at them two or three times: "It's for a film. Would you be prepared to pose naked?" In the avenue de la République, she approached one who replied quite unexpectedly: "If I don't do it now, when will I do it?" ... She was 84.'

intimate feel for an internationally known series of films. In the most extreme cases (*Jane B.*, *Jacquot de Nantes*) the cinema audience has a strangely marginal position with relation to the film, apparently made for a more private and also more emotionally charged purpose than general cinema exhibition. This is, of course, an illusion at least in large part, but it contributes to the power of Varda's films both by indicating that the film was born out of a mutual desire to see this product to completion on the part of film-maker and actors, and by the guarantee which it gives of the authenticity of the material translated to screen. The finished work is experience transcribed and framed, certainly not a reproduction of life; nonetheless it is rooted in reality and the process of converting experience into film is a result of the combined perceptions of all those involved concerning what is important, striking or potentially significant in the raw material before the camera and in their own stock of memory.

References

Biró, Yvette (1991) 'Les Cariatides du temps ou le traitement du temps dans l'œuvre d'Agnès Varda', in *Etudes Cinématographiques: Agnès Varda*, Paris, Lettres modernes, pp. 41–56

Ishaghpour, Youssef (1982) *D'une image à l'autre: la nouvelle modernité au cinéma*, Paris, Denoël/Gonthier

Prédal, René (1991) 'Agnès Varda: une œuvre en marge du cinéma français', in *Etudes Cinématographiques: Agnès Varda*, Paris, Lettres modernes, pp. 13–39.

Varda, Agnès (1994) *Varda par Agnès*, Paris, Cahiers du cinéma

Conclusion

The preceding chapters have I hope left in no doubt Agnès Varda's place as a very important and individual voice in the modern French cinema. Her career pre-dates the start of the Nouvelle Vague, and *La Pointe Courte* shows several of the characteristics which would make that movement famous, five years before its officially recognised start. Through all the changes which French society and French cinema have seen in the subsequent four decades she has continued to produce films which reflect her own preoccupations and her original vision, on the margins of the official production and distribution system even when this has led to financial difficulties. Her *œuvre* is exceedingly varied, comprising documentaries and fiction films, short films and features, and also a large number which lie between the two, since Varda's care to give appropriate formal expression to what she has to say includes a determination not to add padding in order to make up required length. As she said to interviewers at the Glasgow Film Festival in 1996: 'If you feel you're expressing something which is not worth more than ten minutes, why use more?' Some of her films have met considerable public acclaim and gained an international audience, perhaps most strikingly *Sans toit ni loi/Vagabonde*; some remain difficult to see even in France, but all are rewarding.

Together they form a body of work which has considerable formal and thematic coherence, as this book has aimed to illustrate. Varda's considerable creative freedom as her own producer has allowed her an unusual degree of control over the form of her films (although financial and to a lesser extent other institutional constraints mean that such control can never be total). Her films show a deep awareness of the signifying power of every element of the images of which they are made, and of the conjunctions and progressions of these images, their rhythm and direction. Even in her most straightforward fictions (which are, when the count is made, rare) she is never concerned simply to tell a story, but always to reflect on the implications of events through the way in which they are presented. Most of all, throughout her career, she has been concerned with the nature of perception, and the way in which experience is lived by those involved. The change which takes place in objects as they are seen by a human eye, processed by a human brain, and incorporated into the world of a human experience is perhaps the most ubiquitous subject of exploration in all her films. Inevitably, this leads to a questioning of the function of film-making itself; the camera has to be self-aware, and to make the audience aware, not only of its own biases but also of those which spectators are unwittingly carrying with them. This consideration is incorporated into the film's structure, but far from denouncing the bias Varda's films celebrate the great enrichment which such personal investment brings to experience, as well as the dangers which sometimes arise from too easy acceptance of one's own perceptions. 'Taking one's desires for reality' (as the old 1968 slogan has it) – and, conversely, taking reality for one's desires – is a constant motive for action and perception among Varda's protagonists and indeed for the camera itself. Without it vision would become insignificant (indeed, probably impossible) but it also leaves the subject open to disappointment and maybe even to revolt against reality, if she or he is not able to adapt her or his desires.

In her most recent films, Varda has used her interest in the intermixture of desire and 'reality' which underlies perception, first to carry out a long series of explorations of the function of memory, and secondly to create films which are reworkings of the desires and perceptions of specific people, the ostensible subjects and the first intended audience for the films. Varda's work has always been personal in the sense that it springs from an individual vision, but in these films it becomes doubly personal in that they represent an intimate exchange between Varda's perceptions and her desires regarding the other, and the latter's interpretations and preferences, perceptions and desires of themselves.

This book has for obvious reasons concentrated mostly on those films which have had distribution outside France and which the reader may reasonably be supposed to have been able to see. I hope, however, that it has succeeded in placing those films in the context of Varda's work in a wider sense, and in showing that each of her films has many threads which link it to others, previous workings of similar themes or later developments which pick up issues left open in the earlier film. It is important to note that Varda does not reject any of her films, and to read *Varda par Agnès* is to realise to what extent the issues which preoccupied her at the time of her earliest ventures still interest her. In this sense too her work is an unusually coherent whole. The themes selected in previous chapters do not by any means exhaust the richness of interpretation which could be found in the films – and, similarly, the privileging of particular films in the context of certain headings is in large measure a matter of convenience, and every one of Varda's films would undoubtedly yield meaning under every one of the chapter headings. I hope that the reader will feel inspired to look further, on the basis of what has gone before.

Filmography

All screenplays written by Agnès Varda

La Pointe Courte 1954, 89 min., b/w.

Production company: Tamaris Films, France
Script: Agnès Varda and the people of La Pointe Courte
Camera: Louis Stein, Paul Soulignac, Louis Soulanes
Editing: Alain Resnais
Continuity: Jane Vilardebo
Music: Pierre Barbaud and local tunes
Principal actors: Silvia Monfort (she), Philippe Noiret (he)

O saisons, ô châteaux 1957, 22 min., col.

Producer: Pierre Braunberger, Films de la Pléiade
Camera: Quinto Albicocco
Editing: Janine Verneau
Music: André Hodeir, Jazz Groupe de Paris
Voices: Danièle Delorme, Antoine Bourseiller

L'Opéra-Mouffe 1958, 17 min., b/w

Production: Ciné-Tamaris
Camera: Sacha Vierny
Editing: Janine Verneau
Music: Georges Delerue
With: Dorothée Blank, Antoine Bourseiller, André Rousselet, Jean
    Tasso, José Varela, Monika Weber

Du côté de la côte 1958, 24 min., col.

Producers: Anatole Dauman, Philippe Lifchitz, Argos Films
Camera: Quinto Albicocco, R. Castel
Continuity: Anne Olivier
Editing: Henri Colpi
Music: Georges Delerue
Assistant: Michel Mitrani
Voices: Roger Coggio, Anne Olivier, Jean-Christophe Benoît (singer)

Cléo de 5 à 7 1961, 90 min., b/w (brief colour)

Production: Ciné-Tamaris
Assistant directors: Bernard Toublanc-Michel, Marin Karmitz
Camera: Jean Rabier
Editing: Janine Verneau, Pascale Laverrière
Continuity: Aurore Paquiss
Music: Michel Legrand, Agnès Varda
Décor: Bernard Evein
Principal actors: Corinne Marchand (Cléo), Antoine Bourseiller
    (Antoine), Dominique Davray (Angèle), Dorothée Blank
    (Dorothée) – with Jean-Luc Godard, Anna Karina, Eddie
    Constantine, Sami Frey, Georges de Beauregard and others in the
    film within the film

Salut les Cubains 1963, 30 min., b/w

Production: Pathé-Cinema
Camera and animation: J. Marques, CS Olaf
Editing: Janine Verneau
Commentary spoken by Michel Piccoli

Le Bonheur 1964, 82 min., col.

Production: Mag Bodard
Camera: Claude Beausoleil, Jean Rabier
Editing: Janine Verneau
Continuity: Francine Corteggiani
Sound: Louis Hochet
Music: W. A. Mozart, adaptation Jean-Michel Defaye
Décor: Hubert Monloup
Principal actors: Jean-Claude Drouot (François), Claire Drouot
    (Thérèse), Marie-France Boyer (Emilie)

Les Enfants du musée 1964, 7 min., b/w

Production: Pathé-Cinema for TV series 'Chroniques de France'

Elsa la Rose 1965, 20 min., b/w

Production: Ciné-Tamaris, Pathé-Cinema
Camera: Willy Kurant, William Lubtchansky
Sound: Bernard Ortion
Music: Simonovitch, Ferrat, Moussorgsky, Gershwin, Handy
With the participation of: Louis Aragon, Elsa Triolet, Michel Piccoli (reader)

Les Créatures 1965, 105 min., b/w and col.

Production: Mag Bodard, Franco-Suédoise Parc Films, Madeleine Film, Sandrew
Camera: Willy Kurant, William Lubtchansky
Editing: Janine Verneau
Continuity: Elizabeth Rappeneau
Music: Pierre Barbaud, Henry Purcell
Décor: Claude Pignot
Principal actors: Michel Piccoli (Edgar), Catherine Deneuve (Mylène), Eva Dahlbeck (Michèle Quellec), Marie-France Mignal (Viviane Quellec)

Loin du Vietnam 1967

A sequence was made for this collective film on French reaction to the Vietnam war, but was finally not used. Varda's name remains in the credits since she participated in the montage.

Oncle Yanco 1967, 22 min., col.

Production: Ciné-Tamaris
Assistant director: Tom Luddy
Camera: David Myers
Editing: Jean Hamon
Sound: Paul Oppenheim
Music: Yannis Spanos, Richard Lawrence, Albinoni

Black Panthers 1968, 28 min., b/w

Production: Ciné-Tamaris
Assistant director: Tom Luddy

Camera: David Myers, John Schofill, Paul Aratow, Agnès Varda
Editing: Paddy Monk
Sound: Paul Oppenheim, James Steward

Lions' Love 1968, 110 min., col.

Production: Ciné-Tamaris
Camera: Steve Larner
Editing: Robert Dalva
Sound: George Alch
Music: Joseph Bird
With the participation of: Viva, Jim Rado, Jerry Ragni, Shirley Clarke, Agnès Varda

Nausicaa 1970, 90 min., col. (never shown)

Production: ORTF
Script: Agnès Varda
Camera: Charlie Gaeta
Editing: Germaine Cohen
Continuity: Claude Dequier
Music: Mikis Theodorakis
Décors: Michel Janiaud
Greek adviser: Georges Katacousinos
Principal actors: France Dougnac (Agnès), Myriam Boyer (Rosalie), Stavros Tornes (Michel), Catherine de Seynes (Simone), Gérard Depardieu (hippy)

Daguerréotypes 1974–5, 80 min., col.

Production: Ciné-Tamaris, INA, ZDF
Camera: Nurith Aviv, William Lubtchansky
Editing: Gordon Swire
Sound: Antoine Bonfanti, Jean-François Auger
With the participation of the inhabitants of the rue Daguerre and Mystag

Réponse de femmes 1975, 8 min., col.

Production: Ciné-Tamaris, Antenne 2
Executive producers: Sylvie Genevoix, Michel Honorin
Camera: Jacques Reiss, Michel Thiriet
Sound: Bernard Bleicher
Editing: Marie Castro

Plaisir d'amour en Iran 1976, 6 min., col.

Production: Ciné-Tamaris
Camera: Nurith Aviv, Charlie Vandamme
Editing: Sabine Mamou
Sound: Henri Morelle
Actors: Valérie Mairesse (Pomme), Ali Raffi (Darius), Thérèse Liotard
   (voice)

L'Une chante, l'autre pas 1976, 120 min., col.

Production: Ciné-Tamaris, SFP, INA, Contrechamp, Paradise Film,
   Population Film
Camera: Charlie Vandamme, Nurith Aviv
Editing: Joëlle von Effenterre
Continuity: Alice Chazelles
Sound: Henri Morelle
Music: François Wertheimer, Orchidée
Décors, costumes: Frankie Diago
Principal actors: Thérèse Liotard (Suzanne), Valérie Mairesse
   (Pomme), Ali Raffi (Darius), Robert Dadies (Jérôme), Jean-Pierre
   Pellegrin (le docteur Pierre Aubanel)

Quelques femmes bulles 1977, 58 min., col. (video) for Antenne 2

Director: Marion Sarrault
Music: Orchidée
Written and presented by Varda

Mur Murs 1980, 81 min., col.

Production: Ciné-Tamaris
Camera: Bernard Auroux
Editing: Sabine Mamou, Bob Gould
Sound: Lee Alexander
Music: Buxtehude, Carey, Cruz, Fiddy, Healy, Lauber, Los Illegals,
   Parker
With the participation of Juliet Berto and (the artists): Terry
   Schoonhoven, John Wehrie, Arthur Mortimer, Jane Golden, Kent
   Twichell, Richard Wyatt, Willie Herron, Harry Gamboa, Arno
   Jordan, Judy Baca, Cat Felix

Documenteur 1980–1, 63 min., col.

Production: Ciné-Tamaris
Camera: Nurith Aviv
Editing: Sabine Mamou
Sound: Jim Thornton, Lee Alexander
Music: Georges Delerue, Michel Colombier
Principal actors: Sabine Mamou (Emilie), Mathieu Demy (Martin)

Ulysse 1982, 22 min., col.

Production: Garance
Photos: Agnès Varda
Camera: Jean-Yves Escoffier
Editing: Marie-Jo Audiard
Sound: Jean-Paul Mugel
Music: Pierre Barbaud
With the participation of: Ulysse Llorca, Bienvenida Llorca, Fouli Elia

Une minute pour une image 1982, Television series, 170 2-minute spots

Production: Garance

Les Dites Caryatides 1984, 13 min., col.

Production: Ciné-Tamaris
Production manager: Teri Wehn-Damish
Camera: Cyril Lathus
Editing: Hélène Wolf
Music: Rameau, Offenbach

7P., cuis., s. de b… (à saisir) 1984, 27 min., col.

Production: Ciné-Tamaris
Camera: Nurith Aviv
Editing: Sabine Mamou
Sound: Daniel Ollivier
Music: Pierre Barbaud
Principal actors: Marthe Jarnias (the old lady), Saskia Cohen-Tanugi (the mother), Yolande Moreau (the Belgian maid)

Sans toit ni loi 1985, 105 min., col.

Production: Ciné-Tamaris, Films A2
Assistant directors: Jacques Royer, Jacques Deschamps
Camera: Patrick Blossier
Editing: Agnès Varda, Patricia Mazuy
Continuity: Chantal Dessanges
Sound: Jean-Paul Mugel
Music: Joanna Bruzdowicz
Décors: Jean Bauer, Anne Violet
Principal actors: Sandrine Bonnaire (Mona), Macha Méril (Mme
   Landier), Yolande Moreau (Yolande), Stéphane Freiss (Jean-
   Pierre), Yahiaoui Assouna (Assoun), Marthe Jarnias (Tante Lydie)

T'as de beaux escaliers tu sais 1986, 3 min., col.

Production: Miroirs, Ciné-Tamaris
Camera: Patrick Blossier
Editing: Marie-Jo Audiard
Music: Michel Legrand
With several short film extracts

Jane B. par Agnès V. 1986–7, 97 min., col.

Production: Ciné-Tamaris, La Sept
Assistant directors: Jacques Royer, Marie-Jo Audiard
Camera: Nurith Aviv, Pierre-Laurent Chenieux
Editing: Agnès Varda, Marie-Jo Audiard
Continuity: Marie-Florence Roncoyolo, Sylvie Koechlin
Sound: Olivier Scwob, Jean-Pierre Mugel, Alix Comte
Décor: Bertrand Lheminier, Philippe Bernard, Olivier Radot, Jean
   Dewasne of the artist's studio
Costumes: Rosalie Varda
Principal actors: Jane Birkin (herself), Agnès Varda (herself), Philippe
   Léotard (the painter), Jean-Pierre Léaud (autumn lover), Farid
   Chopel (the colonial), Laura Betti (Lardy)

Kung-Fu Master 1987, 78 min., col.

Production: Ciné-Tamaris
Camera: Pierre-Laurent Chenieux
Editing: Marie-Jo Audiard
Sound: Olivier Schwob, Olivier Varenne

Music: Joanna Bruzdowicz, les Rita Mitsouko, les Berurier Noir
Costume: Rose-Marie Melka
Principal actors: Jane Birkin (Mary-Jane), Mathieu Demy (Julien), Charlotte Gainsbourg (Lucy), Lou Doillon (Lou). From an idea by Jane Birkin

Jacquot de Nantes 1990, 118 min., b/w and col.

Production: Ciné-Tamaris
Assistant directors: Didier Rouget, Philippe Touret
Camera: Patrick Blossier, Agnès Godard, Georges Strouvé
Editing: Marie-Jo Audiard
Sound: Jean-Pierre Duret, Nicolas Naegelen
Music: Joanna Bruzdowicz
Décors: Robert Nardone, Olivier Radot
Costumes: Françoise Disle
With the participation of Jacques Demy. Principal actors: Philippe Maron, Edouard Joubeaud, Laurent Monnier (Jacquot 1, 2, 3), Brigitte de Villepoix (Jacquot's mother), Daniel Dublet (his father)

Les Demoiselles ont eu 25 ans 1992, 63 min., col.

Production: Ciné-Tamaris
Camera: Stéphane Krausz, Georges Strouvé, Agnès Varda
Editing: Agnès Varda, Anne-Marie Cotret
Sound: Thierry Ferreux
Music: Michel Legrand, Jacques Loussier
With the participation of: Catherine Deneuve, Mag Bodard, Jacques Perrin, Jean-Louis Frot, Bernard Evein and others

L'Univers de Jacques Demy 1993, 90 min., col.

Production: Ciné-Tamaris
Production manager: Perrine Bauduin
Camera: Stéphane Krausz, Georges Strouvé, Peter Pilafian
Editing: Marie-Jo Audiard
Music: Roland Vincent

Les 101 nuits 1994, 100 min., col.

Production: Ciné-Tamaris
Camera: Eric Gautier
Editing: Hugues Darmois
Sound: Jean-Pierre Duret, Henri Morelle

Costume: Rosalie Varda

Sets: Cyril Boitard, Cedric Simoneau

Principal actors: Michel Piccoli (M. Cinéma), Marcello Mastroianni (the Italian friend), Henri Garcin (Firmin), Julie Gayet (Camille Miralis), Mathieu Demy (Mica), Emmanuel Salinger (Vincent). A galaxy of stars in guest appearances

Select bibliography

Books

Etudes cinématographiques: Agnès Varda, Paris, Lettres modernes, 1991
 Issue no. 179–86 of *Etudes Cinématographiques*, a periodical of
 which each issue is effectively a book. A series of detailed, well-
 researched articles by a number of authors, many well known in
 French film criticism, looking at different aspects of Varda's work
 up to 1991.

Flitterman-Lewis, Sandy, *To Desire Differently*, New York, Columbia
 UP, 1996
 This is a book about French women film-makers which contains
 probably the most detailed study of Agnès Varda's work in English.
 Clearly Flitterman-Lewis is most interested in Varda as an exponent
 of women's cinema, and on this part of her work she is an essential
 reference. Detailed studies of *Cléo de 5 à 7* and *Sans toit ni loi*.

Hayward, Susan and Vincendeau, Ginette (eds), *French Film, Texts
 and Contexts*, London, Routledge, 1990
 The last chapter, 'Beyond the gaze and into *femme-filmécriture*:
 Agnès Varda's *Sans toit ni loi*' (Susan Hayward), is an essential
 study of the mechanics of the gaze in *Sans toit ni loi*.

Revue belge du cinéma, no. 20, été indien 1987: *Agnès Varda*
 A special issue of a periodical. Contains an interview (on *Mur
 Murs*, *Documenteur* and *Jane B.*), several closely argued articles and
 the full text of *Ulysse*.

Varda, Agnès, *Varda par Agnès*, Paris, Cahiers du cinéma, 1994
 A patchwork of texts on Varda's life and films, provides much the
 richest source available for the film-maker's own approach to her
 work. Lavishly illustrated, invaluable.

Articles and interviews

Interview, 'Agnès Varda', *Cinéma 61*, no. 60, October 1961, pp. 5–20

Interview, 'Agnès Varda de 5 à 7', *Positif*, no. 44, March 1962, pp. 1–27

Interview, 'La grâce laïque', *Cahiers du Cinéma*, no. 165, April 1965, pp. 42–50

Varda, Agnès, 'Autour et alentour de *Daguerréotypes*', *Cinéma 75*, no. 204, December 1975, pp. 39–53

Interview, 'Brève rencontre avec Agnès Varda', *Ecran 77*, no. 58, May 1977, pp. 12–13

Interview, *Revue du Cinéma/Image et Son*, no. 369, February 1982, pp. 45–7

Interview, 'En marge de Hollywood, LA au cœur', *Cahiers du Cinéma*, nos. 334–5, April–May 1982, pp. XIII–XVI

Interview, *Positif*, no. 253, April 1982, pp. 40–4

Bergala, Alain, 'Agnès Varda joue et gagne', *Cahiers du Cinéma*, no. 340, October 82, pp. VII–VIII

Chevrie, Marc, 'Tu n'as rien vu à Saint-Aubin', *Cahiers du Cinéma*, no. 358, April 1984, p. X

Audé, Françoise, interview 'Conversation avec Agnès Varda' and article 'Le Diptyque paradoxal', *Positif*, no. 325, March 1988, pp. 2–7

Interview, 'Badminton', *Les Inrockuptibles*, no. 47, June 1993, pp. 76–80

Flitterman-Lewis, Sandy, 'Magic and wisdom in two portraits by Agnès Varda: *Kung-Fu Master* and *Jane B. par Agnès V.*', *Screen*, 34: 4, winter 1993, pp. 302–20

Index